THE T
CARYL

R. Darren Gobert specialises in comparative drama, dramatic and performance theory, and the philosophy of theatre at York University, Canada, where he is Associate Professor in the Department of English and the Graduate Programme in Theatre and Performance Studies. His works include *The Mind-Body Stage: Passion and Interaction in the Cartesian Theater* (2013). He is editor of the journal *Modern Drama*.

Also available in the Critical Companions series from Bloomsbury Methuen Drama:

MODERN ASIAN THEATRE AND PERFORMANCE 1900–2000
by Kevin J. Wetmore, Siyuan Liu and Erin B. Mee

THE PLAYS OF SAMUEL BECKETT
by Katherine Weiss

THE THEATRE OF BRIAN FRIEL
by Christopher Murray

THE THEATRE OF DAVID GREIG
by Clare Wallace

THE THEATRE OF HAROLD PINTER
by Mark Taylor-Batty

THE THEATRE OF MARTIN CRIMP: SECOND EDITION
by Aleks Sierz

THE THEATRE AND FILMS OF MARTIN MCDONAGH
by Patrick Lonergan

THE THEATRE OF SEAN O'CASEY
by James Moran

THE THEATRE OF TENNESSEE WILLIAMS
by Brenda Murphy

THE THEATRE OF TIMBERLAKE WERTENBAKER
by Sophie Bush

THE THEATRE OF CARYL CHURCHILL

R. Darren Gobert

Series Editors: Patrick Lonergan and Erin Hurley

B L O O M S B U R Y
LONDON • NEW DELHI • NEW YORK • SYDNEY

Bloomsbury Methuen Drama
An imprint of Bloomsbury Publishing Plc

50 Bedford Square	1385 Broadway
London	New York
WC1B 3DP	NY 10018
UK	USA

www.bloomsbury.com

First published 2014

The author and publisher would like to thank the Faculty of Liberal Arts and Professional Studies, York University, for the financial support it provided to this work.

British Library Cataloguing-in-Publication Data
A catalogue record for this book is available from the British Library.

ISBN: HB: 978-1-4725-3884-0
PB: 978-1-4081-5452-6
ePDF: 978-1-4081-5454-0
ePub: 978-1-4081-5453-3

Library of Congress Cataloging-in-Publication Data
A catalog record for this book is available from the Library of Congress.

Typeset by RefineCatch Limited, Bungay, Suffolk
Printed and bound in India

In memory of Jill Birnbaum

PERMISSIONS

The author gratefully acknowledges the many authors, publishers, and publications who gave permission to quote from unpublished or previously published material, including Blackwell Publishing/Wiley Books, Bloomsbury Methuen Drama, Caryl Churchill, *Comparative Drama,* Grove Press, Johns Hopkins University Press, Merlin Press, *PAJ: A Journal of Performance and Art, PMLA,* Max Stafford-Clark, *Theater*, and University of Minnesota Press.

Quotations from Caryl Churchill, *Blue Heart* in *Plays: Four* (London: Nick Hern Books, 2008), pp.60–128, appear with the permission of Nick Hern Books Ltd: www.nickhernbooks.co.uk

Quotations from Caryl Churchill, *A Dream Play* in *Plays: Four* (London: Nick Hern Books, 2008), pp.207–65, appear with the permission of Nick Hern Books Ltd: www.nickhernbooks.co.uk

Quotations from Caryl Churchill, *Drunk Enough to Say I Love You?* in *Plays: Four* (London: Nick Hern Books, 2008), pp.267–309, appear with the permission of Nick Hern Books Ltd: www.nickhernbooks.co.uk

Quotations from Caryl Churchill, *Far Away* in *Plays: Four* (London: Nick Hern Books, 2008), pp.129–59, appear with the permission of Nick Hern Books Ltd: www.nickhernbooks.co.uk

Quotations from Caryl Churchill, *Hot Fudge* in *Shorts* (London: Nick Hern Books, 1990), pp.275–304, appear with the permission of Nick Hern Books Ltd: www.nickhernbooks.co.uk

Quotations from Caryl Churchill, *Icecream* in *Plays: Three* (London: Nick Hern Books, 1998), pp.55–102, appear with the permission of Nick Hern Books Ltd: www.nickhernbooks.co.uk

Quotations from Caryl Churchill, *The Judge's Wife* in *Shorts* (London: Nick Hern Books, 1990), pp.147–63, appear with the permission of Nick Hern Books Ltd: www.nickhernbooks.co.uk

Quotations from Caryl Churchill, *Love and Information* (London: Nick Hern Books, 2012) appear with the permission of Nick Hern Books Ltd: www.nickhernbooks.co.uk

Quotations from Caryl Churchill, *Mad Forest* in *Plays: Three* (London: Nick Hern Books, 1998), pp.101–81, appear with the permission of Nick Hern Books Ltd: www.nickhernbooks.co.uk

Quotations from Caryl Churchill, *A Number* in *Plays: Four* (London: Nick Hern Books, 2008), pp.161–206, appear with the permission of Nick Hern Books Ltd: www.nickhernbooks.co.uk

Quotations from Caryl Churchill, *The Skriker* in *Plays: Three* (London: Nick Hern Books, 1998), pp.239–91, appear with the permission of Nick Hern Books Ltd: www.nickhernbooks.co.uk

Quotations from Philip Roberts and Max Stafford-Clark, *Taking Stock: The Theatre of Max Stafford-Clark* (London: Nick Hern Books, 2007) appear with the permission of Nick Hern Books Ltd: www.nickhernbooks.co.uk

CONTENTS

PREFACE AND ACKNOWLEDGEMENTS: THE THEATRE OF CARYL CHURCHILL

The central conceit of the BBC series *Masquerade* was elegant in its simplicity. The episodes shared a setting – a party – and explored the disguises and pretences evoked by the series title and registered in its etymological root, *maschera* or *mask*. But a different cast of characters peopled each instalment; a different group of actors embodied them; a different writer wrote each script. The first was entrusted to Caryl Churchill, already an established playwright but not yet the household name she would become a few years later, after the international success of *Cloud Nine*. Her episode, *Turkish Delight*, aired 22 April 1974. It slyly subverted the central conceit by setting the scene not at a party but just outside one, in the ladies' room. And thus it peered quickly behind the mask to introduce several women taking refuge in the loo, identically dressed in long skirts and skimpy tops, their midriffs bare, in an Orientalist fantasy of eastern beauty. They are the ex-wife, the fiancée, and the call-girl mistress of a well-known politician, who smiles for the cameras at the costume party just outside the door. The ex-wife and fiancée are dressed to please, each believing that she alone knows the politician's harem fantasy of made-up 'Turkish delights'. The less naïve call girl, Angie, works a different angle: blackmail on the client who has done her wrong.

When the harem girls predictably meet in the ladies' room, they express equally predictable antagonisms toward one another. There are two surprises. First, the lavatory attendant turns out to be Angie's aunt, a maid prized for her ability to 'clean right into the corners'.[1] Second, the discord quickly cedes to bonhomie as the women bond over a shared lover who (no surprise here) is beneath contempt. They find common cause or at least common enmity, thrown comically into relief by yet another identically costumed woman who answers their accusatory query about her outfit – '[w]ho were you trying to please?' – with a curt reply: 'Myself'.[2] Eventually ex-wife, fiancée, and call girl unmask their shared paramour and, after deciding that '[w]e won't be his harem any more', help one another improvise new costumes: 'something from a horror film' for Angie, smearing blood and green make-up on her face; a mummy for the ex-wife, assiduously wrapped in toilet tissue; and a radically austere choice for the prim fiancée, who rejects her initial idea, Lady Godiva, in favour of being 'just me with no clothes on'.[3]

Virtually ignored in Churchill scholarship, the script contains all of its author's trademark concerns. Class tensions ripple through the exchanges between Angie and her childless aunt, who anticipate a later Angie and (putatively childless) aunt in Churchill's 1982 masterpiece, *Top Girls*. *Turkish Delight*'s Angie, like *Top Girls*' Marlene, believes she has made it to the top, having transited out of poverty with her guile and smarts. But she, too, seems unaware that her success has required a damaging capitulation to patriarchy. Her aunt, meanwhile, admires the material comforts brought by her niece's profession even as she disapproves, not because of latent feminist instinct but because of a class-marked prudishness that Churchill equally mocks. (The aunt summarises her marital relations thus: 'My Philip didn't have none of these funny ways. "Get layed down, gel", he used to say, then at it and over with, before I hardly knew'.[4]) *Turkish Delight* thus reveals an early fidelity to the politics Churchill famously declared in 1987, when she asserted that 'socialism and feminism aren't synonymous, but I feel strongly about both and wouldn't be interested in a form of one that didn't include the other'.[5] The playwright questions the social forces that keep the working-class women in service, for the materially striving niece is still paid by the hour like her passive aunt, whose loyalty keeps her scrubbing into the corners for lower-paying clients. And Churchill imparts a feminist message even while baring no shortage of female flesh. There is no prurience. On the contrary, by restricting her action to the ladies' room she leverages the power of an all-female representational space and an all-female cast, years before she did so in *Top Girls*. If such representation provides its female viewers 'intense pleasure' (in the words of Elaine Aston[6]), it is because it occurs so rarely in the culture industry, a point that *Turkish Delight* emphasises when men demand entry to the lavatory, perhaps worried that the real fun is happening there. Entry is denied. The politician John – reduced to an economic function by his blunt name – is kept out of the play. And as his harem dissolves, its women find a different kind of community in wronged sisterhood.

As *Turkish Delight* demonstrates, Churchill's work foregrounds issues of class and gender even as it insistently moves outward in unexpected directions. This book mimics that pattern. It keeps Churchill's politics in the foreground even as it explores the many and varied aesthetic pleasures of her peerless career in the theatre. Two fundamental strategies have governed its composition. First, I tether the plays tightly to significant productions. For more than any writer in the contemporary theatre, Churchill has drawn attention to the meaning of the word *playwright*, whose job it is 'to fashion vehicles, just like a cartwright or wheelwright, which an actor can inhabit and travel in'. I quote the Scottish writer and director David Greig, who once described *A Number* as 'a piece of music for the actor to play' and praised Michael Gambon's rendition of the play's Salter for this epiphany. As Greig attested, watching the actor perform Churchill's words 'shifted everything on its axis for me as a writer'.[7] Recognising that the proof is in the playing, the research for this book included voluminous production records: files from the Royal Court, the theatre with which Churchill is most associated, but files, too, from the National Theatre and elsewhere or, across the Atlantic, Manhattan Theatre Club, New York Theatre Workshop, and others. I have also drawn extensively on files from the Public Theater in New York, where Joseph Papp's fastidious record-keeping bequeathed a bounty of archival treasures.

A second strategy concerns chronology. Churchill has always defied it, scrambling time as early as 1962, in her unpublished play *Easy Death*, and many times since: in *Cloud Nine*, with its audacious time jump between acts; in *Top Girls*, with its time-shattering dinner party of historical guests; and so on. There are historical watersheds: Churchill's first play, *Downstairs*, premiered when she was a student at Oxford University; her first professional play, *The Ants*, broadcast on radio; her stage breakthrough with *Owners*; or her first collaborations with the Joint Stock and Monstrous Regiment companies, which catalysed her politics and forged new creative tools. These and other milestones are celebrated as they arise, but they do not structure a chronological narrative. Instead, I offer five interlocking discussions, any of which might serve as an entry into Churchill's work. Each chapter provides close readings of plays and details their composition and rehearsal processes, their initial reception and subsequent scholarly views. But since each chapter lays a different emphasis, each deploys a different reading practice, for many approaches seemed necessary to characterise such a restlessly imaginative and prolific career.

The first chapter explores Churchill's uncanny success at tailoring her form to match her thematic content. In *Turkish Delight*, for instance, she marks the fourth costumed woman as different with a speech prefix ('Other Girl') that uniquely refuses to define her in relation to the party's host (as with 'The Attendant') or the play's unseen politician (as with 'The Call Girl', 'The Ex-Wife', and 'The Fiancée'). But Churchill lands her point about this woman's promising difference not through dialogue but with a formal conceit. Her play abandons its masquerade theme, its trio of wronged women, and its own party setting. It ends instead with the Other Girl, who describes her nightly ritual of checking on her baby and making a cup of tea. She gets the last word: 'I drink the last sweet bit of tea down at the bottom where I didn't stir it, and I go to bed'.[8] I attend to such matters of form while analysing *Top Girls* (1982), *The Skriker* (1994), and *Far Away* (2000), each of which advances its ideas by means of Churchill's signature formal daring. The plays are among the playwright's most vivid landscapes – a term I borrow from Gertrude Stein, another playwright made anxious by chronological narratives and one with whose work Churchill would at least twice engage: once in 1994, when she worked with actors in the National Theatre's Studio on Stein's play *In Savoy, or 'Yes' Is for Yes for a Very Young Man*, and again in 2013, when she lent advice to Katie Mitchell for the director's Stein project, *Say It with Flowers*.

Turkish Delight begins with Angie complaining that she cannot enjoy sex outside of work since 'half way through I think, What's the market value? It's like losing all that money if you do it for love'.[9] My second chapter digs into monetary transactions between partners, not only those transactions dramatised on stage but also those that make the professional theatre possible. Examining contracts and budgets, profits and losses from productions of *Owners* (1972), *Serious Money* (1987), and *A Dream Play* (2005), I analyse how Churchill has navigated an increasingly market-driven theatre industry without reducing her collaborative relationships to (in the coinage of Marx and Engels) the 'cash nexus'. And I understand her borrowings from others in those plays – whether from Joe Orton, Thomas Shadwell, or August Strindberg – in terms of an alternative gift economy to which she has already much contributed, especially in the unique latitude she allows those performing and directing her work.

The third chapter is no less materialist, but its focus shifts from ledger sheets to onstage bodies. Reading *Cloud Nine* (1979) against *Icecream* (1989) and *A Number* (2002), I explore one of Churchill's longest-standing preoccupations: the body, which serves as a repository of cultural memory and a sometimes unwitting inheritor of ideological baggage. Again productions prove instructive. The actors that have inhabited Churchill's roles have each shaped and even subverted them, as, indeed, historical agents have done with the roles bestowed by their sociocultural situation. Even a 'Turkish delight', her midriff on display, might make a surprising feminist statement just by revising the script a little. In *acting*, we therefore find insights into offstage *agency*, especially if we are mindful of the words' shared etymology in the verb *agere*, to do.

Whether in history or the theatre, this doing never occurs in a vacuum and, in Churchill's work in particular, it never happens solo. Accordingly, my fourth chapter turns its focus to collaboration and its attention to the rehearsal room. Analysing the processes that engendered *Light Shining in Buckinghamshire* (1976), *Fen* (1983), and *Mad Forest* (1990), I argue that these plays make visible their collaborative methods in order to rebuke the politics of the outside world – just, indeed, as *Turkish Delight*'s women might do from the political haven of the toilet, once they have shed the cultural cliché of catty competitors and disentangled themselves from the John on whom they have equally relied. Churchill's workshopped plays not only reveal a collaborative aesthetic, in other words, but also model an ethics of social cooperation. For these ethics to be made manifest, however, actors must bring the play to life. They must inhabit the landscape that collaboration has made possible.

When Stein offered her theory of dramatic landscape in 1934, she proposed the theatre as a place where art could fulfil its ultimate function: 'to live in the actual present, that is the complete actual present, and to completely express that complete actual present'.[10] Readers will recognise the terms of contemporary performance theory which Stein anticipates, and to which I turn in my final chapter. There, I explore the ontology of performance and distinguish it from the make-believe of scripts, make-up, ersatz props. We might see the fiancée making just such a distinction in *Turkish Delight* when she doffs her costume and learns to play herself. For the theatre is at its essence much more than masquerade, as Churchill explores in plays such as *Traps* (1977), *Blue Heart* (1997), and *Love and Information* (2012), each interrogating the very nature of theatrical performance.

If each chapter foregrounds three works, each also reaches forward and back to over fifty others: many unpublished and unproduced, some unfinished. Taking this larger perspective, we might better appreciate the playwright's habit of refining her theatrical ideas: *Turkish Delight*'s lavatory attendant and niece, for instance, conjointly anticipate Annie from *Objections to Sex and Violence*, on stage the next year at the Royal Court and emerging into class consciousness after the man whose house she cleans pays her for sex, too. Consonances between historically remote works (for Churchill's career is, as I write, in its sixth decade) prove revelatory. In the young writer's rejected proposals to BBC Radio, for instance, we see the seeds of much later fruit: unrealised projects such as *The Love Salesman* and *The Magic Ring* anticipate general themes and particular details from plays such as *Owners* and *The Skriker*.

Five figures criss-cross the entire book and emerge decisively as critical partners in the playwright's career: Stephen Daldry, James Macdonald, Max Stafford-Clark, Les Waters, and Mark Wing-Davey, who among them have directed thirty-five Churchill premieres and revivals. Some plays, too, surface in multiple chapters, for my five narratives interlock snugly and therefore deliberately press against one another. For instance, Churchill's preoccupation with DNA reveals itself in the third chapter, in my considerations of identity and the body, and again in the fifth, concerning the performances through which both identities and bodies are forged. Similarly, a preoccupation with sharing undergirds both the second chapter, on capitalism, and the fourth, on collaboration. The chapters are designed to amplify and complement one another in such a way that they collectively capture the spirit of her writing, which while often bracingly nonlinear is widely accessible.

Two essays by other scholars appear in the book's sixth section. In plays such as *Light Shining in Buckinghamshire*, Churchill stresses the importance of a polyvocal history, and these other writings bring critical perspectives whose difference from my own can help secure deeper understanding. Working in counterpoint with my analyses, each essay proceeds chronologically. Elaine Aston sets Churchill's work in its broader theatre-historical context, offering a vivid picture of London's theatre scene in the past fifty years. Siân Adiseshiah traces the rise and fall of the Left in Britain, providing a broader political context within which we can situate Churchill's dramatic interventions, including her latest play (at the time of writing) *Ding Dong the Wicked*, which I analyse in my epilogue.

One final characterisation: my goal, necessarily constrained by space, has been to produce a thorough study of Churchill's career distinct in its form and enlivened by its archival discoveries. But this study is never dispassionate. Caryl Churchill is my favourite playwright, and my love for the work has propelled this book and left, I hope, some residue in its prose.

I end with words of thanks to those who have sustained me during the past sixteen months. For convincing me to steer my love and information toward his press, I thank Mark Dudgeon, an unfailingly personable editor. For subsidising my research abroad, I thank the Faculty of Liberal Arts and Professional Studies at York University. For myriad kindnesses that made it all possible, I thank my department chair, Jonathan Warren, and graduate programme director,

Marie-Christine Leps. The study could not have been completed on time without a dedicated team of research assistants: Amanda Attrell, Romilly Belcourt, Meryl Borato, Thom Bryce, Thea Fitz-James, Heather Holditch, and especially Alex Ferrone, who was there at the beginning and there at the end. During archival research I incurred other debts. I acknowledge staff at Brooklyn Academy of Music and New York Public Library for the Performing Arts, especially Jeremy Megraw and Arlene Yu, whose smiling assistance made sorting through stage manager reports or wig receipts seem almost like fun. I acknowledge staff at the V&A Theatre and Performance Archives, at the British Film Institute's National Archive, and at the Manuscripts and Sound and Moving Image divisions of the British Library. Two archivists proved invaluable, and so I particularly acknowledge Gavin Clarke at the National Theatre Archive and Louise North at the BBC Written Archives Centre.

I must also thank Max Stafford-Clark for generous permission to quote from his diaries, an indispensable guide to British theatre of the last forty years bound in elegant volumes often gifted by Churchill herself. I warmly thank her, too, both for allowing use of unpublished material and for bearing my periodic intrusions on her privacy with characteristic grace.

Many people answered queries or proved exemplary theatre companions, among them Ross Arthur, Anna-Alisa Beloüs, Marcia Blumberg, Adrian Bucur, Stephen Cummiskey, Anna Evans, Sheila Ghose, Lora Hutchison, Kaitlin Kratter, Warren Lee, Alisa Palmer, Ria Parry, Janelle Reinelt, Aleks Sierz, Anna Szczepaniak, Sarah Wilson. David Benedict also provided access to numerous London sources, and I count meeting him among the book's gifts to me. Elaine Aston, Bernice Neal, and Hersh Zeifman also read and improved the entire manuscript: they were my first audience and will, I hope, recognise their good influence. And Ross Gascho supported me in countless other ways as he always does, and he had earned my eternal admiration and affection even before he pronounced *Top Girls* his favourite play.

One person remains to be acknowledged. I began writing this book in June 2012, while living in London and thrilled to be in the same city again with my dear friend Jill Birnbaum – an enthusiastic companion for both tennis and theatre that summer, and, as it happens, the sort of committed feminist and un-cynical advocate for social justice that Churchill might celebrate. Shortly after Jill and I and our partners watched the Wimbledon final that July, her health began failing; in October, a hospital stay prevented us from seeing *Love and Information* together, as we had planned. She chose the book's cover in April 2013, but she did not see its completion. I dedicate it, with love, to her memory.

CHAPTER 1
CHURCHILL'S LANDSCAPES

Caryl Churchill once told a journalist that '[p]erhaps I feel the same about theatrical form as an artist feels about paint'.[1] Her analogy explains much. In *Vinegar Tom*, the bold presentational style reveals the play's means of production just as the *impasto* of the abstract expressionist does. In *Fen*, the vivid scenes and characters shade into one another without visible demarcations, as in Renaissance *sfumato*. And in her 2012 play *Love and Information*, sharply drawn dots – the shortest of the sixty-nine scenes is two words long – collectively constitute an epic canvas that exceeds the sum of its pointillist parts. Churchill's analogy figures her medium as a fluid vehicle for unbound expression rather than an agglomerate of genres and conventions: in other words, if theatre is paint, she does what she wants with it. It is therefore apt that Sarah Daniels once called her fellow playwright the Picasso of their craft.[2] The scope of Churchill's techniques has cemented her reputation as the most restless and innovative playwright now working, ever reinventing her style and pioneering new forms. And these forms uncannily match her content, which has evolved in tandem with history: from the threat of nuclear annihilation (in her first published play, *The Ants*) through the collapse of communism (*Mad Forest*) or from the sexual revolution (*Cloud Nine*) to the new biotechnological revolution (*A Number*). As she once told another journalist, 'I don't set out to find a bizarre way of writing. . . . I enjoy finding the form that seems to best fit what I'm thinking about'.[3] Thus Churchill echoes August Strindberg, whose experiments in drama emerged precisely alongside his experiments with painting, and whom Churchill honoured with her adaptation of the expressionist *A Dream Play* in 2005. Equally restless and innovative, Strindberg sought to design new dramatic shapes after bemoaning that 'we have not yet found the new form for the new content, and the new wine has burst the old bottles'.[4] In this chapter, I scrutinise three of Churchill's most radical forms, illuminating how each manages to contain its dramatic content.

Top Girls

Churchill's best known and most-produced play, *Top Girls*, had a long gestation. Gillian Hanna of the now-defunct feminist theatre collective Monstrous Regiment remembers early discussions between the company and the playwright about a project that would bring together women from different historical periods, including Joan, the legendary pope from the early Middle Ages, and Isabella Bird, the celebrated Victorian explorer.[5] Churchill herself told an interviewer that her preparatory work on Dull Gret, the figure from Flemish folklore famously painted by Pieter Bruegel the Elder, began as early as 1977 or 1978.[6] And records from London's Royal Court Theatre show that she was working on a play provisionally called *Famous Women* by 1979.[7] The juggernaut of *Cloud Nine* – the play that established Churchill's international fame and brought her first commercial success – had presumably consumed much of that year and the next, during which time she deepened her experiments in overlapping dialogue by writing *Three More Sleepless Nights*, premiered at Soho Poly on 9 June 1980. But she continued work on *Top Girls*, too, completing a full draft by March 1981. She sent it to Max Stafford Clark, the director of *Cloud Nine* and *Light Shining in Buckinghamshire* before it and by then the Artistic Director of the Royal Court, asking in a letter whether he saw possibility in the project despite its unconventional manoeuvres. He did, and Churchill continued to refine the play even as she began preparations for *Fen* (whose inaugural meeting with director Les Waters took place on 13 December 1981[8]) and as she finished *Crimes*, a teleplay for the BBC. A second draft of *Top Girls* was completed by March 1982 and became Stafford-Clark's primary focus by late May.

Top Girls tells the story of Marlene, a businesswoman in early 1980s London whose success at the titular employment agency depends not only on her intelligence and ruthlessness but also on the working-class sister who has raised Marlene's child as her own. The play dramatises Marlene's bitter fight with this sister, Joyce; her awkward relationship with the disowned daughter, Angie; and her interactions with her work colleagues, Nell and Win, each, like Marlene, a 'high-flying lady'.[9] Marlene has been promoted to managing director over a sexist (and unseen) rival, Howard Kidd, whose wife will accuse her of being 'not natural' and 'one of these ballbreakers'.[10] And we see her celebrate this promotion at a surreal dinner party attended by exceptional women drawn from history (such as Isabella Bird or Lady Nijo, the thirteenth-century concubine turned nun and memoirist) or from legend (such as Dull Gret, Pope Joan, or Griselda, the absurdly docile wife celebrated in Petrarch, Boccaccio, and Chaucer). 'We've all come a long way', Marlene toasts, setting her accomplishments alongside theirs: 'To our courage and the way we changed our lives and our extraordinary achievements'.[11] While most plays respect theatrical tradition by revealing their plots in chronologically ordered scenes, *Top Girls* borrows a device more common to fiction: it reveals its chronological story (its *fabula*, in the terms of narrative theory) in a non-consecutive arrangement of prolepses and analepses (its *sjuzhet*). So the play begins with its dinner party on a Saturday night, before moving ahead to Monday at Top Girls; it then retreats to Joyce's backyard the preceding Sunday and advances again to Monday at the agency. Finally, the play shifts to a year earlier to represent a fraught Sunday-evening visit between the play's sisters.

In chronological order, in other words, the plot begins with Marlene's arrival for this unexpected visit and her dispensing of presents: chocolates and a dress for Angie, perfume for Joyce. ('There's no danger I'd have it already, that's one thing', she responds, dismissing the gift as a bourgeois luxury unknown to her.[12]) And the plot ends after Marlene's promotion and at the office, to which Angie makes her own unexpected visit and where her biological mother assesses her as dispassionately as she would a Top Girls job-seeker. 'She's a bit thick. She's a bit funny. . . . She's not going to make it', she tells Win.[13] The *fabula* gives Marlene the final speech and leaves her on the precipice of greater success – not unlike Margaret Thatcher, whom she worships and whose second electoral victory would come some months after the play's premiere. But the *sjuzhet* of *Top Girls* instead begins with its surreal dinner party, immediately signalling the play's fractured temporality by bringing its subjects impossibly together. And it ends with Angie's somnambulant prophecy about a future in which top girls like Marlene and Thatcher continue to be rewarded: 'Frightening'.[14] By reordering its plot, the play gives Angie the last word over Marlene who, in contrast to her ebullience in the opening scene, is left tired, drunk, and upset over the confrontation with Joyce that comprises the play's final act.

Ordering her plot as she does, Churchill trains attention on this confrontation, which despite Churchill's disclaimer that 'the argument is a drunken one between two angry sisters, not a considered political assessment' nonetheless pitches diametrically opposed politics against one another.[15] In one corner stands Marlene, blind to any interest but her own and certain that 'equality' means only her own ability to compete on equal terms. Thus she resembles Thatcher herself, whose apparent pioneering as the first female Prime Minister of Britain belied more ignominious achievements, such as reversing upwards trends in social mobility.[16] When Marlene snorts that 'I don't believe in class' and 'I believe in the individual', she espouses a philosophy in which 'there is no such thing as society. There are individual men and women', as Thatcher notoriously put it.[17] At the same time, Marlene unmasks her confused logic when she professes to hate a working class which, she simultaneously asserts, 'doesn't exist'.[18] As the incoming director of an employment agency – a pointedly chosen profession – she betrays no sense that individual success relies on collective support, however certain her conviction that 'the eighties are going to be stupendous. . . . For me'.[19] And thus she recalls Thatcher's tone-deaf remark that 'a first class nanny-housekeeper' is essential to a woman's achievement, made as she presided over an exclusively male Cabinet and the most male-dominated Parliament in decades.[20] Churchill slyly registers such egocentrism when the Prime Minister is paid Marlene's ultimate compliment: 'She's a tough lady, Maggie. I'd give her a job'.[21]

In the other corner stands Joyce, hidebound by a crude leftism whose political interventions are reduced to scratching or spitting on the occasional Mercedes or Rolls Royce. Joyce is deaf to Marlene's complaints about their mother's life, made more awful by a drunken and abusive husband whose putatively committed socialism stopped somewhere short of home. And Joyce's reflexive contempt for the middle class – foreshadowed in her ungracious response to Marlene's perfume – runs through the scene, as when Marlene enquires about the estuary near their childhood home, with its mud and lapwings. 'You get strangers walking there on a Sunday', Joyce concedes. 'I expect they're looking at the mud and the lapwings, yes'.[22] As the exchange attests, *Top Girls* contains some of the best naturalistic dialogue of Churchill's career, sensitive not only to the fault-lines of class and the power dynamics they shift but also to the subtextual cover under which most arguments brew. When Angie reveals that a neighbour has killed his wife, for instance, Joyce declares him a '[s]tuck up git'.[23] And by coupling Mr Connolly's homicide with his class pretensions, she passive-aggressively indicts her sister. But she delays an upfront attack until her interlocutor has praised Thatcher, after which Joyce's epithet 'filthy bastards' can rhetorically subsume Mr Connolly and Marlene, too.[24] Perhaps because Joyce's politics are closer than Marlene's to Churchill's, critics have been reluctant to recognise that 'Joyce's repetition of leftist truisms is not all that different from Marlene's continual invocation of right-wing rhetoric', in the words of Janet E. Gardner, a welcome exception to this reluctance.[25] These critics acknowledge Joyce's sacrifice in raising Marlene's child, which worsens her privation and precipitates her miscarriage and consequent barrenness. But they have been slower to see Joyce as a suspect mother who casually calls Angie 'stupid' and 'a big lump' and reacts disproportionately to the girl's refusal to come in from the garden: 'Fucking rotten little cunt. You can stay there and die'.[26]

Far from using Joyce to 'embod[y] the socialist feminist response to Marlene's bourgeois feminist stance' (as one critic asserts),[27] Churchill pitches Joyce and Marlene in an insoluble opposition that mimics Thatcher's intransigence and the uncompromising leftist positions that helped cement her first majority victory in 1979. Class exploitation has of course facilitated Marlene's ascent on the corporate ladder: she uses not only her sister, who provides unpaid childrearing, but also the typists, clerks, and secretaries whose own typically female and non-unionised labour she sells to corporate clients. But Joyce – whose views Marlene may justifiably see as parroting their father's – stops short of this insight about the entanglement of class and gender, and she, like her sister, prefers a crude class warfare she expresses as hatred for the women whose houses she cleans: 'the cows I work for and their dirty dishes with blanquette of fucking veau'.[28] Her unsisterly stance is Manichean, as an exchange with Marlene makes clear:

> **Joyce** . . . nothing's changed and it won't with them in.
>
> **Marlene** Them, them. / Us and them?
>
> **Joyce** And you're one of them.
>
> **Marlene** And you're us, wonderful us, and Angie's us / and Mum and Dad's us.
>
> **Joyce** Yes, that's right, and you're them.[29]

Joyce shares Marlene's view of exploiters and exploited locked in a symbiotic discord. And her professed politics is not one of rethought social relations like Abiezer Cobbe's in Churchill's *Light Shining in Buckinghamshire* but a passive resentment over her own exploitation. In *Crimes*, the dystopian teleplay that Churchill wrote for the BBC between drafts of *Top Girls*, the psychopathic protagonist Jane Banks explains that 'I didn't want to be frightened. I wanted to be frightening'.[30] Borrowing Angie's last word in *Top Girls*, Jane thus neatly summarises the options that Joyce and Marlene alike see before them. They bequeath this worldview to Angie, on whose worth they agree; she betrays their influence when she celebrates Marlene as special precisely because '[m]y mother hates her'.[31] Each is a product of her times. It is no accident that Jane Banks, who appears in the year 2000, tells us in her opening monologue that she was born in 1982, the year of *Top Girls*' premiere.

Trevor R. Griffiths has identified Churchill's fondness, apparent in *Top Girls*, for 'bring[ing] two or more discursive structures into collision, trapping her audiences into working out the nature of the pressures and events that are shaping her characters' predicaments and reactions'.[32]

And the formal innovation of placing Marlene and Joyce's discursive collision at the play's end intensifies its loaded irresolution. ('Goodnight. Joyce –', Marlene begins. But Joyce interrupts: 'No, pet. Sorry'.[33]) Audience members are left to imagine a world that escapes the false binary of frightened and frightening encouraged in Thatcher's Britain. 'I quite deliberately left a hole in the play rather than giving people a model of what they could be like', Churchill explained, even as she suggested that, if the action were to continue, Angie might 'get a job as a bricklayer in a feminist collective'.[34] Churchill's facetious suggestion articulates a possibility which *Top Girls* delimits only in the negative space of its deliberate hole. Joyce's politics could hold promise if she were less 'limited and bad tempered' – the assessment is Churchill's own[35] – and if it could make room for a feminism based on broader political, economic, and social equality rather than the individual self-interest which Marlene promotes. But context circumscribes achievement.

For the same reason, it is difficult to imagine Marlene's promotion over Mr Kidd if we doubt Nell's claim – however sexist its formulation – that 'Marlene's got far more balls than Howard'.[36] Churchill wrote the play while thinking about female barristers, whose industry culture compels them to imitate male colleagues as a minimum precondition for success.[37] It is worth remembering that the professional theatre also clung to its sexist traditions, especially when Churchill entered it in the early 1960s. A letter in the archives of the BBC records the playwright's agent, Peggy Ramsay, lauding her play *Lovesick* for having abandoned its writer's 'feminine delicacy' (presumably because of the play's cavalcade of sexual quirks and its male protagonist, Hodge). '[T]his play could very easily have been written by a man', Ramsay wrote to the director John Tydeman, who ultimately directed it and six more of Churchill's radio plays.[38] The agent intended high praise. She had accepted Churchill to her roster in February 1961, when Churchill was only twenty-two and before the agency had consolidated its position as the most formidable in Britain.[39] The same year, the playwright married David Harter, and the next decade would bring three children and multiple miscarriages. Yet Ramsay – who unabashedly preferred male clients – regarded Churchill and her fellow pioneer Ann Jellicoe as 'honorary men'.[40] She ignored the unique material challenges they faced, engendered more often by culture than biology. Another detail from the archive tells: while *Lovesick* was ultimately broadcast on 8 April 1967, the delivery of its final draft was delayed when the playwright's sons contracted mumps.[41]

Churchill, in other words, experienced firsthand how other women could work to maintain a masculinist status quo, even as she broke important barriers on their behalf: she became the first female resident writer in the Royal Court's history, for example, after her appointment by Oscar Lewenstein in 1974. But unlike Marlene she used her success to combat the biases of her industry rather than acquiesce to its default interests. And therefore she persisted in her experimentation with feminist forms – an experimentation galvanised by *Vinegar Tom*, her collaboration with the feminist collective Monstrous Regiment. '[M]y whole concept of what plays might be is from plays written by men', the playwright attested, identifying 'the "maleness" of the traditional structure of plays, with conflict and building in a certain way to a climax'.[42] Hence *Vinegar Tom*'s fractured narrative arc, with its final-scene shift to the music hall where its cross-dressed performers lampoon misogyny in song and dance and tops and tails. And hence the upset chronology of *Top Girls*, which narrows from its transhistorical dinner party to its pithy prophecy about women's frightening future: a rebuke not only to those like Marlene and Thatcher but also, we might say, to those like Ramsay, who judged the play inferior to Churchill's all-male *Softcops* and felt that *Vinegar Tom*'s women seemed like lesbians – not, one assumes, a note of praise.[43]

Faced with *Top Girls*, Stafford-Clark wrote in his diary: 'Structure difficult . . . how do we kn[ow] it's a y[ea]r earlier? Pity Angie's end: "She's not going to m[a]k[e] it" isn't at the end'.[44] It would be easy to fault him for initially preferring a chronological trajectory that Churchill herself dismissed as masculinist. In fact, the playwright found a remarkably sympathetic reader in her male director, whose journals reveal his commitment to first understanding and then theatrically realising her feminist vision. Preparing for rehearsals, he grappled with the dialogue, which contrary to previous reports was already overlapped in Churchill's script.[45] He considered myriad ways to double the sixteen roles in order to cover them with a cast of seven, and he puzzled over whether Lady Nijo should be represented by an Asian actor such as Megumi Shimanuki or self-consciously presented by the blonde Lindsay Duncan, his ultimate choice to play Nijo and Win. He auditioned scores of actors, including both Miriam Margolyes and Julie Covington from *Cloud Nine* as well as Judy Davis, then at the Court performing in Terry Johnston's *Insignificance*. After rehearsals began on 19 July, he helped Churchill to refine her script. For instance, she devised a new opening moment rather than plunging the audience immediately into the dinner party with Isabella's line 'I sent for my sister Hennie to come and join me'.[46] And she tightened Act 1, eliminating much of Joan's Latin recitation and all of Nijo's story of meeting the Emperor again later in her life. The director and cast calibrated the volume of the act's intricately entwined dialogue in order to direct the audience's attention more effectively as the scene progressed. According to Lesley Manville – cast as Patient Griselda, Nell, and a young job-seeker called Jeanine – it was 'a technical nightmare'. But '[i]t was also very bonding', leaving some of the women friends for life.[47] The only unworkable discord arose between Lynn Dearth, cast as Marlene, and Stafford-Clark, who drafted the actor a letter on 14 August, near the end of the play's four-week rehearsal process: 'I cannot agree that some minor criticisms about certain specific areas of your performance in the play constitute fundamental disagreement. . . . C[aryl] and I both hope . . . we can start work on Monday in a state in which we're both as free from tension as possible'.[48]

Days later, he replaced her with Gwen Taylor – at forty-three, the veteran of the cast, although she played the younger sister to Deborah Findlay's Joyce – who stepped into the demanding role even as the show was set to open. Churchill had lost a lead actor at the very end of the rehearsal process for *Owners*, too, a decade before, when Stephanie Bidmead had inherited the role of Marion (Marlene's acquisitive precursor) from an indisposed Jill Bennett. But whereas Bidmead struggled with the role, Taylor joined the *Top Girls* ensemble seamlessly, as audio tapes from the 1982 production attest. Due to the casting change, the first preview was delayed until 23 August, and the production opened five days later, when Stafford-Clark's diary records this judgement: 'Best play I've ever directed'.[49] Yet *Top Girls* played to only 65 per cent of capacity, and critics responded with befuddlement. Praise fell on the cast, which also included Selina Cadell, Lou Wakefield, and Carole Hayman (a member, too, of the *Light Shining in Buckinghamshire* cast some years earlier). But the *Telegraph* and *Times Literary Supplement* impugned the play's structure, declaring it 'inchoate' and 'untidy'.[50] '[C]larity could be achieved by more straight forward story-telling', pronounced *The Times*, as if Churchill were not posing a challenge to linear development but instead were uncertain that Monday follows Sunday.[51] There were exceptions, in whose praise we also see signs of the times: the *Observer*'s Robert Cushman lauded the play but condescended to wonder how the director felt at rehearsals, surrounded by all those women.[52] Universal acclaim in London would eventually arrive, but it would be delayed until the play returned to the Royal Court in January 1983, after a successful New York run: a transatlantic crossing from criticism to canonisation taken by *Cloud Nine*, too, similarly reprised after a rhapsodic response stateside.

When the British production of *Top Girls* transferred to New York – it began previews at Joseph Papp's Public Theater on 21 December 1982 and opened on 29 December – it was revisiting a country that had in some sense inspired it. In 1979, on a trip to Massachusetts for a student production of *Vinegar Tom*, Churchill had been struck by how young American women perceived the success of female executives as an index of feminist achievement.[53] Her bewilderment at this phenomenon spawned Marlene, who joined the cast of characters (such as Lady Nijo and Dull Gret) on whom Churchill had been working since her discussions with Monstrous Regiment. America therefore looms portentously in *Top Girls*: Marlene boasts of her American vacation and endorses Ronald Reagan; Win praises the American way of life; and Angie, idolising Marlene, preserves her Grand Canyon postcard and baldly announces that 'I want to be American'.[54] Clearly the play resonated in New York, where it opened to capacity business and almost universally terrific reviews. (The exception was Frank Rich of the *New York Times*, who found it 'fascinating' but disliked the deliberate hole left between Marlene and

Joyce. 'Even in England, one assumes, not every woman must be either an iron maiden or a downtrodden serf', he wrote.[55]) Since the British actors appeared as part of an Equity exchange, the American dates were strictly limited; as the show played, Papp and Stafford-Clark cast an American company that began work on 24 January 1983 and opened on 24 February.[56] (Churchill herself conducted rehearsals for the week that Stafford-Clark was needed in London to prepare the show's Royal Court reprise.) But this second iteration underperformed, playing to 55 per cent of box office capacity, and drew more muted praise. The British cast was considered stronger and more cohesive; the American cast was deemed unbalanced by the blazing performance of Linda Hunt as Pope Joan and Louise – a performance much missed during Hunt's periodic absences from New York (once for a full two weeks), to do film work as her contract allowed.

The play won Best Play and Best Ensemble Obies for both casts in 1983 – the award committee's definition of 'ensemble' unusually expanded to include Stafford-Clark. And the next two years would see multiple regional productions in the United States as well as productions and translations worldwide: in Australia, Denmark, Finland, Greece, Holland, Japan, New Zealand, Norway, Sweden, Switzerland, West Germany, Yugoslavia, etc.[57] In the years since, it has been Churchill's most revived play, with major London productions in 1991, 2002, and 2011, and many more regionally. It received a Broadway revival in 2008, directed by James Macdonald and starring a cast including Mary Beth Hurt, who (according to Stafford-Clark's diary) had been considered for the play twenty-five years earlier. It is tempting to see the play's success in various temporal and geographic locations as testimony to its universal message. But we also remember that each production of *Top Girls* conveys its particular insights and unique resonances. In 1982, when Angie's friend Kit declared her desire to be a nuclear physicist, its significance surely loomed larger. In 2008, the name of Act 1's restaurant was not 'La Prima Donna' but 'La Casa Blanca' – an unsubtle nod to Hillary Clinton, whose historical primary race with Barack Obama was being fought even as the show opened on 7 May. On the occasion of Stafford-Clark's first revival of the play in 1991, he had noted that:

> [i]f I were to revive the play again, whether or not I intended to make certain changes to the production, the intervening years would change the play, as the context would change. But the dilemma that's posed in the final scene between Joyce and Marlene . . . is as pertinent today as it was ten years ago. I imagine that dilemma won't go away.[58]

His remark gained credence after he revived the play again in 2011. In the hindsight of nearly thirty years, Marlene appeared more clearly as a historical figure herself, her shoulder pads as much a vestiary relic as Patient Griselda's hennin. More fruitfully, then, we might look to these varied productions to see how the seemingly transhistorical oppression of women is crosshatched with historically contingent concerns, highlighted differently in every performance context.

This crosshatching is the technique, and indeed the meaning, of *Top Girls*' bravura first act, which consciously or unwittingly recalls Judy Chicago's landmark art installation from 1979, 'The Dinner Party'. In it, a triangular table is set for thirty-nine famous women, each represented by her name (embroidered on the table runner) and a complement of cutlery, glass, napkin, and plate.[59] Both works collapse spatio-temporal boundaries, drawing guests from throughout history and across the globe: the Japanese Nijo, for example, or Egypt's Hypatia, the mathematician and philosopher for whom Chicago sets a place at the table. And both works erase the distinction between real and represented by including historical guests alongside fictional figures, such as Churchill's Griselda or Chicago's Kali, the Hindu goddess. Differences outnumber similarities, however. Whereas Chicago's women are absent and thus silent, Churchill's are raucously present, more like Trimalchio's in *Satyricon*. They speak on top of one another; they drink to excess; they eat the meals that have been prepared off stage (a fake steak for Hayman's Gret, production records reveal, owing to the actor's vegetarianism). Leitmotifs emerge, of course: dead lovers, lost children, and a socially unsanctioned ambition that takes Marlene to America, Joan to Rome, Gret to Hell. But whereas Chicago's installation placidly equates the women in neatly organised place settings, essentially reducing each to a vulvic plate,

Churchill's play demonstrates as much subjective difference and intrasexual discord as harmony, especially as her dinner guests jockey for the audience and Marlene's attention.

The art installation rests on its 'Heritage Floor' comprised of 999 tiles, each dedicated to an additional woman: these include both Pope Joan and Isabella Bird, for instance. And thus Chicago visually represents how a foundation laid by others can support women's accomplishment. A tougher thinker, Churchill recognises that this accomplishment may be bought at a larger cost to feminism. However extraordinary her cross-dressed achievement, for example, Joan affirms the sexism of the office when she is elevated to pope, and her alienation from her own body provokes her failure to recognise her own pregnancy. Thus Isabella's retort that 'I always travelled as a lady and I repudiated strongly any suggestion in the press that I was other than feminine' unwittingly endorses rather than rebukes Joan's patriarchal politics. (Marlene's assent is both comical and pathetic: 'I don't wear trousers to the office. I could but I don't'.[60]) Lady Nijo casually attests to her era's misogyny – 'they beat their women across the loins so they'll have sons and not daughters'[61] – but she does not challenge it. And, indeed, she affirms her inferiority to the Emperor to whom she was gifted at fourteen (he discards her) and to her gift-giving father. When Marlene insists that Nijo was raped by the Emperor, her judgement seems surely correct. But it also indexes her failure to understand the different contexts that have shaped each woman's unique experience of patriarchy, for Nijo's reply – 'of course not, Marlene, I belonged to him' – is disturbing but not inaccurate.[62] By bringing the women together, Churchill highlights the gaps among them, emphasised, too, in their frequent failure to listen and their sometimes competitive or dismissive responses when they do. When Isabella condemns the 'barbaric practices in the east', for instance, her judgement complements Nijo's assessment of Christians, whom she considers 'Barbarians'.[63]

The act also indexes a larger failure. Situating herself at the end of a long line of female overachievers, Marlene reads their experience as a narrative progression, with her rise to managing director its apotheosis.[64] But the play, by formally refusing a teleological structure, contradicts not only her egocentrism but also her view of history. Marlene may seem to express a feminist impulse in bringing the women together and encouraging sororal bonding. But, finally, her accomplishment as managing director is not feminist by Churchill's definition: Marlene stands not on women's shoulders but on their backs. And thus she finds a disturbing fit with her guests. They have taken more challenging roads than they might have, to be sure, and they have impressively navigated survival under an oppressive patriarchy. But they have done so by absenting themselves (as Nijo does when she becomes a wandering nun), surrendering (as the servile and rewarded Griselda does), or just joining in (as Joan does with her elevation to pope or, in the telling Italian, *papa*). Marlene's choice from this menu is clear. It finds a metonym when she orders dessert: 'I'd like profiteroles because they're disgusting', she tells the mute waitress, comically adumbrating her finally misogynist careerism, reliant entirely on having more balls than her competitors.[65] Churchill implies that Marlene may suffer for her capitulation as her dining companions have suffered for theirs: none more than Joan, stoned when her duplicity is uncovered after her ill-timed labour during a papal procession. Far from emphasising that they've 'come a long way' as Marlene claims, then, Churchill instead questions a liberal feminist detour that looks a lot like a sexist retrenchment.

As Linda Fitzsimmons has highlighted, one voice emerges from the cacophony to offer an alternative vision.[66] Dull Gret's dialogue is at first mostly limited to blunt grunts interjected into the interwoven dialogue of her dining companions: '[p]ig', she replies to Isabella's remark about horsemanship; '[s]ad', she concurs when Nijo and Joan and Isabella and even Marlene each admits to thinking or wishing that her life is over.[67] But when Gret begins a lengthy monologue about her assault on Hell, the other women uncharacteristically listen up:

> **Gret** I'd had enough, I was mad, I hate the bastards. I come out my front door that morning and shout till my neighbours come out and I said, 'Come on, we're going where the evil come from and pay the bastards out'. And they all come out just as they was / from baking or washing in their

Nijo All the ladies come.

Gret aprons, and we push down the street and the ground opens up and we go through a big mouth into a street just like ours but in hell. I've got a sword in my hand from somewhere and I fill a basket with gold cups they drink out of down there. You just keep running on and fighting / you didn't stop for nothing. Oh we give them devils such a beating.[68]

No acquiescence for Gret. She acts for herself, of course, madder than hell on behalf of the many children she has lost, but she significantly fights alongside others, too, who leave their baking and washing to adopt a revolutionary cause that stops for nothing and – with its vision of women fighting alongside one another in a collective endeavour – looks like feminism. Some critics have seen this feminist action as parodic, recognising that Bruegel's painting mocks a greedy shrew who 'could plunder in front of hell and return unscathed' in the Flemish proverb.[69] But others have recognised that Churchill rewrites a male myth. Bruegel's Gret, like Chaucer's Griselda, is 'a man's creation, as you see' – in the words of *Cloud Nine*'s Betty, who similarly finds that 'what men want is what I want to be'.[70] Churchill, in an act of feminist re-visioning, invents a Gret of her own whose intervention in the underworld models possible interventions on earth: Gret pointedly likens hell to 'the village where I come from'.[71] Her story of resistance seems to galvanise its audience. Nijo had previously joined with Lady Mashimizu and all the ladies to ambush the Emperor after he violated court custom and allowed his attendants to beat his concubines. She here revisits that action while rooting for an even more ambitious warrior, her dialogue overlapping Gret's not in competition or contradiction but in concert. 'All the ladies come', she summarises approvingly. 'Take that, take that'.[72]

For now such spontaneous cooperative action is deferred. And this deferral is connected to the structural hole (and perspectival blind spot) that the third act will leave exposed. Whatever their experience of gender oppression, the dinner guests mimic Marlene by ignoring the concerns of class limned by their stories. Patient Griselda tells a tale of hideous exploitation that is finally about her peasant family's assent to whatever the marquis's noblesse obliges. After Isabella piques Nijo with her comment on the east's barbaric practices, she clarifies that she meant to rebuke only the 'lower classes'. (About them, Nijo responds, 'I wouldn't know'.[73]) It is no accident that Churchill sets the garrulous talk of her dinner guests against the unceasing labour of the waitress, who dispenses Frascati and brandy, Waldorf salads and steaks, zabaglione and Marlene's disgusting profiteroles without speaking a single word or hearing one of thanks. When Stafford-Clark first read *Top Girls*, he worried in his journal that the 'Dinner for Dead' (as he called it) didn't sufficiently 'reverberate thru the play'.[74] But, as he later understood, the waitress – in her usual reliable and silent way – provides the pivotal link. In her unsung labour, she leads us into the second act and the agency where work is sold. There we hear of men interviewing for the higher-flying assignments but see only female job-seekers: Jeanine, advised to remove her wedding ring at interviews; Louise, looking to secure belated recognition by abandoning her sexist employer; Shona, whose undented confidence as she recounts sales trips in her Porsche is revealed as a fraud, her impersonation of masculine success a failure. And the waitress leads us, too, to the third act's kitchen, that site of so much unpaid female labour and the considered setting of Joyce and Marlene's final confrontation.[75]

Stafford-Clark made manifest the ties between *Top Girls*' first and later acts through his skilled use of doubling. The audience's first experience of the play's women – substantial, since the first act typically lasts forty minutes – haunts their reappearance in different guises. For example, when Lady Nijo lauds Marlene for being promoted '[o]ver all the women you work with. And the men', she instigates a hierarchical and competitive discourse that will predominate at the agency itself, where Marlene encourages Jeanine to be 'in at the top with new girls coming in underneath you' and where Win will declare one of Nell's suitors 'beaten'.[76] In all three of Stafford-Clark's productions, audiences would have recognised Win as played by the same actor as Lady Nijo. And just as Nijo's privileged ascent as the Emperor's concubine was arrested, so too the ironically named Win will find no upward room in the Top Girls hierarchy. 'Marlene's filled it up', she commiserates with

Nell, whom we recognise as the actor who had played Griselda.[77] We see the waitress, too, now trying to bluff her way to class transit as Shona. Pope Joan reappears as Louise, who thinks she 'pass[es] as a man' at an office where she is the only woman – '[a]part from the girls', she clarifies, delimiting the corral that keeps clerical help separate from management. She now seeks new work at an agency that enshrines the same cute diminishment in its very name, her resentful rationale betraying the fact that she hasn't passed as a man at all: 'I've seen young men who I trained go on, in my own company or elsewhere, to higher things. . . . They will notice me when I go'.[78] Dull Gret, meanwhile, reappears as the inarticulate Angie, perhaps harbouring some revolutionary potential of her own as a feminist bricklayer or in some other capacity left unrepresented in the play's open ending.

The play's open-endedness is foreshadowed in Act 1, which puts the play's formal innovations on display all at once. It showcases Churchill's use of overlapping dialogue – a now-ubiquitous technique that she has solid claim to inventing – governed by her script's slashes (when a new speech begins as the previous speech continues) and asterisks (when a third speech begins simultaneously). It showcases her radical use of time, which here unlooses women from history. Joan, the probably apocryphal ninth-century pope, ends the act by reciting from Lucretius' *De rerum natura*, a pre-Christian poem not widely known until the fifteenth century and one which, Stephen Greenblatt's *The Swerve* has argued, made modernity possible. As Joan recites, Nijo and Isabella join in:

> **Joan** O miseras / hominum mentis, o pectora caeca!*
>
> **Isabella** Oh miseras!
>
> **Nijo** * Pectora caeca.[79]

'O wretched minds of men, O poor blind hearts!', they intone, as Joan recites a thematically resonant passage which extols the pleasure of hearing another's miseries. '[T]o see what ills we're spared is sweet', Lucretius wrote.[80] Marlene has recapitulated these ills already, posing a non sequitur exclamation – 'Oh God, why are we all so miserable?'[81] – whose chance theological enquiry papa cannot answer. Joan's speech falters. It concludes inconclusively – 'nos in luce timemus something terrorem'[82] – by invoking the inchoate fear (*timor*) and terror (*terrorem*) that even the enlightened (*in luce*) like Joan experience. Then she vomits in a corner. She says nothing more until she reappears as Louise or Angie or, in a future production, some other of *Top Girls*' women, still shadowed by a frightening patriarchy.

Churchill has insisted that the doubling in *Top Girls*, unlike in *Cloud Nine*, is insignificant; she wrote the play for a cast of sixteen.[83] But as Elaine Aston has argued, having only one actor remain stable throughout the play – Marlene – anchors and amplifies her character's male-identified subject position. Thus she throws into relief the possibility for subversion that the other onstage bodies possess, with their shifting significations and slippery subjectivities.[84] Doubling serves as the feminist counter to straightforward identification just as the play's chronology works to undermine a male-oriented teleology. It is revealing, certainly, that no major production of the play has foregone doubling. And it is revealing, too, that new doublings have unearthed new possibilities. On Broadway, for instance, Martha Plimpton played both Pope Joan and Angie – each aspiring to a self-destructive model of masculine power but in over her head. Mary Beth Hurt played both the waitress and Louise, who complains of being overlooked and articulates her difference from a new kind of working woman. Thus Louise seemed to comment precisely on the waitress's situation in Act 1, her resonances amplified by the plain fact that Hurt was by the far the oldest cast member.

In Churchill's *Perfect Happiness*, directed by Tydeman and broadcast for radio on 30 September 1973, the housewife Felicity declares that 'I completely fail to understand why girls today are so unhappy' before bestowing unwanted advice on the younger Leanne and Margo, who work for her husband Geoffrey.[85] The exchange devolves into Felicity's accusations of adultery, answered by the younger women's story about murdering their boss, later revealed as a cruel joke. 'There's more to us Leanne than you might think', Felicity calls after them at the play's end, feeling herself wronged by their assumptions about her class privilege.[86] (Churchill specifies her upper-middle-class voice.) But there's more to them, too, which Felicity refuses to see. The play thus emphasises the class tensions that rive the female community, entangling class and gender concerns which, Churchill shows, can never be untangled. *Top Girls* does likewise. But in its radical form, it opens up into an uncharted space of possibility, daring its audiences to find their own models 'of what they could be like', as Churchill explained.[87] In Stafford-Clark's televised version of *Top Girls* for the BBC – first broadcast on 2 November 1991 – he interfered with this form, re-cutting the play so that we begin at the Top Girls agency before heading to the dinner party. There, the director showed Marlene and her guests expanding their party to make room for the woman who had served them; at the end of Act 1, they offer the waitress a drink. Such a scene intends to celebrate the pleasures of women's company: Churchill's final innovation, much lauded by feminist critics, is to have an all-female cast, as she had done for the first time in *Perfect Happiness* or in the 1974 teleplay *Turkish Delight*. But the inclusion of the waitress lent a sense of communitarian hope that we may not deserve, even decades later.

The Skriker

Marlene belongs in a company of Churchill characters whose buoyant theatricality, thrilling to watch, mitigates their alarming amorality: see, too, Jane Banks in *Crimes*, the rapacious Marion in *Owners*, the ruthless Scilla in *Serious Money*. In both theatricality and amorality, however, all pale next to the eponymous creature of Churchill's *The Skriker*. Over the course of the play, the Skriker – a '*shapeshifter and death portent*' – will transform itself into guises including an ill old woman, a petulant child, a thirty-something male suitor, and, most delightfully, a couch. But it appears first in its own fairy shape ('*ancient and damaged*') and home ('*Underworld*').[88] These pithy stage directions throw down a gauntlet to Churchill's designers, who are given no other aid in imagining the Skriker's milieu and appearance. And they throw into relief the torrential monologue the creature immediately unleashes: 'Heard her boast beast a roast beef eater, daughter could spin span spick and spun the lowest form of wheat straw into gold, raw into roar, golden lion and lyonesse under the sea, dungeonesse under the castle for bad mad sad adders and takers away. Never marry a king size well beloved'.[89] The torrent continues for another four pages, culminating in the Skriker's declaration that 'Ready or not here we come quick or dead of night night sleep tightarse', after which the scene transforms into a mental hospital, where a pregnant teen named Lily visits her friend Josie, recently committed after killing her baby.[90] But the creatures of the Underworld – where we had already seen Johnny Squarefoot, '*a giant riding on a piglike man, throwing stones*'[91] – are not left behind. For in the hospital there is also a Kelpie, '*part young man, part horse*'.[92] Alternately charmed and terrified, the girls find their lives penetrated by the Skriker, who magically grants their sometimes unwitting wishes. 'You'll begin to get a taste for it', the Skriker predicts.[93]

Formally, Churchill's play is a palimpsest. It overlays the recognisable world of contemporary London with a dark spirit-world of fairies and monsters drawn from English folklore. Each world has its language: the humans speak naturalistically; the spirits communicate only in dance, gesture, and (in an operatic Underworld banquet) song. Between the two realms moves the Skriker, the play's most linguistically and physically demanding role. In its human manifestations, it speaks intelligibly, even plainly. (Appearing to Lily as a tipsy American in a hotel bar, it admits: 'I'll level with you, ok? . . . I am an ancient fairy, I am hundreds of years old as you people would work it out'.[94]) Elsewhere, as in the opening monologue, it uses 'a damaged language', as Churchill explained in the invaluable 'Translator's Notes' she provided to the play's foreign adaptors: 'a bit like someone with schizophrenia or a stroke, where the sense is constantly interrupted by the other associations of words'.[95] This damaged language gets tangled in phonemic associations, so that *boast* begets *beast* begets *beef*, for instance, or *spin* gives rise to *span* and *spun*. (Meanwhile, that which is spun puns on the already punned bun said to be the *lowest form of wheat.*) More often its associations are semantic, so that the imperative *Never marry a king* leads the schizophrenic tongue to *king size* and to *size well*, as in the Suffolk nuclear power stations. Or the exclamation

Ready or not here we come – a hide-and-seek alert to London mortals about malevolent fairies on their way – leads to the exhortation *come quick*, to the Biblical opposition *quick or dead* (undone in the play, where both mingle), and then to the discomfiting idiom *dead of night*. These phrases join with the crude epithet *tightarse* to re-frame some childhood words of comfort (*night night* and *sleep tight*) as ironic warnings to those whom the Skriker will haunt.

As the opening juxtaposition of Underworld and mental hospital makes clear, spatial illogic governs. The physical setting, as the Skriker's summary of television technology would have it, is 'happening *there* and it's *here*'.[96] And the linguistic geography is at once intelligible and mislaid, whether relocating the Arthurian county of Lyonesse *under the sea* or associating the sea's Dungeness crabs with an earthly *dungeonesse under the castle*: home to *bad* or *mad adders* and thieves (i.e. *takers away*), and policed (as London's Tower is) by a *beef eater*. The Skriker's first appearance at the hospital occurs immediately after a trancelike moment in which Josie '*doesn't reply*', and therefore the creature is effectively associated with the girl's mentally unstable perception.[97] But even as it forces us to question what we see, it validates the insane evidence. After all, the spectators have perceived the Skriker, too – and even Johnny Squarefoot and the Kelpie, invisible to Josie – and thus are made to share the ambiguous state which the play likens to madness and from which it provides no release. We are trapped in the paradox that Lily uncovers when she wishes Josie wasn't mad. On one hand, Lily's wish causes the Skriker's disappearance and thus confirms Josie's madness. On the other hand, the efficacy of the wish confirms the Skriker's existence, and, after Lily declares that 'I wish you [i.e. Josie] were like before I wished', the fairy just as quickly returns.[98] The play's unsettling first-edition cover – a Man Ray photograph of Luisa Casati – therefore proves illustrative, its multiple exposures forcing us to reconcile contradictory perspectives that are discernible even in the play's most naturalistic moments. When Josie explains from her hospital room that the food's not healthy, for example, she equally describes the feast she is offered in the Underworld, consumed at treacherous cost.

In spite of its ricocheting connotations, the Skriker's speech conveys a denotative meaning. In the opening monologue, it situates itself as the magical gnome in the English folktale 'Tom Tit Tot': it performs magic for a king's bride, and thus it forestalls the sure death brought on by her mother, who boasted her daughter could spin straw into gold. Payback is sought, but punishment is averted when the daughter correctly names the gnome. ('Tom tit tot! Tomtom tiny tot blue tit tit! Out of her pinkle lippety loppety, out of her mouthtrap', the Skriker summarises.[99]) However, the story's apparently happy ending gets tangled in the telling: with tales of a dismembered woman who searches for her body parts, of a midwife who defies a fairy edict and puts magic ointment in her eyes, of forbidden food eaten ('bit a bite a bitter bread and he was crumbs'[100]). Mashing these and other plot points together, the Skriker demonstrates the thesis of Vladimir Propp's iconic *Morphology of the Folktale*: it makes apparent the structural similarities that undergird all folktales, with their wishes granted and punishments meted. And thus, too, the Skriker foretells its interactions with Josie and Lily, whose divergent ends – a horrifying survival for one, damnation for the other – limn the limited and decidedly grim conclusions that most folktales offer.

Skriker syntax snakes forward with non sequitur associations and snaps back to regain semantic sense. And thus it mimics the play's form more generally, which collapses not only stories but also time itself, just as *Top Girls*' first act had done. The plot seems to progress from the Skriker's first appearance in the hospital to Lily's final appearance in a distant future, before two of her descendants. But this teleology is undermined by the Skriker's (and Churchill's) storytelling, which contains all of its beginnings and endings already in the first monologue. That is, the play's events 'loop back upon themselves . . . in a continuous, complex chain of events', as one critic has written.[101] So the chopped-up hag invoked in the opening appears in person later, when Josie has been transported to the Underworld: 'Where's my head? where's my heart? where's my arm? where's my leg', she sings.[102] An early line – 'My mother she killed me and put me in pies' – perplexingly intrudes into the Skriker's speech but recurs with greater contextual sense when the Dead Child appears singing the same words, their 'me' now relocated onto a less puzzling speaker.[103] And the meal that causes a 'crumbling to dust' in the opening monologue proleptically tells Lily's end after she 'bit off more than she could choose. And she was dustbin'.[104] This report, however, precedes Lily's ingestion of the food, which is deferred past the final curtain: the play's last moments show her reaching toward the proffered morsel. Fairy time, we see again, operates on its own logic. Josie feels she has spent years in the Underworld only to find a mere minute has passed when she returns to earth; Lily loses generations of her life during an apparently brief Underworld trip, just like the groom whom the Skriker's first speech invokes, who expends a century in a second of experiential time. When the Skriker appears (in the guise of a man) to court Lily, Josie will attack it with a knife; bleeding, it will calmly remove its shirt to reveal an unsullied one underneath.

The Skriker, I am suggesting, contains all in its fairy maw without regard for either chronology or causality. Remember Tom Tit Tot or the Dead Child, each with an 'I' on the Skriker's tongue. In a similar way, the play incorporates Churchill's literary predecessors across genres and from high and low: the Skriker's deformed speech includes shards from John Dryden's 'Alexander's Feast', T.S. Eliot's *Four Quartets*, the Frank Loesser musical *Guys and Dolls*, and many others.[105] *The Skriker* also draws into orbit many of Churchill's own preoccupations at once. Environmental concerns loom as in earlier works: *Not Not Not Not Not Enough Oxygen* (with its suggestive title), for example, or *Lives of the Great Poisoners* (which elevates the inventor of refrigerant chlorofluorocarbons to its titular pantheon, alongside Medea and Hawley Crippen). In *The Skriker*, we learn that the creature's damage originates in environmental devastation. Whereas people used to honour fairies as nature spirits by 'leav[ing] cream in a sorcerer's apprentice' – a reference to the superstitious saucers left to forestall fairy fury – now '[t]hey poison me in my rivers of blood poisoning makes my arm swelter'.[106] (Elsewhere it is blunter, lamenting that '[y]ou people are killing me, do you know that?'[107]) In its characteristic way, *The Skriker* looks forward as well as back. As Sheila Rabillard has shown, the play foreshadows Churchill's libretto for Orlando Gough's climate change opera *We Turned on the Light*, premiered on 29 July 2006 at the Royal Albert Hall. One shows us Lily's descendant, a deformed girl who '*bellows wordless rage*' at her great-great-grandmother even while she is assured that 'they couldn't helpless'.[108] The other shows us a great-great-granddaughter confronting an ancestor, who explains our environmental heedlessness by arguing that '[i]t's hard to love people far away in time'.[109]

The play also incorporates its writer's interest in mental illness, looking forward to *Love and Information* (with telling subtitles such as 'Schizophrenic' or 'Shrink') and going backward to the earnest Dr Weber in *Schreber's Nervous Illness*, based on Daniel Paul Schreber's memoirs. (Directed by John Tydeman, the play was first broadcast for radio on 25 July 1972.) Mental illness gained metaphoric weight later that year, in *The Hospital at the Time of the Revolution*, in which the teenaged Françoise's disturbance cannot be uncoupled from Algeria's colonial rule: her illness manifests the psychic damage of racism, just as the Skriker's speech does when it channels Enoch Powell's notorious 'rivers of blood' into a seeping ecological devastation, a '[p]oison in the food chain saw massacre'.[110] When Françoise's parents visit their sins upon a blameless girl, meanwhile, they announce their kinship with *We Turned on the Light*'s great-great-grandmother, with *Fen*'s Angela, with *Far Away*'s Harper. For Churchill's child characters are traditionally prey, as they are for *The Skriker*'s Black Annis, Jennie Greenteeth, Nellie Longarms, and RawheadandBloodyBones, each legendary for harming the young. The Skriker's ultimate target is Lily's gestating child. 'Look at it floating in the dark with its pretty empty head upside down, not knowing what's waiting for it', she casually tells the pregnant teen, offering herself sardonically as a fairy godmother.[111] And thus *The Skriker* subsumes Churchill's trademark concerns with gender and class, too. Lily and Josie resemble *Top Girls*' Angie: working-class girls whose economic disempowerment renders them vulnerable to the dangerous glamour of Marlene or the Skriker. (The latter's curse on Josie, in turn, literalises a simile from *Light Shining in Buckinghamshire*, whose Cobbe declares that '[w]ords come out of my mouth like toads'.[112])

Josie spits toads after denying the Skriker's request for a kiss; Lily grants it and is instead made to spit pound coins. It is another trope of fairy tales, present in 'Frau Holle' by the Brothers Grimm or 'Les Fées' by Charles Perrault: the unkind action of one girl brings punishments; the kind action of another brings rewards.[113] Churchill's interest in such fairy tales – seemingly the play's oddest feature – in fact represents another longstanding preoccupation. When the Skriker offers Lily a ring in the hotel bar, for example, it reanimates an abandoned play from 1962, *The Magic Ring*, which concerned a fairy whose ring grants its wearer's wishes but brings malign consequences. (The project was rejected by a BBC script reader and went uncommissioned.[114]) Fairies flit around *Fen*, too, evidence of the fenpeople's superstitious ways but also given curious validation when, after her death, Val emerges into a hallucinatory dreamscape and meets a girl killed by a boggart's curse. A forbidden cowslip has been picked, she learns, a parallel to the warning issued to Josie in the Underworld: never pick a flower. One critic has therefore suggested that *The Skriker* inverts *Vinegar Tom*, approaching its themes of poverty, humiliation, and prejudice from an upside-down perspective. If *Vinegar Tom* equates to Thomas Shadwell's *The Lancashire Witches*, Claudia Barnett summarises, *The Skriker* is her *Macbeth*: it admits the supernatural witchery for which Churchill's earlier characters were falsely persecuted.[115]

The Skriker also takes up Churchill's decades-long preoccupation with expanding the boundaries of theatre, which she has attributed to her interest in the *Tanztheater* of German director Pina Bausch and the English troupes which Bausch inspired, including Second Stride.[116] In *Midday Sun* – premiered at ICA on 8 May 1984 – Churchill had collaborated with other artists on an installation of dialogue, music, and dance. She and Second Stride choreographer Ian Spink continued this fusion of expressive arts two years later, when together with other collaborators they recast Euripides' *Bacchae* as *A Mouthful of Birds*. They also made *Fugue*, a teleplay in which dialogue is almost completely superseded by movement, and whose performers included Sally Owen, *Midday Sun*'s choreographer. (It was broadcast on Channel Four on 26 June 1988.) In 1991, she, Owen, and Spink collaborated with Orlando Gough on *Lives of the Great Poisoners*, her most ambitious multimedia project to date. Spink would claim that these earlier dance-theatre works influenced *The Skriker*.[117] But if the play looks like an apotheosis – drawing into its capacious mouth not only Spink's movement and Judith Weir's music but also performers such as Philippe Giraudeau and Stephen Goff[118] – it is important to remember that Churchill had begun writing it many years earlier. As she has explained, *The Skriker* 'went on as a background thing between other projects, the thing I was always going back to and puzzling away at'.[119] And thus 'the thing' came to assimilate many of her themes and tropes (it even steals a line from *Icecream*[120]) and in the process transformed them into the Skriker's various shapes: the supernatural of *A Mouthful of Birds*, for instance, or, more obliquely, the world of finance from *Serious Money* (1987), whose City setting *The Skriker* initially shared.[121] When it finally appeared in 1994, the resulting play could be aptly described as 'both a logical consequence of her previous work and entirely, startlingly, *sui generis*'.[122]

Churchill had worked on the play for eight years before she sent it to Max Stafford-Clark, as she had done with *Top Girls*. His first impressions are recorded in his diary of 4 December 1991, which declared 'it's wonderful'[123] but fretted that it was unstageable: he wondered, for example, how toads and money could be made to come out of actors' mouths, how airborne fairies could be made to dance, how the Skriker could be made to shape-shift without using multiple actors (as at least two later productions would[124]). 'I think I just h[a]v[e] a failure of imagination', he worried, adding that 'Nick Hytner w[oul]d know how to do it'.[125] He and Churchill continued to discuss the play over several months, during which time his reservations intensified and their relationship became strained. She worried that he didn't appreciate the play, whose theatrical demands continued to puzzle him, and by early July 1992 his diary would record a judgement that validates this worry: he acknowledged its 'powerful theatrical vision' but wrote that 'I c[a]nnot really get into it . . . I find it obscure beyond belief'.[126] As a result, *The Skriker* wended away from the director's Out of Joint company (founded after he left the Royal Court) and to London's most prominent public theatre, the National – a somewhat ironic landing for Churchill's weirdest and most demanding play. There, in the Cottesloe Theatre, it would begin previews on 20 January 1994 in a production realised by a trio from *A Mouthful of Birds*: Les Waters directed, Annie Smart designed, Ian Spink choreographed.

The working method differed substantially. Whereas the earlier script was generated during a workshop, using the method I describe in the fourth chapter, *The Skriker* came to the process complete and underwent only minor revisions during rehearsals. (For example, Josie's name was changed from Cassie.[127]) These rehearsals, meanwhile, unfolded mostly in parallel studios: while Waters worked with the actors – Sandy McDade as Josie, Jacqueline Defferary as Lily – Spink worked with the dancers, including Giraudeau and Goff.[128] Moving between as the Skriker was Kathryn Hunter, whose acclaimed work with Theatre de Complicite would have prepared her for the Skriker's intense physical demands. When the show opened, Hunter's performance would be universally acclaimed as 'brilliant', 'mesmerising', 'a glowing tour de force'.[129] But most critics concurred that Churchill's wild imagination had gone unmatched by her other collaborators: Waters's direction was deemed 'too emotionally withdrawn', Spink's choreography 'risible', Smart's design (most damningly) 'mildly decorative'.[130] The worlds of the fairies and humans, it was thought, had been insufficiently synthesised. The reception was no doubt bruising for the playwright: the play was 'disproportionally important' to her; it had been allowed an unusually long rehearsal period, in which she was closely involved; and it was her first time at the National, which had an enormous success in the same season with Tom Stoppard's equally intellectually minded (though considerably less strange) *Arcadia*.[131]

Perhaps recognising *The Skriker*'s unrealised potential, the Public Theater planned a production with a different creative team led by director Mark Wing-Davey and designer Marina Draghici, whose work on Churchill's *Mad Forest* had earned Obie Awards for both in 1992. So *The Skriker* – now embodied by Jayne Atkinson and with Philip Seymour Hoffman in its fairy entourage – reappeared in another place and time, beginning previews on 26 April 1996 and opening on 15 May at the Public's Newman Theater, *Top Girls*' home over a decade earlier. Whereas Smart's set was almost minimalist, a sliding white box cleverly repurposed from scene to scene, Draghici's was all excess, its rococo aesthetic achieved with glittery trash gathered from the Public's cast and employees. Whereas Waters had de-emphasised the metaphor of mental illness, Wing-Davey amplified it, compelling his company to watch Frederick Wiseman's documentary about the insane, *Titicut Follies*, alongside their research in English folklore. (A rehearsal report from the show's stage manager notes that the film paled next to the 'total insanity' of the show's rehearsals.[132]) Like his London predecessors, however, Wing-Davey struggled with the play's demands. He had hoped to synthesise the human and fairy worlds by directing both himself – assisted by choreographer Sara Rudner, a former Twyla Tharp dancer – but by the end of rehearsals he was forced to split the work with assistants, who worked simultaneously in different rooms. Despite this improvised solution, early previews had to be cancelled. The show could not be finished on time.

When it did open, *The Skriker* sold robustly despite polarised reviews: exalted by some critics ('astonishing', declared the *New York Times*) and eviscerated by others ('far more numbing than "Springtime for Hitler"', countered the *Wall Street Journal*).[133] But because the Newman Theater was rented to the Gay and Lesbian Film Festival, slated to open on 6 June, *The Skriker* could not be extended despite box office interest. As a result, it played only four weeks, causing one disgruntled critic to bemoan that the play 'deserved better treatment' and another to note that 'I suspect that seldom has so much effort been put into a project that, from the outset, had no chance of extending or moving'.[134] Blame was placed on artistic director George C. Wolfe, who was producing the Public's first Churchill show since the death of Joseph Papp. (It would be the last during Wolfe's tenure: Churchill returned only with *Drunk Enough to Say I Love You?*, produced by his successor, Oskar Eustis.) In rehearsals, *The Skriker* had been undermined by temporal pressures of the theatre industry, exacerbated (as production records reveal) by several actors' chronic lateness. And after its delayed debut, it was undermined by the same pressures, an ironic fate for a play predicated on time's elasticity.

Exploring the play's shape-shifting form, I have so far avoided the question of what, exactly, *The Skriker* means. In compendia of fairies and folklore, we read of a creature wandering invisibly through Northern England: Shriker or Skriker, its graphemic variation just like those that govern Skriker speech.[135] The goblin is thus associated to a word from Lancashire dialect meaning 'complain', itself no doubt related to the Middle English word for 'shriek'.[136] We find this word used in both the history of theatre and the history of fairies. In the mediaeval Wakefield cycle, for example, Noah complains of his wife that '[f]or all if she stryke, / [y]it fast will she skryke', and in Spenser's *Faerie Queene*, the knight Calepine hears of yet another child under threat when a 'little babe did loudly scrike'.[137] The Skriker must relate in some way to the '*horrible shriek*' that punctuates the sound design and signifies Josie or Lily's movement from one world to another, even as (because of stage magic and *The Skriker*'s spatial disjunction) they don't really move.[138] Otherwise, the name, like the play, remains hard to pin down. Churchill herself would only admit that it is 'about damage – damage to nature and damage to people', an oft-quoted remark as specific and cryptic as her opening stage directions.[139]

Since Elin Diamond's terrific article 'Feeling Global', something like critical consensus has emerged around Diamond's central thesis: that the play gives monstrous shape to the forces of globalisation, to 'the awesome schizophrenic accumulation of energy [in] capitalism', as the French philosophers Gilles Deleuze and Félix Guattari characterised it.[140] According to this reading, the play's spatial and temporal illogic mimics the space-time compression which the geographer David Harvey has identified as central to late capitalism.[141] Everything has become commoditised, Harvey tells us, its value determined through market exchange in an economy of global capital flows, which might recall Lily's torrent of coins as well as her irritated throat. Capital may disappear in an instant (as Lily's does) or move, at the push of a button, from the Hong Kong Stock Exchange to Euronext. It's here and it's there. Thrumpins, brownies, and bogles, apparently from the past, make visible the shadowy economic forces that now seduce and oppress, forces which remain beyond our control and even apprehension. But Churchill makes us see the illusion-shattering underbelly, where the Skriker's frenzied party ('Your wealth, Josie, happy and gory', it toasts) will culminate in gloomy silence and with Josie on her knees, scrubbing the floor.[142] World and Underworld become coterminous as in Churchill's very first play, *Downstairs*, where the detested realm of the title cannot be kept at bay and intrudes on the snobbish upstairs family's lives. The lavish Underworld feast, meanwhile, is revealed as just another commodity in a globalised economy: perhaps shiny, actually hideous, probably toxic. 'Don't eat.

It's glamour', a ghost warns.[143] Global capitalism rests on the fairy tale of plenty for all, even as it co-opts us into doing its evil bidding, whether buying goods made by labour deadly to the environment and the workers or, in Josie's case, doing the killing herself while 'trying to keep the Skriker sated seated besotted with gobbets'.[144]

The benefit of this reading is that it helps us to locate the elusive *Skriker* alongside Churchill's other plays from its years of gestation. For instance, it explains the connection among *Fen*'s thematic emphases (on labour, on the environment) and its hallucinatory dreamscape. It makes visible *Serious Money*'s financial setting, which revisions to *The Skriker* had repressed to the play's unconscious. It dramatises a postmodern world like that in *Icecream* or *Hot Fudge*, where even killing can be packaged as a commodity: 'I like the kind of war we're having lately. I like snuff movies', the Skriker announces.[145] And, as in *Lives of the Great Poisoners*, it weaves a micropolitics of poisonous family relations into a macropolitics in which Mother Earth meets matricide. The problem with this reading is that it cannot possibly accommodate all of the Skriker's intoxicating weirdness, the promises of 'sleep slope slap' or threats of 'slut bitch slit' about which even Churchill's cheat sheet for translators says little.[146] As an argument, it tidily incorporates our inevitable mystification: there is no escape from the schizophrenic energy of capitalism. Doing so, however, it undermines *The Skriker*'s particular cunning. When Wing-Davey expressed his hope to make the play eighty per cent intelligible, he clarified that Churchill herself understood 'somewhat less' than all.[147] Facetious or not, the director tapped something essential in *The Skriker*, Churchill's most exhaustive and inexhaustible play. It works expressionistically, to be sure, giving form as it does to whatever unconscious drives or murky forces of history or ideology. But part of what it expresses must always elude understanding for its visceral impact to register.

Far Away

After *The Skriker* came a rare break from writing that lasted three years, roughly coincident with the period between Tony Blair's ascension as

Labour Party leader in July 1994 and his election to Prime Minister in May 1997. In a perspicacious article, Elaine Aston has explored this coincidence, suggesting that Blair's New Labour embrace of market capitalism may connect to Churchill's struggle, after *The Skriker*, to complete a state-of-the-nation play that she had promised to Stafford-Clark's Out of Joint company: *Britannia and the Bad Baby*, which he described as an 'epic and satirical piece for ten actors, dealing with "freedom"'.[148] A crisis of politics apparently occasioned a crisis of creativity. As the era seemed to portend the end for traditional leftist politics in Britain, so it undermined the traditional leftist playwriting we see in Churchill's *Light Shining in Buckinghamshire* or *Serious Money*, for example, with their debts to the great Marxist playwright Bertolt Brecht.[149] And thus *Britannia* faltered, with its similarly epic shape and Brechtian stagecraft. Strange, short plays began to emerge instead: the libretto for *Hotel*, the gnomic *This Is a Chair*, the self-destructing *Blue Heart*, all from 1997. Aston argues that these texts represent not only the working through of Churchill's writer's block but also her navigation of a new political landscape. *This Is a Chair*, for example, refigures the relationship between drama and politics as inscrutable, even absurd, with each scene's action bearing no relation to the Brechtian caption that frames it. ('**The Labour Party's Slide to the Right**' announces a scene in which Ted and John confront their sister Ann in her flat, causing her boyfriend to leap from the balcony.[150]) Churchill's search for a different mode of political engagement ultimately engendered an invigorated theatrical form fitted to twenty-first-century concerns. And a new chapter in Churchill's stagecraft was inaugurated with *Far Away*, premiered at the Royal Court's Theatre Upstairs on 24 November 2000.

The play comprises a triptych of short acts, each separated by several years. The first act dramatises a late-night conversation between a young girl, Joan, and the aunt, Harper, at whose house she is staying. Joan can't sleep; Harper assures her that '[i]t's the strange bed'.[151] We apprehend that Joan has recently arrived, but the reason remains a mystery as the economical, even taciturn dialogue continues. The girl eventually reveals that she has been outside, stepped in a pool of blood, and seen her uncle hitting people while herding them into a shed. But

Joan tells what she has seen as reluctantly as Harper explains it, each of them engaging in an evasive rhetoric that admits nothing inessential. Finally Harper will be forced to concede that Joan has 'found out something secret', and, 'trusting [her] with the truth now', she explains that the people were traitors.[152] 'I'm on the side of the people who are putting things right', she declares.[153] The play chills. Because of its flinty storytelling – like its characters it reveals nothing more than it has to – we are left uncertain about the conflict violently unfolding immediately outside the house. Its parties are identified only as 'us' and 'them', but without *Top Girls*' clear class distinctions and with no context given apart from Harper's dubious claim to righteousness. Thus, *Far Away* recalls Churchill's teleplay *The Judge's Wife* – first broadcast on the BBC on 2 October 1972 – in which the Judge's sister-in-law learns of two sides in perpetual social struggle: 'two camps, Barbara, mine and theirs. Either you are with, or you are against'.[154] With her similarly uncompromising rhetoric, Harper at once disciplines and seduces her niece into taking a position against 'them'. She chides that '[t]here might be things that are not your business when you're a visitor in someone else's house' and (less veiled) that 'sometimes you get bad children' who end up in lorries, but ultimately her assurance that traitors deserve punishment convinces the girl, keen to 'help uncle'.[155] (As the sadistic Headmaster in Churchill's *Softcops* puts it, terror 'makes us love our duty'.[156]) 'You're part of a big movement now to make things better', her aunt responds, even as she and Churchill remain mum on the scene's abiding mysteries, such as Joan's parents – themselves, one may imagine, beaten in a shed somewhere not so far away.[157]

The second act shifts to a millinery, where a now-adult Joan works on her 'first professional hat' alongside a co-worker, Todd; over the course of four scenes, their creations proceed from inciting design choices ('I'm starting with black') to completion, when they are '*enormous and preposterous*'.[158] But their workplace conversation, as pared-down as Harper and Joan's night-time chat, continues to traverse the play's political concerns. Eventually we learn that their product is contracted for 'parades' – one of which the audience witnesses in the act's fifth scene, which shows a '*procession of ragged, beaten, chained prisoners, each wearing a hat, on their way to execution*'.[159] 'It seems so sad to burn them with the bodies', Joan laments.[160] The shadowy politics of the first act, in which Harper engaged in a covert operation to transport detainees, give way to images of a terror state whose college graduates might find employment adorning any number of parades or show trials, broadcast on nightly television: another nod to *Softcops*, whose Pierre proposes '[d]ifferent coloured hats' for his model prisoners, on display in the Garden of Laws.[161] Meanwhile, Joan has moved from innocence to experience while perfecting her art, tracing a degraded *Künstlerroman* narrative. Elin Diamond has noted that *Far Away* is Churchill's only representation of artists (although we must discount the unproduced 1961 play *Portrait of an Artist*, about the death of a famous sculptor), and thus the playwright seems to implicate art in the state's spectacularised executions: it provides a temporary toxic glamour as in *The Skriker*'s Underworld.[162] Todd celebrates the 'joy' of his genre's ephemerality. 'You make beauty and it disappears, I love that', he says, precisely tracing the defining feature not of millinery but of performance itself – always evanescing as it recedes into memory, as I discuss in my fifth chapter.[163] 'It's like a metaphor for something or other', he summarises, minutes after the unmistakably metatheatrical parade of hatted prisoners.[164] Thus the hats are made to 'silently scream out the horror that results when aesthetics loses all concern for the material reality from which it works', as Una Chaudhuri has seen.[165]

The play's third act moves forward in time again, to an argument between Harper and Todd about the now all-encompassing battle outside. The first act's Manichean opposition – 'right' us *versus* 'traitor' them, with its delineated if unidentified sides – cedes to a war of the world in which Portuguese car salesmen might take sides against dentists or mosquitoes or the weather. As Harper and Todd bicker about the loyalties involved in this conflict – one in which Todd 'never liked cats' and Harper finds 'crocodiles are always in the wrong'[166] – they demonstrate the same unbending righteousness in which Harper had instructed Joan as a girl. But it is now rendered absurd in a conflict of perpetually shifting allegiances among ever more atomised and ill-defined groups: children under five, musicians, the Spanish. Harper and Todd bicker, too, about Joan, who despite Harper's imperative that '[y]ou don't go walking off in the middle of a war' has done just that.[167] In order to visit her now-husband, Joan has navigated on foot the world's internecine landscape, in which 'everything's been recruited, there were piles of bodies and if you stopped to find out there was one killed by coffee or one killed by pins, they were killed by heroin, petrol, chainsaws, hairspray, bleach, foxgloves, the smell was where we were burning the grass that wouldn't serve'.[168] Note the 'we', deployed as Joan stakes a claim against the apparently pacifist grass – one more hedge against the moral high ground claimed by 'our' side. Recounting her journey, Joan reveals the danger and yet the necessity of any action whatever in a Balkanised world of perpetual conflict. Both danger and necessity reveal themselves in *Far Away*'s final image, of Joan stepping into a river with murky allegiances: 'The water laps round your ankles in any case'.[169]

Churchill finished writing *Far Away* in 1999 and chose as its director Stephen Daldry, then the Artistic Director of the Royal Court. The decision caused further upset with Max Stafford-Clark, who had once reasoned that he could resign from the Court and start his Out of Joint company partly on the grounds that 'Caryl will g[i]v[e] me what she has anyway'.[170] Yet despite feeling 'pissed off and upset' about *Far Away*, Stafford-Clark ultimately responded with magnanimity, rationalising in his diary that 'someone as unremittingly inventive as Caryl needs to be reinvented by her director as well'.[171] Daldry might have been uniquely suited to this reinvention, especially if it was initiated three years earlier, as Aston has argued: *This Is a Chair* – premiered on 25 June 1997 at the Duke of York's – had been his first time directing Churchill's work. Three years later, Daldry and his artistic associates read and debated *Far Away*: a double bill with Harold Pinter's *Mountain Language* was considered; potential curtain-raisers or afterpieces discussed; Churchill's wish to stage the play in the smaller Theatre Upstairs rather than the main space questioned. Katie Mitchell, then one of the Court's Associate Directors, admitted that she would 'kill' to direct it: a thematically appropriate formulation, whether witting or not.[172] Mitchell saw the play as an 'insoluble' one that 'creates its own landscape' – an apt painterly image – while Stafford-Clark surmised that Churchill had 'developed her own response to a political agenda which she h[as] discovered she c[a]nnot effectively address any more'.[173]

As she had in *The Skriker*, Churchill had apprehended a changing political reality and devised a new dramatic landscape in order to reflect or even anticipate it. Therefore, when the playwright Simon Stephens declared *Far Away* the 'strongest theatrical response to 9/11', his formulation was felicitous however wrong chronologically: even as Churchill's play preceded the terrorist attack on the World Trade Center, she had astutely characterised the politics it quickened.[174] Old oppositions of left and right faltered in a world permeated by a shape-shifting fight against transmogrifying enemies. Soon the United States would be plunged into a 'war on terror' whose slippery rhetoric matched its askew aim. The administration of George W. Bush would launch its verbal salvoes against a stateless al-Qaeda, nineteen of whose members had executed the attacks in New York and Washington, even as America instead bombed the nation of Iraq, unconnected to 9/11 and indeed an erstwhile American ally by virtue of a shared animosity toward Iran, at once Iraq's longtime enemy and its bedfellow in Bush's infamous rhetorical construction 'the axis of evil'.

Such illogic suffuses *Far Away*, whose formal landscape captures with eerie precision the twenty-first century and its competing quandaries. In the season which I write, American Secretary of State John Kerry has praised a military coup for 'restoring democracy' in Egypt by deposing the country's first freely elected president.[175] And Bush's successor Barack Obama has waived a provision of American federal law in anticipation of arming select terrorist groups fighting a putatively shared enemy, the Syrian dictator Bashar al-Assad. We are not far away, it turns out, from a world in which unambiguous ethical dicta – 'crocodiles are always in the wrong', for instance – sit in an ambiguous ethical landscape whose 'enemies' elude precise identification. The names we give them are only provisionally accurate ('children under five' grow older) or mutually exclusive (a dentist might also be Bolivian), and, as we have seen again in Iraq or Syria, national and tribal and religious identifications confuse and negate one another even as their various insurgencies rage. Slippery identity categories, so crucial in defining a 'them' to oppose during wartime, implicate us in Harper's taunt to her niece: 'Maybe you don't know right from wrong yourself'.[176] Bombarded with rhetorical constructions about whom to fear – whether a shapeless al-Qaeda, mercurial leaders such as al-Assad, or 'Chilean soldiers' lurking upstream[177] – we experience the very affective states that *Far Away* interrogates. As a result, we become prey to other rhetorical constructions such as those that placate Joan, whether Harper's formulation 'I'm responsible for you' or synonymous assurances used to justify National Security Agency spying.[178]

When Stafford-Clark first read the play in December 1999, he had described it as an 'elliptical political fable', and thus he captured the play's formal challenges even as he declared himself 'relieved' not to be directing it.[179] For *Far Away*, with its disparate yet rhetorically connected three parts, represents a political problem of here-and-now urgency even as it emanates its title's fable aura. The apparent contradiction produces the play's signature disquiet, which Daldry honoured in the premiere production. Audiences were first confronted with an old-fashioned front cloth representing a cottage nestled in a pastoral landscape and augmented by the sounds of birds and streams. (The set and costumes were designed by Ian MacNeil, Daldry's then-partner; the sound, by Paul Arditti, working with Churchill for the fifth time.) But in light of the theatre's constrained space, the distant idyll was in fact disconcertingly close – and thus the play's spatial logic and titular irony imposed themselves immediately.[180] The curtain rose on Harper (played by Linda Bassett), lightly singing the nineteenth-century hymn 'There Is a Happy Land, Far Far Away' on MacNeil's spare and hard-to-date set, her song's putatively soothing qualities offset by the dark lighting (by designer Rick Fisher) and the restless Joan (Annabelle Seymour-Julien) with her resonant opening line: 'I can't sleep'.[181] Soon talk of cowering prisoners and spilled blood established the play's subjects, seemingly far away but in fact roosting close to home: insoluble conflicts and the violence they engender. These were thrown into chilling relief by Act 2's workplace banter as the older Joan (Katherine Tozer) and Todd (Kevin McKidd) made hats, their flirtation and kindnesses – as when they argued over who should take the nicest decorative beads – jarringly juxtaposed with the spectacularised atrocities they worked to serve.

Honouring Churchill's spare aesthetic in the play, Daldry and his designers conveyed its menace simply. A blackout followed Joan's question '[w]hy was uncle hitting them?', after which Harper calmly re-lit an onstage lamp.[182] A simple repetition of costumes cued the change of Joans. The sound of swarming bees accompanied the transition from Act 2 to 3. The prisoners processed quietly and sombrely, their membership drawn variously from a group of nearly thirty volunteers. (Churchill's text specifies only that '*five is too few and twenty better than ten. A hundred?*'[183]) At the play's conclusion, Daldry ensured that Tozer would strike an inconclusive note by rehearsing an additional line at the end of Joan's monologue, which he cut before the show opened. After she pronounced the play's final, iambic 'in any case', the front cloth crashed down as if its counterweights had been cut, an abrupt transition like those that end the first and second acts. 'The play just needed to be left hanging there', as Tozer put it.[184] With this suspended conclusion, Churchill left the audience to discern *Far Away*'s lessons. The play's box office success suggested hunger for the challenge: performed at the Royal Court twice nightly to meet demand, the play nonetheless sold out; it then transferred to the Albery Theatre in the West End on 18 January 2001, where it played for another eight weeks. The next year, the production was remounted at New York Theatre Workshop with a new cast: Frances McDormand as Harper, Chris Messina as Todd, Marin Ireland as the older Joan, and Alexa Eisenstein and Gina Rose alternating as the younger Joan. Opening on 1 November 2002, this run, too, sold out and extended, with Frances McDormand replaced on 27 December by Kathleen Chalfant, a gifted stage actor well known for her political engagement.

If the New York production intensified the play's menace, Daldry's adjustments helped: the theatre's fire curtain accommodated the pastoral painting, so its fall was deafening and swifter; Catherine Zuber's extravagant hats improved upon their predecessors, amplifying their silent screams. Extra-theatrical reasons mattered more. Between the London and New York premieres, the 9/11 attack had claimed almost 3,000 victims, and Bush had coined the phrases 'war on terror' and 'axis of evil' whose anxiety-inducing rhetoric *Far Away*'s had foretold.[185] (When Todd's boss at the hat factory addresses his labour complaints with the platitude '[t]hese things must be thought about', Churchill links its curious efficacy to the terrorised environment in which her characters live. After all, when Joan tells Todd in the same exchange that '[y]ou make me think in different ways', she offers a chilling reminder that her childhood made her think in different ways, too, its lessons discernible in her nonchalant hatmaking.[186]) In other words, the culture had caught up with Churchill's prophetic vision; as Simon Stephens would note, recent history had in fact transformed the play into social realism.[187] This transformation may also explain the play's reception, as mixed as *Top Girls'* had been. While some of the initial London reviews pronounced the play 'unmissable' and 'devastating', others found it 'less than convincing' and 'disappointing'.[188] But like the cat that Joan evokes in the first act – 'it gets in if the door's not properly shut. You think you've shut the door but it hasn't caught and she pushes it open in the night'[189] – the play wormed its way under the culture's skin, where like an anxious threat it restively lurks. *Far Away* is now one of Churchill's most celebrated plays, having received too many major productions to recount: among them, its Paris premiere in 2002 at Peter Brook's Théâtre des Bouffes du Nord, starring *The Skriker's* Kathryn Hunter, and a 2004 production at the Sheffield Crucible, starring Hunter's *Skriker* castmate Jacqueline Defferary.

One production, at the Odyssey Theatre Ensemble in Los Angeles in 2003, specified the play's setting as 'Somewhere in America' in its programme.[190] Another, at the Project Arts Centre, Dublin in 2004, costumed its hatted prisoners in the orange jumpsuits the world now associates with Guantanamo Bay's 'non-compliant' detainees.[191] Such directorial choices testify to a desire for clear answers – 'a desperate longing for the absolute', as Pope Joan had put it in *Top Girls*[192] – that the play everywhere frustrates. In earlier plays, Churchill had prefigured some of her later themes. From *The Ants*, first broadcast on BBC Radio 3 on 27 November 1962, we learn that 'there's always [a war] somewhere' as the play's child protagonist learns to kill what he has previously loved: the 'horrid self-righteous' ants (in his grandfather's description) that will reappear in *Far Away* as one of the groups to be opposed, along with Moroccans.[193] From *Seagulls*, a 1978 play premiered only in 2002, we learn that dolphins can be trained as weapons of war, anticipating the weaponised pigs and deer and even butterflies that *Far Away* describes in its third act. From *Crimes*, first broadcast on 13 April 1982, we learn that 95 per cent of the future population has been imprisoned. For example, the elderly Mrs Drake, charged under the eerily prophetic Prevention of Terrorism Act for disobeying a police officer, conjures a mental image that *Far Away*'s hatted prisoners would later embody. But the politics of each of these earlier plays is comparatively simple. In *The Judge's Wife*, the storytelling logic is circular and closed, obsessively returning to the central scene of Michael Warren shooting the unnamed Judge and to its us *versus* them theme: 'Your violence will be met by violence and we are stronger than you', the Judge declares.[194] In *Far Away*, by contrast, the politics and plotting are more complex. They may be marked by the same senselessly repetitive violence: the final scene of the second act shows Todd and Joan beginning new hats for new condemned. But the play's tripartite structure (three acts, three speaking roles) hedges against the binary rhetoric to which *The Ants* and *Crimes* and Todd and Joan submit, and it resists, too, the easy impulse to see state malfeasance at the root of our anxious global state, as directors in Los Angeles and Dublin did.

The play chastises this urge to find a blameworthy enemy: Churchill described Joan as 'trying to do the right thing' and instructed Bassett to make Harper more sympathetic.[195] Instead, it re-engages its audiences in a universal citizenry menaced by state and non-state terror alike, numbed into unfeeling by the kind of trauma that Todd describes: 'I've worked in abattoirs stunning pigs and musicians and by the end of the day your back aches and all you can see when you shut your eyes is people hanging upside down by their feet'.[196] In Daldry's production, the second-act prisoners cut across the divisions on which conflict relies. They were both young and old, both male and female, both black and white. Their chains forced the kind of community which theatre, less coercive, might encourage, but which life during wartime inhibits. ('I know a cat up the road', Todd claims, about to mount a feline defence. But Harper scolds him: 'No, you must be careful of that'.[197]) Katherine Tozer – who had previously played *Top Girls*' Griselda in a 2000 production of *Top Girls* – has testified that *Far Away* was '[d]evastating' and took a toll, with its 'gruelling message' and 'terrifyingly light style of playing'.[198] But so too has her castmate Linda Bassett testified to a balm against *Far Away*'s terrors: at the Albery Theatre, the cast forewent individual dressing rooms in favour of a shared space. 'The world was so bleak that we had to look after one another', she told me.[199] The cast thus mimicked Churchill's gesture of bringing her audiences together in the small Theatre Upstairs, each spectator inevitably touching others in a way unlikely Downstairs, with its plush fixed seating. To be sure, Churchill exposes the theatre's potential to capitulate, which we have seen in the Nuremberg Rally, the Moscow Show Trials, or Act 2's hat parade. But she also demonstrates its reparative potential, on display when box office proceeds were donated to the Stop the War Coalition (4 November 2000 at the Royal Court) or to the Inad and Al-Kasaba Theatres in the West Bank (22 February 2001 at the Albery).[200] For art, Churchill knows, is never divorced from the world it seeks to reflect, the world it seeks to shape. Perverse confirmation of this insight arrived in a scene as chillingly absurd as *Far Away*. In 2002, months after Al-Kasaba hosted the Nobel Prize-winning playwright Wole Soyinka, the theatre's offices were ransacked by the Israeli army.[201]

In 1960, in one of the few explicit statements she has given about her aesthetics, Churchill noted that writers 'see the world in a mess and don't know how to do anything about it. We mistrust causes and abstract words spelt with capital letters'. But even though playwrights 'don't give answers', she stresses, they can and must 'ask questions':

> We need to find new questions, which may help us answer the old ones or make them unimportant, and this means new subjects and new form. . . . The imagination needn't have the same limits as factual knowledge; we may make cautious philosophical and scientific statements, but we do not have to feel, visualise and imagine cautiously.[202]

Feeling and visualising and imagining her way through the more than fifty years since, Churchill has repeatedly offered new dramatic forms in order to press the philosophical, scientific, and especially political questions of her time. Yet even as the playwright has transformed her dramatic landscapes over her career, she has consistently warned audiences about threats (whether of sexism, capitalism, or terror) to their environment and survival. One of her earliest plays dramatises a woman's worry when a storm threatens, calmed by the husband who issues the titular consolation: *You've No Need to Be Frightened*. The unnamed wife with her night-time anxiety might remind us of *The Skriker* and its own wake-up call, or of *Far Away*'s Joan, roused by a dead-of-night shriek (her word) and standing in nightgowned incomprehension before her aunt, just like the frightened Angie at the end of *Top Girls*. James Nicola, the artistic director of New York Theatre Workshop, told a journalist that *Far Away* represented 'Caryl's dealing with her love of her grandchildren and thinking, "What do I say to them about this horrific world that we live in, and how can I prepare them for it without frightening or intimidating them?"'[203] Another question given dramatic form.

In other words, Churchill refuses the role imposed on *The Skriker*'s Lily, mute before her condemning descendants. And she refuses to understate the danger, as Harper does when she dismisses Joan's night-time scare as an owl instead of acknowledging the person screaming. But like the husband in *You've No Need to Be Frightened*, who prepares his wife for a future after he has left, Churchill offers comforts. Theatre might help us to visualise and to feel with the same imagination as the playwright does in her shape-shifting work. Theatre might awaken us to dangers and also lend shelter against them. For theatre encourages community – one lesson of *Far Away*, as the cast discovered in their dressing room – and community like all politics is a group effort. It is therefore significant that Churchill continues to push the world of contemporary theatre forward – her landscapes inspiring fellow innovators such as the American dramatist Tony Kushner, who has called her 'the greatest living English-language playwright' and recounted his desire to transcend her influence.[204] His British contemporary Mark Ravenhill, too, has expressed the challenge and the hope: 'I read *Top Girls* at least once a year and I weep. One day, I think to myself, one day I'll write something as good'.[205] If the emphasis on goodness remarries aesthetic form to commendable ethics, it also issues an urgent reminder. Unlike Joan's hats, Churchill's beautiful landscapes never forget the urgent contexts and the precarious times in which they have been formed.

CHAPTER 2

DERIVATIVES; OR CAPITALISM AND THE THEATRE

In Churchill's teleplay *The After-Dinner Joke* – directed by Colin Bucksey and broadcast on the BBC on 14 February 1978 – the protagonist, Selby, undergoes a classic journey from innocence to experience. At the beginning of the play, she resigns from her secretarial position in order to 'do good', as she explains to her boss, called Price in the script but Shanks in the televised version.[1] She is instead convinced to remain on the payroll while working full-time as a charity organiser, beginning an education as instructive as Wilhelm Meister's in Goethe's iconic eighteenth-century novel. A series of short scenes indebted to Monty Python – the description is Churchill's[2] – chart Selby's progress. They take her not only across England but also to the Middle East, where she learns of world-class private hospitals with doors open to global tourists but closed to ill villagers – such as the unspeaking Arab gardener, for instance, whose watering keeps the hospital gardens blooming even in the middle of the desert. And she travels, too, to the developing world, where she is comically kidnapped by guerrillas looking to secure land reform in their unnamed country.

Eventually, Selby comes to understand that capitalism bleeds into every corner of the international economy and global community. As her co-worker Dent instructs, charity is finally 'the figures at the bottom of the columns. Whether to buy the freehold of the gift shops. Whether to leave our latest bequest in Imperial Tobacco'.[3] She learns that the causes of world poverty reside in systems of global trade, with their capitalist origins in colonialism. But the final joke is that the English themselves might be bought and sold as they had bought and sold others. In one of the play's most acid scenes, a television ad shows discarded camels charitably donated to the now-owned inhabitants of Kensington and Chelsea, grateful for the crumbs, and – in a blistering send-up of ubiquitous 'adopt a child' promotions – strikers at a car factory seek rich Arab families to adopt them. The developing world may seem to be England's perennial victim, its colonial wounds festering but dressed with charity because (as a government minister explains) 'if we let these countries get too poor they won't be able to buy our goods'.[4] But so too might England capitulate to the same logic: an oil sheikh, bored of London shopping with his wives, buys the Marks and Spencer chain instead. It is the final joke on the English 'top people' (as the play characterises them) of the kind that contribute anecdotes to Oxfam's charity book *Pass the Port*, whose for-sale after-dinner jokes Churchill satirises.[5] At the end of the play, Selby is rescued from her guerrilla captors and, back home, accepts Price's offer of a management position in his empire. She has realised that there is no escape from big business, and a final silent scene shows her '*sitting behind a large desk*'.[6]

In this chapter, I explore the meanings of capitalism – the ramifications of private and public property, the dynamics of borrowing and lending, the complications of globalisation – in Churchill's plays. I focus on three works in which her debts to other playwrights are most apparent, whether cheekily borrowing from other playwrights or freely adapting public domain text. The use of other writers' styles, words, and plots in these plays proves thematically congruent, since like Bertolt Brecht (the modern theatre's most insatiable appropriator) she condemns the capitalist principle of private ownership. But other critical dividends can be yielded by examining major productions of the plays, and especially by examining the transactions that facilitated them. For while they show how ownership is inimical to good social relations (including those among co-workers such as producers, actors, and directors), in production they reveal the inescapability of property – that is, of entities to be owned – in the worlds of state-sponsored, not-for-profit cultural production and private commercial production alike. In other words, I explore how Churchill's thematic concerns take on metatheatrical resonances and extra-theatrical implications: how the plays comment on themselves as well as the world off-stage. To do so, I peer backstage. The BBC changed the ending to *The After-Dinner Joke*, for instance, instead having Selby take a hiatus 'from the business side of things' – and thus allowing for the possibility of a break from capitalism.[7] It is instructive to learn, too, that the BBC cut bits from *The After-Dinner Joke* to be repackaged as sketches for Comic Relief programming, the very sort of feel-good response to African famine that the play satirises.[8] Whether Churchill approved either the script changes or her words' reuse remains unclear from the programme's production records in the BBC Archives. But it would not have mattered. The network owned the property, after all, thanks to a contract that paid the writer £1,700 for her work.[9]

Owners

The month that *Owners* premiered, December 1972, also saw the broadcast on BBC Radio 3 of Churchill's radio drama *Henry's Past* and the first production of her play *Schreber's Nervous Illness* (which, while broadcast for radio earlier that year, was given a lunchtime production at the King's Head, the estimable pub theatre in Islington, on 5 December). Nonetheless, *Owners* has been regarded as inaugurating Churchill's career, since it was her first professional stage production and the first play included in the first volume of the multi-volume edition of her work. As she has written, 'my working life feels divided quite sharply into before and after 1972, and *Owners* was the first play of the second part'.[10] *Owners*' opening was originally scheduled for November but delayed by a last-minute change of lead actor: the play was ready for dress rehearsal when Jill Bennett, also preparing to play Alice in *Henry's Past*, became injured. (The fourth wife of the playwright John Osborne, Bennett was injured when Osborne – certainly drunk if not high on the prescription drugs he abused in those years – deliberately crashed their car during one of their routine arguments.[11]) In *Henry's Past*, Bennett was replaced by Sheila Allen. In *Owners*, Bennett was replaced by Stephanie Bidmead, and on 13 December 1972, after a week of previews, the play opened at the Royal Court Theatre Upstairs. Nicholas Wright directed.

Owners mixes some pressing social concerns of its time with farcical, even absurd elements. It centres on Marion, a thirty-something North

Londoner, and her fraught relationships with Worsely, her amoral employee; Clegg, her butcher husband; Alec, her disaffected lover; and Lisa, Alec's hard-pressed wife. Recently out of a mental hospital, Marion seems to have regained her equilibrium by developing a pathological acquisitiveness. Perpetually consuming – she declares of her clothes that 'I love to throw them away. And get new ones'[12] – she earns her living by purchasing Islington properties and selling them off for profit, thus taking advantage of the area's gentrification (which in the early 1970s was rapid, and which Churchill saw firsthand as a resident).[13] But Marion's rapacious consumption intrudes on her personal life, too. For instance, when her husband feels his patriarchal prerogative threatened by their childlessness, she buys him not only a new butcher shop, Clegg and Son, but also a baby to inhabit the filial role. This latter purchase not coincidentally undermines the marriage of Alec and Lisa, whose building Marion has acquired and whose flat she tries to force them from with the aid of Worsely. Thus Churchill focalises the play's social concerns. Meanwhile, Worsely's self-loathing and multiple unsuccessful suicide attempts provide some of the play's funniest lines and most absurd elements.

Owners demonstrates the capacity of ownership to foment discord, either between competing claimants to property or between those who own and those who do not. We see this view most obviously in the play's treatment of real estate. Marion makes her living, after all, by pitting prospective buyers against one another and, more insidiously, by scaring away value-depressing tenants with the help of her henchman. When, in the play's second scene, Alec and Lisa return to their flat to find it burgled, we learn it was an inside job: in his capacity as a potential buyer, Worsely had been given the key by the building's unwitting owner. But Worsely presents himself to the couple as their charitable saviour, offering two hundred pounds to help them procure a safer home. The ruse seems to work with Lisa, the play's most guileless and sympathetic character. She asks: 'You want to give us two hundred pounds? For nothing?. . . . You're very kind. Are you sure you can spare it?'[14] In fact, by encouraging them to vacate their tenancy, Worsely serves only Marion's interests. In any case, he explains, a new landlord will bring them a rent hike: 'Under the new act your rent here will of course be adjusted to a fair rent'.[15] He alludes to the real-life Housing Finance Act of 1972 that, however well-intentioned, permitted rent-controlled tenancies to be adjusted according to the property's rateable value. The market, in other words, was allowed to determine a price, even if its ostensibly 'fair' dictates proved inhumane to the urban poor it displaced.

What Churchill reveals in this scene is that social interactions such as those between Lisa and Worsely are akin to social initiatives such as the Housing Finance Act: vehicles through which those who own acquire more in a system that privileges owners. And thus the toxicity of ownership in the play extends well beyond real estate. When Lisa and Alec remain after the property changes hands, she complains that the new landlady, Mrs Arlington, treats her as 'something that goes with the house'.[16] The line cuts doubly. On one hand, the tenants' fungibility is underscored by Worsely's attempt to force them out in the first place; such a tenant is an objectified *something* that will eventually *go* as the house changes hands (each time to a more affluent pair) and as new 'fair rents' are set. On the other hand, the Arlingtons exploit Alec and Lisa's babysitting labour as if they were not fungible adornment but rather the property's fixed chattels. Churchill describes Mrs Arlington as 'someone who has never met difficulties' – a quietly devastating description in light of the play's thematic concerns. If there is '[n]o need to send her up', as Churchill instructs, it is because people like Lisa are subjugated by the principle of ownership rather than by this or that particular buyer.[17]

These concerns are obviously consonant with Churchill's socialist leanings; as she told an interviewer at the time, 'on a simple political level I think owning is stupid'.[18] And from the 'ownership of property and things' it is a short step to 'the idea of owning and controlling people' – as Churchill claimed in another interview from the period, in which she excoriated the 'whole idea of Western individualism, and capitalism, and progress'.[19] *Owners* compresses and theatricalises this progress as Marion's acquisitions extend quickly and logically from houses to Lisa and Alec's baby. The play also reveals the inescapability of property's logic – its subordination of human interests to acquisitive values – buoyed as it is by Britain's political and judicial systems. (A few years after *Owners, Light Shining in Buckinghamshire* would dramatise the seventeenth-century moment that inaugurated capitalist property rights in Britain: the right, as Worsely puts it, for a man to 'do what he likes with his own'. As he tartly summarises, 'the law's not for morals so much as property. The legal system was made by owners'.[20]) It is no accident that Lisa continually if unwittingly accedes to this logic no matter how it disenfranchises her. In response to Worsely's offer, she consults first with her own landlady ('If you're an owner, dear, you expect to own') and then with Marion ('Since you know about property'), the very owner whose rapacity most threatens her.[21] Lisa's vulnerability is underscored in her first scene, in which, befuddled, she concedes: 'I'm sorry, but I'm not used to property at all'.[22]

If human interactions in the play are transactional, their value market-driven, no social relationship can remain uncorrupted: not only landlords and tenants but also neighbours, lovers, co-workers, and spouses betray the logic of property. Marion declares ownership over Alec on the basis of their prior relationship – 'You were mine then and you always will be'[23] – and disturbingly her logic holds when Alec falls back in with her. Jealous of Marion's acquisition, Clegg responds by bedding Lisa, cautioning her afterwards that (like many disenfranchised people, then as now) she pays a debt that is not her own. 'I've plenty more owing', he declares. He continues by invoking *Exodus* 21:24 and *Romans* 12:19, thus cementing Churchill's connection between Christianity and acquisition: 'An eye for an eye. A mouth for a mouth. A cunt for a cunt. Vengeance is mine. I will repay'.[24] For Lisa the transaction has a different value. She believes that she is paying a ransom that will return her child, whom she had signed over to Marion shortly after declaring, poignantly, that 'I'm not worth nothing'.[25] But Lisa's sexual investment in Clegg pays no dividend. And too her threats to sue are quickly quashed. 'Have you a home that would impress a judge?', Marion reasons.[26] For Lisa is decidedly not an 'owner'. A harried mother of two other children, she makes her meagre living performing what Adam Smith called unproductive labour: she washes hair in a salon. And she repeatedly ignores the principal rule of the market, which Marion states baldly: 'The more you want it the more it's worth keeping', she says of the baby.[27] The baby, meanwhile, fattened by Clegg up to fifteen pounds, is likened to the choicest product at the butcher shop, the place of commerce and consumption where Churchill begins and ends the play – thus marking both the ubiquity of buying and selling and the lack of progress this ubiquity ensures.

The baby is also leverage in Clegg and Marion's marital negotiations. The husband understands their marriage bond in pecuniary terms, telling Alec that 'She is mine. I have invested heavily in Marion and don't intend to lose any part of my profit'.[28] Meanwhile, his wife has bought him off, given him the child in order to discharge a matrimonial duty (as she sees it) through outsourcing. In the manner of the capitalist economy she exploits, she co-opts the productivity of the working class and manages to produce without labour of her own. Not for the first time, Marion thus claims a patriarchal position: after all, men also have children without the pain of labour. And so Churchill ties her socialist and feminist themes together. Patriarchy, we see, is complicit in the capitalist logic of ownership, an idea neatly encapsulated in the baby's purpose: he becomes the son in 'Clegg and Son' just as Clegg was under his own father. (That they sell meat, living beings chopped into saleable objects, is surely no coincidence.) Patriarchal succession is assured as the property is handed down from one male generation to another, as indeed property was in Britain, as elsewhere, for centuries. In Churchill's view, the historically recent right of women to own property does not strike a blow for feminism so much as extend a patriarchal prerogative to women like Marion who now may own and so treat others like objects. Thus the playwright pointedly sets the play's third scene in a strip club, where Marion boasts that '[i]f you want a girl, Clegg, I'll buy you one'.[29] Churchill's interests in class and gender coalesce, as they do in *Vinegar Tom* and many other plays. (Race too hovers somewhere near *Owners*' edges: Clegg's dog is called Sambo.)

In an early but still much-cited article on Churchill, Alisa Solomon wrote that the 'psychic emotional and ethical experience' of the playwright's characters is 'the inexorable result of their socio-political organization; their social being determines their thought'.[30] This claim holds especially true in *Owners*, whose protagonist – like Marlene in *Top Girls* – is encouraged by her society to exploit the advantages of capitalism without regard to its corrosive effects on women. Marion claims not to feel this irony: 'Most women are fleas but I'm the dog', she declares, merrily reiterating one of Clegg's insulting terms for her.[31] But we must remember that she has just left a mental hospital. Her always new clothes are 'coming undone, slightly askew', and despite her voraciousness – she is shown continually eating, whether chocolate, bananas, or grapes – she stays always thin.[32] Even in her metabolism, in other words, she mirrors the acquisitive society she symbolises. It consumes without discernible benefit, its unacknowledged psychosis barely under control. Her self-interests are in fact self-destructive, feeding a patriarchal logic that works against her; when Clegg attempts to 'buy' her assassination, tellingly he uses a cheque that Marion has herself signed. Thus Churchill suggests that people do not 'own' themselves but are determined by (and enslaved to) a fundamentally disenfranchising capitalism. She makes this satirically clear in the increasingly absurd suicide attempts of Worsely, whose control over his own destiny is so meagre that neither slashed wrists nor hanging, neither a fall from great height nor a shot to the temple, manages to kill him.

A kind of resistance is proposed through Alec, the sole character who (in the astute assessment of Elaine Aston) has 'no investment in a materialist economy'.[33] He responds to the burglary by saying '[i]f he wants the things that much, perhaps let him have them' and to Marion's request for his apartment by saying 'I don't at all mind leaving if you want it very much'.[34] His decisive actions in the play number two. First, he disconnects the intravenous drip keeping his senile mother alive; second, he runs back into the burning house (torched on Marion's orders) in a failed attempt to save the Arlingtons' baby. While he resists a world of property and ownership, the precise usefulness of this resistance remains unclear, seeming to lead to annihilation – even if he achieves a kind of agency that is denied Worsely, with his inviolate dedication to property. (He surmises that even one's life is 'God's property not yours'.[35]) At least, Churchill seems to say, Alec's decisions do not feed the ferocious acquisitiveness that threatens civil society, as the forces of government, the law, and the courts do. And religion. Churchill declared that Alec represented Marion's opposite – 'the more passive Eastern idea of simply being' – as opposed to Christianity, which the playwright associated with Western individualism and capitalism'.[36] Thus the epigrams to the play juxtapose a Zen poem to 'Onward Christian Soldiers', Marion's favourite song as a child. Even her name is biblical, reminding us of another woman famous to literature who had a child without labour and gave her husband a son not biologically his own.[37]

Owners' anti-capitalist themes have been glossed by several critics since the play's premiere, most concisely and well in a 2009 article by Jean E. Howard.[38] What have gone unexplored are some of the extra-theatrical resonances and implications of this critique. In thinking of these, we should first consider the play's oddity in the Churchill canon. Whereas much of her work seems *sui generis*, *Owners* atypically bears resemblances to other plays. The central plot conceit mirrors that of Steve Passeur's 1930 work *L'Acheteuse* – less remembered now, certainly, than it was in the early 1970s – in which the protagonist, Elizabeth, 'purchases' her husband Gilbert by paying his debts and in which the central relationship is sustained, as Marion and Clegg's is, by mutual hatred and the wife's capital. (One telling difference: while Passeur's play, tinged with misogyny, ends with Elizabeth's preparation to kill herself, Churchill's ends with Worsely's last botched suicide attempt and Marion's chilling declaration that 'I'm just beginning to find out what's possible'.[39]) The tone of *Owners*, meanwhile, self-consciously mirrors that of Joe Orton, Churchill's contemporary and erstwhile Islington neighbour. (He lived a mile away, at 25 Noel Road, until his brutal death in 1967.) Churchill has said that *Owners* was written after she had 'reread Orton's [*Entertaining Mr*] *Sloane*, which may have done something to the style'.[40] This formulation understates the debt Churchill incurs in the play, which mimics Orton's grisly outrageousness and his characteristic blend of social critique, farcical plotting, and black-as-night tone. He is echoed, for example, in *Owners*' first scene, in which Clegg and Worsely discuss the former's plan to kill Marion:

Clegg I must find the right tool for the job.

Worsely Is the idea to kill her at all costs or do you count on getting away with it?

Clegg I hadn't planned on being caught, no.

Worsely Then a knife might be too much of a clue.[41]

Owners is full of such exchanges where we hear Orton's distinctive approach, which piles punchline on punchline to often antic effect, even as the subjects of discussion (murder, suicide, mental illness) seem decidedly uncomic.

Critics have sometimes explained *Owners*' echoes of other playwrights with reference to its early place in the Churchill canon, suggesting that such echoes provide evidence of a still-fledgling talent. But we should recall that, on her estimation, *Owners* was her twentieth play to be written and that its themes were present already in 1962's *The Love Salesman* (with its telling title), an unrealised project that Churchill had pitched without success to BBC Radio.[42] Moreover, the play nudges us outward to other plays in self-conscious ways: Clegg, for example, describes himself as 'more an Othello than a Hamlet'.[43] The play thus engages in a sly metatheatricality that directs us precisely toward those elements that seem *derivative*, in the sense of freely deploying other sources. This appropriative method fits a play that argues insistently that 'ownership' is toxic to social relations. By noticing borrowings from or references to Passeur, Orton, or Shakespeare, readers and theatregoers are recalled to their investment in a discourse (unknown to Shakespeare, certainly) that deems tropes, ideas, or idioms to belong to this or that writer in the first place. Partaking in an economy of sharing, *Owners* rebukes this discourse. At the same time, one of Churchill's principal themes is that this discourse completely pervades our society, and so too we find that even plays cannot escape its logic or indeed its legal consequences.

Theatre scholars, especially those who share Churchill's politics, sometimes naively reinforce the myth that theatre is a distinctly collaborative art-form in which the contributors (actors, designers, directors, etc.) selflessly work together to produce work that belongs to no one individual in particular. And certain theatre companies, including Churchill's frequent collaborators at Joint Stock, reinforce this collectivist story. However, a stroll through the archival records of almost any play in the modern theatre tells a somewhat different tale. Plays are, in fact, private property: they belong to specific agents who often act as limited companies (as is the case with Churchill since the early 1980s, when Caryl Churchill Ltd was incorporated). And they pay dividends to other invested agents, such as producers. Moreover, claims of ownership can be fraught, as the prodigious litigation surrounding *A Chorus Line* or any number of other plays might tell us. (Less acrimoniously, Ian Spink admitted that '[i]t did feel very strange' that only David Lan and Churchill would earn royalties after *A Mouthful of Birds*, their 1986 multidisciplinary collaboration with Spink and Les Waters.[44]) At every step of the theatre-making process, notions of ownership are in fact omnipresent. For example, the production files for *Owners* begin with the legal document that engendered it, a contract by which Churchill undertook to write a play for the commissioning producer, Michael Codron, who had also produced *Entertaining Mr Sloane*. Acting as a limited company, Codron bought an option to produce the play before it was even written. As is typical in such contracts, this option spells out not only the fees payable and the duration of the agreement but also the royalty percentages on profits and the ownership shares of subsidiary rights, such as those for film or television productions; these the purchaser owns in exchange for his or her financial commitment. The investment belongs to the class called *derivatives* since its value will depend on another value, that of the play. Even before a word is written, then, a play such as *Owners* is deemed to have a sole owner (Churchill, per the initial Memorandum of Agreement) even if its rights are 'owned' by Codron, in the words of a letter from her agent, Peggy Ramsay, to the Royal Court.[45]

I do not suggest that Churchill is hypocritical for participating in a discourse of ownership that she claims to find repugnant; as *Owners* makes clear, this discourse is so ubiquitous that no playwright or producer could get any work done without relying on proprietary contracts or without assigning rights and apportioning proceeds. The contract that Churchill signed with Codron is routine, little different than that governing this book, for which I, too, paid fees to at least one of Churchill's publishers for the rights to quote snippets of her dialogue. And it is hard to imagine less toxic business transactions than those between Codron and Churchill or Codron and the Court. Four months after contracting with Churchill, and at her request, Codron paid the rest of the owed commission but agreeably transferred his interest to the Court by means of a sub-licensing agreement, retaining options on any subsequent transfers and subsidiary rights. At the same time, contemplating the concept of ownership behind the scenes, as it were, may enrich our understanding of how the concept is represented on stage – perhaps particularly when the offstage story involves a more remunerative property with more deeply invested investors (as is the case with the aptly named *Serious Money*). Artistic expression and legal ownership are not as separable as we sometimes like to believe, even in the cases of collaboration, of non-commercial theatres such as the Royal Court, or of finally benevolent producers such as Codron.

Looking at *Owners*' initial reviews, one is struck by how the discourse of property reveals itself again and again. Reviewers from almost every major British paper admired the play, with the *Observer*'s Robert Brustein in particular praising Churchill's 'singular . . . creative gifts' and 'poetic imagination'.[46] But the production, they felt, did not capitalise on the play's value. Blame is apportioned: some to the lead performance of Stephanie Bidmead (Charles Lewsen, writing in *The Times*, cattily suggested that Jill Bennett return in her wheelchair to take over) but most to the director, with reviewer after reviewer singling out Wright's flat direction and overly fussy production, with its too-frequent scene changes.[47] (Churchill would later blame herself for the excessive settings, calling *Owners* a play with 'lots of furniture'. 'I learned from Max Stafford-Clark not to do it, and I set my next play in one place'.[48]) After the show closed, Ramsay wrote to the playwright that 'I was dreadfully unhappy about the production of your play Upstairs and have still not got over it. I find it difficult to even talk to Nick Wright'.[49] Ramsay's 'your' of course reinstates the principle of ownership that Churchill's play finds toxic; she worried that the market value of both script and playwright would fall. As an agent, Ramsay was not wrong to worry. We might compare, for example, the dividends paid by Codron's investments in *Entertaining Mr Sloane* and *Owners*. Ramsay's client Orton saw his play transfer from a small commercial theatre, the New Arts Theatre, to a bigger West End space; it enjoyed a Broadway run a year later; and both the television and film options were exercised. By contrast, *Owners* did not transfer after its initial run. And its first American production, which opened on 14 May 1973 at the now-defunct Mercer-Shaw Theatre in New York, was forgotten so decisively that it is almost never mentioned in Churchill scholarship.[50] Thus critics habitually erase Terese Hayden's small-scale show from their chronologies, call *Cloud Nine* Churchill's New York debut, and see the 1993 New York revival of *Owners* as the play's American premiere.[51]

Owners would go without a major revival until 6 April 1987, when a production directed by Annie Castledine opened at the Young Vic in London. That production undoubtedly had thematic resonance, happening as it did on the brink of Thatcher's complete deregulation of the rental market: she managed her long-sought goal of abolishing remaining rent controls in 1988. But the Young Vic producers also made some savvy market calculations about the property (i.e. performance rights) they had purchased. Their revival lured audiences by casting a minor celebrity, singer Loudon Wainwright III, rather against type as Worsely. More importantly, it capitalised slyly on the playwright's name. In the intervening years, of course, Churchill had become a star in contemporary theatre, having written commercial successes in *Cloud Nine*, *Fen*, and *Top Girls*. The Young Vic producers no doubt bet that Churchill's star would be burning even more brightly when its production of *Owners* opened. They were correct. By that time, *Serious Money* had settled in at the Royal Court, bringing with it publicity, critical acclaim, and box office receipts (and thus derivative payments to its producers and royalties to its author) that would dwarf any that the Court or Churchill had ever seen.

Serious Money: A City Comedy

Robert Brustein once praised Churchill's ability to shape leftist politics into un-polemical and dramatically vivid plots and characterisations by describing *Owners* as a 'Marxist critique unblemished by Marxist ideology'.[52] Churchill extended this critique fifteen years later, providing an even more vivid dramatisation of how capitalism reduces social relationships to what Marx and Engels call the 'cash nexus'.[53] The play is *Serious Money*. It too premiered at the Royal Court, on 27 March 1987 (after six previews); the production was directed by Max Stafford-Clark, the Royal Court's Artistic Director and by then Churchill's most frequent collaborator. Similar ideas undergird *Owners* and *Serious Money*, but the latter's context of production – Britain in 1987, eight years into the society-transforming tenure of Margaret Thatcher – transformed and intensified these ideas. *Owners*' obsession with real estate, for example, looks almost quaint in retrospect. 'You don't make money out of land, you make money out of money', as Zac Zackerman explains in *Serious Money*.[54] Shifting our emphasis from houses (with their grounding use-value) to the entirely abstract value of currency, Zackerman's insight colours not only the play's plot but also its formal structure, its set design, and even its production and reception.

The ungrounded quality of stock market capital may explain the impossibility of summarising *Serious Money*, which seems always to elude the spectators' grasp. It tells the story of Scilla Todd, a dealer at the London International Financial Futures Exchange (Liffe) who investigates the sudden death of her brother, Jake, a securities dealer who had been selling insider information and helping to arrange 'fan clubs' of buyers to support hostile corporate takeovers. But Scilla's investigation is dropped with a conspicuous lack of ceremony when she realises the 'serious money' Jake has made. Deciding that she wants a piece of the illegal action herself, she insinuates herself into her brother's shady international circle: Jacinta Condor, a Peruvian businesswoman; Nigel Abjibala, a Ghanaian 'importer'; Billy Corman, a British corporate raider; and Marylou Baines, an American risk arbitrageur (i.e. one who buys undervalued shares immediately before corporate takeovers). Scilla's amorality and her comfort with a crass new brand of financial players, such as her bond-dealing friend Grimes, set her apart from the rearguard boys' network of landed stockjobbers and brokers, such as Frosby and her father, Greville. (Scilla denounces her father's 'pomposity', while Greville finds his daughter a 'monstrosity'.[55] Their divergent reactions to Jake's scandal-tinged death encapsulate their differences: Greville claims that 'I'd rather he'd been a failure', but Scilla reasons that 'insider dealing' is 'not a proper crime like stealing'.[56])

Meanwhile, Corman makes a hostile bid for a company with a pointedly allegorical name: Albion. This takeover is stymied by Albion chairman Duckett's white knight investor, Biddulph, and by Gleason, a minister in Thatcher's cabinet who first unleashes the Department of Trade and Industry on Corman and then, in exchange for his acquiescence, bestows a knighthood. Zackerman, Jake's American friend, loosely connects these players: as a multinational banker, Zac aids Corman in raising capital and, more generally, scouts for ruthless talent like Scilla in order to 'turn the best of them into new market makers'.[57] What makes these plot strands difficult to keep track of is not only the doggerel verse that Churchill adopts and wilfully abandons, or the speed it encourages ('it does have the effect of driving the play incredibly fast which seems very right for it', she said[58]), but also the scenes' cacophony. One example: the second scene involves '[t]hree different dealing rooms simultaneously' with eight actors on stage.[59] In light of Churchill's trademark overlapping dialogue, up to five characters speak at the same time. The goal – as in 1994's *The Skriker* or 2012's *Love and Information* – is more affective than thematic. Here, the narrative seems subordinated to the play's mimicry of the market's stupefying rush.

Like *Owners*, *Serious Money* draws attention to itself as a play through theatrical references: Shakespeare appears again, his *King Lear* suggesting themes of ownership and kinship, and Brecht's signature devices – including estranging verse, songs, doubling, and indirect discourse – are all deployed.[60] *Owners*' plot echoes of Passeur and Orton are replaced by *Serious Money*'s explicit citation: a second-act scene from Thomas Shadwell's 1692 *The Volunteers, or the Stockjobbers* begins Churchill's play. But she has excised a character (the rogue Nickum) and one of his pointed lines ('[t]hese Stock-Jobbing Rogues, are worse than us Sharpers'[61]). And thus she has vacated the scene of Nickum's suspicion of the market and brought Shadwell's setting into

Thatcher's. Her citation serves to stress the longevity of London's stock exchange and its equally longstanding amorality, as Shadwell's characters discuss not only their wares (stock in a producer of mousetraps, for instance) but also their manipulation of the market – their 'lowing and heightening' in order to 'turn the penny' whether their product 'turns to use or not'.[62] Thus too Churchill situates her play in a long tradition of the 'City Comedy', her multivalent subtitle. (The genre dates to the late-sixteenth century, when playwrights such as Ben Jonson began satirising the follies of London citizens, and when Elizabeth I opened the City's first stock market, the Royal Exchange.) Unlike the reader of its script, *Serious Money*'s audience is given no clue where these archaic-sounding lines come from, and so Churchill thumbs her nose at the notion of this or that playwright's 'property' just as she had, more subtly, in *Owners*. But if the metatheatrical flourishes of *Serious Money* recall those in *Owners*, so too does an extra-theatrical irony: like its predecessor, *Serious Money* is a legally protected property whose rights can be bought and sold. The play was not a commission; since her arrangement with Codron, Churchill has rarely accepted them. But when she finished writing, she sold the play's rights – including worldwide performance, film, and television rights – to the English Stage Company (i.e. the Royal Court), making possible the play's first production.

Churchill wrote *Serious Money* at a particularly heady moment for capitalism and certainly a more propitious one than either 1692 (when *The Volunteers* debuted and when stockbrokers were not allowed into the Royal Exchange) or 1972 (when *Owners* premiered and when London trading was decidedly parochial, with women and foreigners banned from the floor). Months before she began research for *Serious Money*, the entire financial services industry of the UK was radically transformed by the so-called Big Bang of 27 October 1986, when Thatcher's government deregulated the London Stock Exchange in favour of 'self-regulation'. Fixed commission charges were abolished; the long-held distinction between brokers (who buy and sell shares for clients) and jobbers (who maintain inventories of such shares for brokers) was dissolved; and the in-person trading floor was replaced by electronic trading. 'Yobs' like Grimes replaced landed jobbers like

Frosby. Moreover, the percentage that foreign investors could own of a given listed company was increased from 29.9 per cent to 100 per cent, thus exponentially increasing the volume of trades and encouraging multinational corporate takeovers such as Corman's of Albion. As legislative fetters to investment fell, so did national barriers; torrents of global capital entered the exchange along with Jacintas, Nigels, and Zac Zackermans. Market forces alone set the tempo. And thus London came to vibrate on the same dizzying frequency as the world's other financial centres, chief among them New York. Zackerman puts it this way: 'The financial world won't be the same again / Because the traders are coming down the fast lane'.[63]

The intoxications and excesses of this period are well reflected in its cultural artefacts, including Martin Amis's bluntly named *Money*, Tom Wolfe's serialised bestseller *Bonfire of the Vanities*, and Oliver Stone's hit film *Wall Street*. The theatre, too, reflected an increased cultural interest in business and its workings: in New York, David Mamet's *Glengarry Glen Ross*, Joe Cacaci's *Old Business*, Dennis McIntyre's *Established Price*, June Shellene and Richard Fire's *Dealing*, Jerry Sterner's *Other People's Money*, and Richard Dresser's *The Downside* would premiere within a three-year period. (The last starred J. Smith-Cameron, who would memorably incarnate *Owners*' Marion in its 1993 revival at New York Theatre Workshop, directed by Churchill's frequent collaborator Mark Wing-Davey.) With the exception of Mamet's play, these artefacts are probably less well remembered than the era's real-life dramas, which riveted audiences on both sides of the Atlantic: in Britain, for example, the stunning arrests of the so-called 'Guinness Four' (who took advantage of market deregulation to help Guinness in its takeover of the Distillers Company); in the United States, the conviction for insider trading of Ivan Boesky, whose infamous defence of greed found its way into both *Wall Street* and *Serious Money* and whose $100,000,000 'fan club' role in the Guinness takeover testified to the irrelevance of national borders in the post-Big Bang market.

If *Serious Money* is informed by this context – Corman's broker cautions him to 'Remember Guinness' and the arbitrageur Marylou is described as 'second only to Boesky'[64] – so too was it engendered by this context. First, the play began its life in London's financial district, the City. Starting on 22 September 1986, Churchill, Stafford-Clark, and a number of others spent two weeks talking to traders in various markets and watching them work on the floor.[65] (They were, Churchill said, 'very helpful'.[66]) Armed with this experience, the improvisations of the workshop actors, and months of research into the financial industry, Churchill began writing the play after Christmas and had finished a draft, eventually reworked, in time for rehearsals, which began 15 February 1987. Second, the Thatcherite ideology behind the Big Bang also affected theatres such as Stafford-Clark's Royal Court, as new cultural policy opened state-subsidised theatre to market forces. Shortly after Thatcher's election in 1979, her Arts Minister had announced that

> [t]he arts world must come to terms with the fact that Government policy in general has decisively tilted away from the expansion of the public to the private sector. The Government fully intends to honour its pledge to maintain support for the arts as a major feature of policy, but we look to the private sphere to meet any shortfall and to provide immediate means of increase.[67]

Accordingly, arts organisations were compelled to find corporate sponsors instead of relying on the Arts Council to make up their budget deficits. The result was devastating for fringe companies and taxing even for more established groups such as the Royal Court. An extraordinary entry in Stafford-Clark's diary reveals that the first read-through of *Serious Money* took place on the same day he met with Thatcher about arts subsidies at 10 Downing Street, where he was surprised to find her 'by far the brightest, the best briefed and by far the sharpest' of the Cabinet there assembled.[68] Churchill's scepticism about such confluences is clear. She signed a denunciation of Thatcher's cultural policy and within two years of *Serious Money* would resign from the Royal Court's advisory council after it found a particularly unsavoury corporate partner in Barclays Bank.[69]

Tory cultural policy was motivated not by hatred of the arts or even the politics of its purveyors, 90 per cent of whom, Peter Hall once estimated, loathed Thatcher.[70] Rather, it desired that market forces judge artistic success. No longer would the arts be recognised as 'worthless and priceless', in Howard Brenton's unexcelled description.[71] An organisation looking to avoid selling itself in a marketplace of corporate sponsors could do so only by selling its product at sufficient prices, and to sufficient numbers of sufficiently wealthy consumers, in the entertainment marketplace. The result is to compel an acquiescence to capitalist logic: the theatre participates in a market economy in either case. The Royal Court's situation in 1987 clearly demonstrates this double bind. *Serious Money* opened to mixed reviews from the dailies – 'pure genius' said the *Telegraph*; 'no advance on *Top Girls* or *Cloud Nine*', said the *Financial Times*[72] – but the public reaction was unequivocal. The run sold out, taking in over £145,000 at the box office. This success could potentially relieve the push toward corporate sponsorship. The Court, which after all owned the play's options, could maximise *Serious Money*'s value and earn additional much-needed capital. But doing so required a commercial production and external investors, anathema to leftist theatre artists. (Monstrous Regiment's Pam Brighton, who had directed Churchill's *Vinegar Tom* in 1976, was particularly harsh, denouncing *Serious Money* as 'bourgeois' and 'in total conflict' with the goals of a socialist theatre.[73]) The left-wing playwright John McGrath – Churchill's Oxford classmate and the man who introduced her to her agent – articulated the bind at a 1988 symposium dedicated to condemning Thatcher's effects on British theatre: 'There are practitioners who will say that running *Serious Money* for six months in the West End is the only way to enable other forms of work to take place', he said, concluding grimly that '[i]t's a fact of life'.[74] Vera Gottlieb, one of the symposium's organisers, conceded of this new fact of life that 'Thatcherism *has* worked on its own ideological terms'.[75] It is amazing to read Stafford-Clark's journals from the time. Where angst about casting, programming, and rewrites used to dominate, we find pages teeming with financial worry, and box office projections and production budgets obsessively rehearsed.

So the English Stage Company's rights to *Serious Money* were re-sold to a separate limited company (Royal Court Productions Ltd) in order to facilitate a commercial production. And so the play opened again, on 6 July 1987, at Wyndham's Theatre, with a slightly different cast: Stafford-Clark retained some of his principal players such as Linda Bassett (who played Marylou Baines; Corman's broker, Etherington; and his public relations guru, Dolcie Starr) and Meera Syal (Jacinta), but lost others such as Lesley Manville (Scilla) and Alfred Molina (Zackerman). A few months' time and commercial success had burnished the play's reputation; the new reviews were less equivocal. But so too did critics develop a new preoccupation. It was anticipated by actor Daniel Webb – he replaced Gary Oldman in the roles of Grimes and Corman – when he was interviewed for the play's opening and predicted that the West End would attract a different kind of spectator: 'It'll be interesting to see what kind of audiences we get'.[76] Within weeks most newspaper items about the show focused on these new audiences. 'It's now a bit like going to see *The Resistible Rise of Arturo Ui* with a coach party of SS men', wrote Thomas Sutcliffe in the *Independent*. '[R]ather as though coachloads of Venetian Jews had driven up to applaud Mr Shakespeare's play about a vengeful Jewish usurer', wrote Jeremy Kingston in *The Times*.[77] Stafford-Clark told a journalist that 'I'm cautiously optimistic . . . that we may be going to make serious money'.[78]

A play about the world of finance, born in the world of finance, *Serious Money* keeps distance from the world of finance only with its relentlessly ironic tone. The villainous Corman revels in his plans for an inefficient company ('sack them all, put in new staff'[79]), little different, as it happens, than his plans for a well-run company. But the playwright is careful not to grant undue sympathy to Corman's victim, Duckett, who betrays his similarity to Corman when he complains that 'I've sacked the finance director and the chief of marketing who'd both been with the company ten years. I've closed two factories and made five hundred people redundant. No one can say I'm not a hardhitting management'.[80] Churchill also lampoons the art/business merger that Thatcher promoted, mocking not only consumers such as Merrison (who buys a Matisse for seven million dollars) but also the artists who collude with corporate interests. Duckett's public relations strategy – summarised by Etherington as 'You're a sweet English maiden, all shining and bright. / And Corman's the villain intent upon rape'[81] – crucially involves his commissioning of a sixty-foot public art project, a mural whose very title, Urban and Rural, connects pastoral Albion to the City. Finally, Duckett is just another bush league villain struggling to keep up with the international bad guys: he sponsors provincial orchestras, but Corman becomes chairman of the board of the National Theatre. When Zac praises London – 'I go to the theatre, I don't get mugged, I have classy friends'[82] – we hear Churchill's warning about 'the investment potential of high culture', as Daniel Jernigan has aptly described it.[83] The playwright's blistering critique sits somewhat uneasily alongside Stafford-Clark's fundraising boast that 'we got some of our backing from people we met in the City'.[84] Accepting too much City money, either wittingly (by seeking investors) or unwittingly (at the box office), the Wyndham's *Serious Money* gained some uncomfortable meanings that its script does not invite. We should recall that Shadwell's stockjobbers also sold a patent for 'bringing some Chinese Rope-Dancers over' for London's theatrical edification.[85] By the time of Thatcher's Britain, even a strikingly anti-capitalist work such as *Serious Money* could be transformed into an investment vehicle. Its investors started receiving dividends after only six weeks, by which time the Wyndham's capitalisation had been recouped.[86] It continued to play for a year and remains the most-seen single production of Churchill's career.

In *Serious Money*, Scilla instructs us in the futures market: 'On the floor of Liffe the commodity is money. / You can buy and sell money, you can buy and sell absence of money'.[87] Speculating about future values of complete abstractions – 'you don't have to take delivery of anything at all'[88] – and hedging these speculations in markets and time zones all over the world, investors elude even the boundaries of time and space. Churchill's action neatly encodes this idea by anarchically ricocheting from past to future and by collapsing spatial borders: recall the global make up of its gallery of rogues or its second scene, with its simultaneous speakers and settings. Peter Hartwell's set design followed suit, providing a *palais à volonté* that served as everyplace at once, its only signifiers being the banks of phones and monitors on which trades are always being conducted somewhere in the world. One of the play's most telling scenes shows Jacinta flying first class, beautifully capturing the groundlessness of capital. In production, there was no plane or indication of flying; rather, Jacinta narrated her emotional and financial investments in England, Peru, Switzerland from centre stage, while the '*metal exchange starts quietly trading copper. When* **Jacinta** *finishes speaking the trading reaches its noisy climax*'.[89] Time and place are irrelevant. All that matters 'is the massive sums of money being passed round the world', as Zac summarises. Reminding us of *Owners*' Marion, he adds that 'trying to appreciate their size can drive you mental'.[90]

Churchill demonstrates the maddening disorientation caused as global capital exchange comes to dominate the economy – a theme, too, of *Icecream*, her next play with Stafford-Clark and Hartwell. Her treatment of spatial and temporal dislocation echoes Frosby's lament that 'Since Big Bang the floor is bare, / They deal in offices on screens. / But if the chap's not really there / You can't be certain what he means'.[91] The concurrent transformations in arts funding and market regulation might explain the unexpected sympathy Churchill betrays for the old-guard traders, displaced by the barbarians at the market gates. It is true that Churchill has fun satirising an old boys' network represented by Frosby, Greville, and the American banker Merrison, forced out of Klein Merrick. But we are clearly meant to relish Merrison's revenge-driven takeover of Corman Enterprises, which he orchestrates through an absurdly small company, Missouri Gumballs. And she shows Greville and Frosby's relationship as one of the few in the play not motivated by money. The play's conclusion clarifies these sympathies. While the venal City and the collusive Conservatives exonerate and indeed reward Corman, the obsolete Greville is 'put in prison to show the government was serious about keeping the city clean'.[92] Frosby's difference from the trading parvenus, meanwhile, finds thematic and formal expression. Eleven rhyming couplets tell the fate of the play's characters, but he gets the odd (twenty-third) line, which doesn't scan poetically: 'Frosby was forgotten'.[93] His conclusion – as close as the play comes to poignancy – is followed by the play's rousing sung finale, in which the Grimeses and Scillas and Cormans celebrate the champagne and cocaine and Maseratis that Thatcher's reign has afforded them, all the while commanding the audience to 'send her victorious for five fucking morious / five more glorious years'.[94]

The play debuted prior to an election campaign, and on 11 June 1987 – between the Court and Wyndham's runs – Thatcher was in fact re-elected. But if she wasn't finished, neither was *Serious Money*, which crossed the Atlantic that autumn. Following a pattern established by *Top Girls* and *Fen*, the move was initiated by the Public Theater's formidable producer, Joseph Papp, following negotiations with the British and American actors' unions: George C. Wolfe's *The Colored Museum* headed to the Royal Court later that season so that eight members of Churchill's British cast, including Bassett and Burt Caesar, could come to New York. (The secondary company of traders, including a young Sophie Okonedo, were replaced by American actors, including Julianne Moore, later to land a leading role in Churchill's *Icecream*.) Once again, a contractual exchange of property was required. American rights, previously sold by the English Stage Company to Royal Court Productions Ltd, were co-licensed to the Public, which came to own a share of future North American productions until its option expired in February 2006. Installed at the Public's Newman Theater, *Serious Money* opened again on 3 December (after a week of previews) to very good reviews and some grousing about the British cast's American accents. (The surprising exception was Clive Barnes, Churchill's loudest New York champion for over a decade. 'I have come to expect more', he wrote.[95]) The run played at 99.68 per cent of capacity, making the Public over $230,000 in a month.

The play's resonance in New York is hardly surprising. The City zeitgeist began on Wall Street, as Zac himself explains, and the plot explicitly features America's leading-edge market manoeuvres such as the junk bonds that (Etherington laments) were not possible in Britain 'just yet'.[96] Stateside, the financial industry remained ubiquitous in entertainment – Stone's *Wall Street* opened during Churchill's Newman run – and on newspaper front pages, which chronicled the recently launched investigation of 'junk bond king' Michael Milken. Indeed, the play seemed timelier than ever: six weeks before the New York opening, the Black Monday crash of 19 October demonstrated anew the madness-inducing power of the markets, as exchanges all over the world fell like dominoes, haemorrhaging huge percentages of their value. These market realities also buffeted the conditions of the play's production. The Public, one of America's largest not-for-profit theatres, lost two million dollars of its endowment. (In an incredible irony, the era also saw the resignation of one of the Public's board members, Ivan Boesky, who had donated at least $138,000 to Papp's theatre.[97]) Financially vulnerable, the theatre must surely have looked to the example of the for-profit Royal Court Productions Ltd, whose show at Wyndham's was still playing in the West End with a replacement cast, still paying healthy dividends. Papp had had successes with both *Top Girls* and *Fen*, which he continued to run with American casts after their time-limited Actors' Equity exchanges had ended, and therefore a New York remount of *Serious Money* was quickly in the works. But this time Papp moved well out of the not-for-profit arena. For the first time in either of their careers, Stafford-Clark and Churchill were headed to Broadway (and a 1,058-seat house) thanks to a $700,000 capitalisation from the Shubert Organization, then as now one of Broadway's powerhouse producing organisations.

Churchill has bemoaned the critical tendency to dwell on *Serious Money*'s reliance on financial-industry audiences, arguing 'I think that it has been exaggerated by the right-wing press . . . it wasn't a simple case of the City liking it'.[98] At the same time, she overlooks how her own production team, including Stafford-Clark, promoted this very narrative. In New York, too, as in its previous iterations, *Serious Money* tried to maintain an ironic critical distance from corporate interests even as it flirted dangerously with them. One cast member taunted the yuppies in the audience, telling a journalist: 'We mock them, but they're so vain they come to see it anyway'.[99] Behind the scenes, a stage manager wrote in one of the show's daily reports that an audience member 'left during Act 1 to throw up. . . . Perhaps the sight of very rich people vomitting is an encouraging response to this play' – pegging spectators as consumers, purged by a product they need but didn't expect.[100] Paul Moriarty and Allan Corduner (the sole member of the cast to appear in all four runs thanks to a special arrangement with Actors' Equity) took a different line, appealing to the savvy of New York audiences who, they implied, might better get the joke. 'It was like party time in London. People used to get shampooed up with champagne before they came in, and rock with laughter at it all', said Moriarty. 'What distressed us after a while was the fact that we were being given these great gales of laughter by the very people whom theoretically we were satirizing . . . [W]e felt they had missed the irony entirely', said Corduner.[101]

In fact the irony was evolving. Behind the scenes, the 'very people' satirised were courted ever more assiduously, as the producers targeted Wall Street in promotional and fundraising schemes. The Securities Industry Association hosted one evening's performance at the Public, using the night to raise money for its Economic Education Foundation, whose trustees included financial-industry stars from Goldman Sachs and Salomon Brothers; the *Financial Times* hosted another, for a guest list that included representatives from the Federal Reserve, Merrill Lynch, and Morgan Stanley. (Asked to attend, Churchill declined.) And the opening night party for the Broadway transfer, 9 February 1988, was held on the trading floor of the Commodity Exchange or Comex, where the Broadway cast had received its on-site training in the market's workings. Correspondence between the producers and Comex reveals the diligence with which the event was conceived: invitees including Meryl Streep, Glenn Close, and Kevin Kline were to be taught how to trade; tickers and monitors were to play as the event's festive backdrop. If the producers believed such an event was congruous with Churchill's carefully constructed satire, Alan Brody, the chairman of Comex, was savvier. Asked by the *New York Times* about his unexpected new friendship with the theatrical community, he answered with a sly jab: 'Don't read too much into this party. We're doing it as a fund event for the traders'.[102]

Whatever the pretended relationship between the exchange and the production, Brody revealed a blunter truth: the creative work of the actors was being leveraged if not co-opted, the value of its cultural glamour seen clearly by Comex and purchased 'for the traders'. (Again Churchill was absent. She told the journalist she found the opening night venue 'puzzling'.[103]) As with *Owners*' Worsely and Lisa, a patina of social interaction covers a dynamic that is, finally, economic. We are reminded of Marx and Engels's description in *The Communist Manifesto* of how the bourgeoisie whittles down possibilities for social relations until there is 'no other nexus between man and man than naked self-interest, than callous "cash payment"'.[104] In *Serious Money*, Baines and Corman send one another gifts ostensibly of friendship, but she in fact encourages Merrison in his takeover of Corman Enterprises when her economic interests are served. Greville introduces Zackerman by calling him a 'colleague', but this apparent collegiality masks a brute material reality. 'Klein have taken over Daddy', as Scilla correctly sees. 'How long will he last?'[105] Meanwhile, in one of the play's most ferocious scenes, Scilla and Grimes arrive unbidden at her father's house. As Grimes peruses the estate ('If you want to sell the house I can pay cash'), Scilla demands information about Zac's serious money ('Fuck off. I want my share'), ignoring Greville's paternal entreaties.[106] Even the bonds of family prove no match for the logic of acquisition: once Goneril and Regan own the kingdom, Lear too is resigned to obsolescence. When Corman meets Thatcher's cabinet minister Gleason at the National Theatre during the interval of *King Lear*, Churchill lands one of Act 2's cleverest satirical jibes. But this meeting and the play's opening night party at Comex share discomfiting significations.

On the page, *Serious Money* underwent only minor changes in its move to Broadway. For example, the line 'Biddulph's running Albion and is big in ITV' was changed to 'Biddulph's running Albion but the price fell in the crash', and a reference to Northern England was given a clarifying couplet with an American reference: 'The north of England's the home of the painter Lowry / But for unemployment it's kind of like the Bowery'.[107] However, the production underwent greater changes in its metatheatrical and extra-theatrical resonances. The idea of an ensemble cast was jettisoned. As the New York press breathlessly reported (and as Stafford-Clark's diary confirms), Isabella Rossellini was considered as Jacinta, Kevin Bacon as Corman, Richard Dreyfuss as Zac.[108] Papp dampened speculation by saying, 'It's moving because of Caryl Churchill. She's the only big name we need'.[109] In reality, a big name was sought and found in Kate Nelligan, rocketed to fame by David Hare's *Plenty* and her film career. Cast in Linda Bassett's roles, she was guaranteed the best dressing room, a minor but telling detail. (Also cast was Alec Baldwin, whose *Married to the Mob* and *Beetlejuice* were filmed but still unreleased and who had already begun work on Mike Nichols's *Working Girl*: an explanation, perhaps, both for the producers' enthusiasm and Stafford-Clark's puzzlement at the actor's preferential contract terms. '[B]y no means a star', was the director's 1987 assessment.[110]) Production records confirm that the Royal Court paid the original cast more or less equally. But by Broadway, Corduner – so indispensable to the show that all agreed he could not be recast – earned only a third of Nelligan's salary. The secondary company of traders, meanwhile, was re-evaluated; three of them, let go. (Moore was asked to stay but declined.)

Privately, Stafford-Clark fretted that the show had lost its collective spirit and intimated that Nelligan's lack of interest in her fellow actors resulted inevitably from the show's new material reality. In his journals, he inveighs against a 'vain & self regarding' Broadway culture, complaining that '[a]ny theatrical debate in US is immediately subsumed by the far greater issue of. . . . Is it a hit?'[111] He bemoans that 'union regulations and producers' greed' made 'the working conditions of the industry . . . manifestly absurd'.[112] But the play's records suggest his attraction to Broadway and its prospect of serious money. His agent, Peter Murphy, bickered volubly with the producers about salary, per diems, and especially lodgings: they had rented Stafford-Clark an apartment on Park Avenue, but he preferred to stay at the storied Algonquin Hotel. One contentious issue concerned the royalty pool set up to apportion box office proceeds to parties including the director. Murphy separately negotiated a guaranteed take of every week's box office for his client, which led to a particularly exasperated exchange of letters. As officials from the Public Theater and the Royal Court commiserated, the concept of a mutually shared royalty pool was undermined if some of its parties were guaranteed minimums. '[I]t is grossly unfair that certain pool members be eligible for guarantees and some not', wrote one.[113] Stafford-Clark's profits would have exceeded that of the English Stage Company, the organisation he himself stewarded and the first shareholder in the play's rights. Many issues – including the director's demand that his name never appear in a font size smaller than Churchill's in the show's publicity – were not fully resolved until after the show began previews.

'[S]exy greedy *is* the late eighties', Dolcie Starr declares.[114] And in her formulation we find a key to the play's complex dynamics both on the page and on stage. Money-making initially seems a displacement activity in *Serious Money*, most obviously in the rousing 'Futures Song' that ends Act 1, with its double entendres about financial rogering. Scilla dresses up sexily to deliver a 'Kissogram' but only to infiltrate Corman Enterprises. Corman advises: 'A deal like this, at the start you gently woo it. / There comes a time when you get in there and screw it'.[115] A Liffe dealer jokes about the similarity between a clitoris and a Filofax: 'Every cunt's got one'.[116] But sex is not a metaphor. Rather, finance expresses the urgency and inescapability of an erotic drive. Money arouses. Its desire, like the markets, proves insatiable; the thrusts and flows of global capital, relentless in their penetration of national and personal barriers. The Big Bang provides no release. Instead, it unleashes an acquisitive lust that propels us toward destructive, compulsive behaviours, just as Marion had discovered in *Owners*. The dangers are clearly signified: Aids, which hovers over the entire play, stands in for capital's incurable toxicity even as it augments sex's taboo appeal.

Linking sex, money, and aggression more sure-footedly than Bret Easton Ellis's *American Psycho* would manage, *Serious Money* exposes its era's signature dynamic: simultaneous attraction and repulsion toward the play's titular subject. The original workshop was driven by a fascination with the City, whose traders' energy inspired Churchill as much as their greed appalled her. At the Royal Court, the show advertised the very conspicuous consumption that the script condemns, relying for its props on fifty companies, including Moët et Chandon, Christian Dior, Asprey, Gucci, and Jindo Fur Salon, which supplied Syal with Jacinta's mink and fox coat. To capitalise a commercial production at Wyndham's, *Serious Money* asked the City. In the play's reception, the push and pull continued. We see repulsion in Churchill's mockery of the financial industry, returned in a caustic *Telegraph* article that derides the play's attitude toward yuppie bankers.[117] But a countervailing attraction is intrinsic to satire, which tends to flatter its victims. The playwright Howard Barker warned Stafford-Clark early in the process that 'the inside dealers, city wheelers will be flattered and tickled', and so it proved.[118] The erotically charged 'tickling' of a rich and repellent partner seems a sign of the times. When Stafford-Clark's journals from the period expose both his contempt for Broadway (its greedy producers, its conservative audiences, its pabulum offerings) as well as his unvarnished desire for its approval, there is no contradiction.

Reading the play's New York production files – teeming with financials, with budgets surpassing projections and box office revenues falling short of them – it is hard not to be reminded of *Owners*' lessons about the seductions of property. With profits the motive, Broadway discourages a joint stock ethos and tacitly endorses the acquisitive values of individual ownership: witness the haggling over the play's royalties, and the false equity of the 'pool' concept as individual pieces are sliced. By contrast, Churchill's aesthetics and politics promote an economy of sharing. In *Serious Money*, she borrows text from Shadwell and dramaturgy from Brecht. Behind the scenes on Broadway, the playwright stayed out of the financial fray: her own contracts had been negotiated by Ramsay upfront, in early 1987; the potentially lucrative film rights went unsold after she insisted that Stafford-Clark, who had never made a film, be allowed to direct. One suspects that Churchill's much-mentioned shyness only partly explains her aloofness from the Royale Theatre (now the Bernard B. Jacobs), where she saw the show for the first time only on 16 February 1988. Four nights later, *Serious Money* closed, fifteen performances and less than two weeks after the Comex party. The show never grossed in excess of its running costs, estimated to be $140,000 per week, and the Shubert Organisation lost its entire capitalisation.[119]

The play had been developed as a collective venture in the Joint Stock way, produced by a state-subsidised, non-commercial theatre, the Royal Court; it ended up in the most expensive for-profit theatre market in the world in a production whose budget was itself serious money (over $86,000 on the initial print ads alone) and whose opening night saw it fêted at the exchange its script pillories. This journey may demonstrate Churchill's principal point about capital, able to penetrate even the unlikeliest corners. As Jernigan writes:

> Churchill constructs a metatheatrical form that is uniquely capable of describing the newly multinational process involved in putting on a theatrical production. She creates a dramatic experience that does not merely break the fourth wall by enfolding the audience into itself, but also recognizes that the fourth wall has already been broken from the other side, as contemporary theater finds itself in the precarious position of being enveloped by multinational business. Churchill provides us with a theater that understands how theater itself has become another component of the corporate enterprise.[120]

And so *Serious Money* may represent the triumph of Thatcher's cultural policy, which emulated that already in practice in the United States. (When *Blue Heart* went to the Brooklyn Academy of Music in 1999, for instance, Churchill would object to the sponsorship of tobacco giant Philip Morris.[121]) It's a fact of life: in the season in which I write, 2012–13, the wealth management firm Coutts has underwritten *Love and Information*, Churchill's latest play at the Royal Court, whose namesake limited company has transferred three different shows – Laura Wade's *Posh*, April de Angelis's *Jumpy*, and Nick Payne's *Constellations* – to the West End. Capitalism prevails. In hindsight it comes as no surprise that *Serious Money* followed the capitalist economy's characteristic pattern: a bullish success giving way to a spectacular and expensive crash.

We must therefore be cautious about seeing *Serious Money*'s quick closing as a 'failure', since surely Churchill asks us to consider success in terms other than those of financial enterprise. It is largely unremembered that, despite a dust-up between Papp and the *New York Times* (who sent a second-string reviewer to the re-opening), the Broadway reviews proved even more positive than those for the Public run, with both Baldwin and Nelligan singled out for praise. The latter was nominated for a Tony Award. The stage manager's daily report for the last show notes: 'A great audience and a wonderful show. . . . We closed in glory'.[122] In London, the play won both a Best Play Olivier and an *Evening Standard* Award (Churchill's first in both cases); two days after the Broadway closing, she accepted the Susan Smith Blackburn Prize for playwriting (her second, after *Fen*); in May 1988, she received an Obie Award for playwriting (her third, after *Cloud Nine* and *Top Girls*).

In 1987, Neil Collins, one of the financial community's best-known journalists, had assessed Churchill's understanding of her exceedingly complex subject as 'far more informative than a dozen text books'.[123] The depth of her understanding became clearer in 2008, when the global financial crisis clarified the consequences of buying and selling debt – 'the absence of money', Scilla calls it.[124] In hindsight, Churchill seemed to have predicted the dangers of an unregulated market and foreseen the global reach of its potential devastation. High-profile revivals followed. In 2009, Jonathan Munby directed the show at Birmingham Rep. In 2010, Eda Holmes directed at Canada's Shaw Festival (a context that recognised both Churchill's socialism and her Shavian provocation). In 2012, Cheryl Faraone directed off-Broadway, in a production that mixed professional and student actors; it was revived in the same space during the summer of 2013. But none transferred to a commercial venue, perhaps understanding that 'satire of big business for the commercial theatre is a self-contradiction', as one critic has put it.[125] Retrospect certainly made clear how for-profit conditions of production could ramify the play's significations. *Serious Money* clearly condemns the all-encompassing reach of multinational capital (and specifically its intrusion into the world of art), but its original production in fact facilitated this intrusion by seeking investors and by marketing itself as cheeky fun for the global financial services industry. Thus its producers may have blunted the play's political edge by acceding to the very logic that Churchill cautions us still to resist.

A Dream Play

Churchill's preoccupation with capitalist ownership receives a surprising side-light from *A Dream Play*, her 2005 version of August Strindberg's 1901 creation *Ett Drömspel*. One of the most radical works in the dramatic canon, Strindberg's play mimics the form of a dream. As he wrote in the preface: 'Everything can happen, everything is possible and probable. . . . The characters split, double, multiply, evaporate, condense, dissolve and merge'.[126] The conventions of time and space that govern reality are abandoned. Time slows and accelerates; settings metamorphose. Cause and effect uncouple. The plot juxtaposes mundane details, such as a man waiting in vain for his fiancée, with metaphysical preoccupations: the central story involves the Vedic god Indra, whose daughter has come to live among mortals. Taking the name Agnes, she marries an idealistic lawyer and grapples with a fundamental paradox: earth is a paradise and yet its people live in misery. She encounters recognisable social problems – allowing Strindberg to address his characteristic concerns with class struggle and gender relations – but in a shifting and surreal dreamscape where, for example, an organ plays human voices or a coal mine appears on the shores of the Mediterranean. (One character sees this location as heaven, another as hell, thus encompassing the radically subjective perspectives of a shared dream.) Eventually Agnes returns to the heavens, where she promises to report the agonies gathered in her shawl: 'Farewell! Tell your brothers and sisters that I remember them / where I go now, and in their name / I bring their lamentations to the throne. / Farewell!'[127] Churchill's version renders this speech in its characteristic diction, compressed and colloquial: 'Goodbye. Tell people / I won't forget them. / I'll tell the gods / what being alive is'.[128]

A Dream Play is one of several translations Churchill has undertaken. In the late 1990s, she wrote English versions of three plays by the Belgian playwright Maurice Maeterlinck: *The Intruder* (based on *L'Intruse*, 1891), *The Death of Tintagiles* (*La Mort de Tintagiles*, 1894), and *Interior* (*Intérieur*, 1895). All remain unpublished and unstaged. Her version of Seneca's *Thyestes* premiered at the Royal Court Theatre Upstairs on 7 June 1994, directed by her frequent collaborator James Macdonald; he used contemporary closed-circuit television monitors to mediate the action of Churchill's text, largely faithful to the Latin. She also translated *Félicité* by the contemporary Québécois playwright Olivier Choinière: *Bliss* premiered on 28 March 2008, also in the Royal Court's Upstairs space, in a production directed by Joe Hill-Gibbons. Unique among these projects, *A Dream Play* saw Churchill working from a literal translation, since she reads no Swedish. But it stands out for more significant reasons. As in her work with Maeterlinck and Seneca, Churchill updated the imagery. For example, Strindberg's coalheavers are replaced by building workers. His cabbages, symbolising cheap food that the poor are forced to eat too often, are replaced by lentils. (See, too, the unnamed protagonist in 'she bit her tongue', who subsists on 'lentils all week' in order to afford fancy dates with her married lover.[129]) However, while her other translations follow their sources closely, *A Dream Play* radically compresses Strindberg, eliminating scenes and stripping those that remain down to their essences. Churchill cut seemingly integral symbols, such as a beautiful flower in need of deep dirt to thrive: a signature image, it appears throughout Strindberg's writings, becoming literalised in *The Ghost Sonata*'s Hyacinth Girl. She also cut the meaning of life, which Indra's daughter reveals to The Writer; in Churchill's version, Agnes unintelligibly whispers the revelation. The result is spare dialogue resembling that of Churchill's other twenty-first-century plays. When The Writer describes the disappointments he has caused his family and friends, for instance, he bemoans that he 'completely fucked up everyone who loved me'.[130] The cumulative effect of these deletions and compressions is first to accelerate the play and second to ground it in a contemporary world while maintaining its fantastic dream-images. One change is representative. Strindberg's play begins in the heavens, with Indra's daughter standing on the topmost cloud in the sky talking to her father. Churchill's play begins after this prologue: Agnes is already on earth and in conversation with a Glazier, outside a 'tower with a flower bud on top'.[131] Retaining the surreal setting of Strindberg's first scene, Churchill too begins and ends in the same place. The 'bud bursts into a giant chrysanthemum' at the play's end.[132]

Churchill notes that 'I'd thought of [Strindberg] as misogynistic and depressive and mostly concerned with miserable relationships and disastrous families'.[133] And English-language audiences in general betray a similarly limited perspective, perhaps because of the dominance of *Miss Julie* among Strindberg's English-language productions. In fact, his work shows astonishing range. He produced novels, short stories, poetry, memoirs, and non-fiction (such as the startlingly radical manifesto 'Woman's Rights', which he released alongside a feminism-inflected story collection, *Getting Married*). Churchill has steadfastly focused on one genre and its near relations, such as radio plays and teleplays. But comparing their dramatic output, we see the two playwrights as close kin: as soon as a stylistic innovation threatens to resemble a customary style, each renovates his or her playwriting idiom. Strindberg's historical verse dramas such as *Master Olof* led to experiments in naturalism such as *The Father*, which gave way to the dream-play experiments he began with *To Damascus* and the radical expressionism of chamber plays such as *The Pelican*. Churchill's career has roamed stylistically from the loose verse of *Having a Wonderful Time* to the minimalist prose of *Drunk Enough to Say I Love You?*; from the rococo puppet fantasy of *The Marriage of Toby's Idea of Angela and Toby's Idea of Angela's Idea of Toby* to the elliptical, sung-through *Hotel*; from the historical *Light Shining in Buckinghamshire* to the dystopian fantasy *Not Not Not Not Not Enough Oxygen*. What unites Churchill's work as it unites Strindberg's is a commitment to leftist politics. Outside Sweden, many are unaware that Strindberg's death was met with public demonstrations – his coffin accompanied by Social Democratic marchers carrying red banners – and by stony silence from the aristocratic Swedish Academy, whose refusal to confer a Nobel Prize was seen to rebuke his politics.[134]

A Dream Play shares motifs with Churchill's other plays, especially, despite the tonal gulf between them, *Owners*. Western acquisitiveness operates under the cover of a co-opted Christianity, which is contrasted to Eastern spirituality: Churchill placed a Zen epigram at the top of her play; Strindberg's began with a Buddhism-inspired dialogue between the Vedic god and his daughter before she descends to witness the inequalities that make the earthly paradise a misery for its inhabitants. The first mortal Agnes meets is the Glazier, who shares his richly symbolic profession (and apparent lack of work) with Churchill's Alex. Most significantly, we find *Owners*' central concern featuring prominently in *A Dream Play*. Consider this exchange between Indra's daughter and her mortal husband in Churchill's version:

Agnes Is it true they're [the building workers] not allowed to swim here?

Solicitor They can try to drown themselves. But then they get beaten up at the police station.

Agnes Can't they go further down the coast and swim in the countryside?

Solicitor It's all fenced off.

Agnes No, I mean where it doesn't belong to anyone.

Solicitor It all belongs to someone.

Agnes But not the sea?

Solicitor Everything. You can't moor a boat without being charged for it. Good, isn't it?

Agnes Why don't people do something about it?

Solicitor Some of them do but they end up in prison or a psychiatric ward.[135]

With everything reduced to property, discipline and madness beckon. The husband tells Agnes that '[t]he great and the good, the law-abiding citizens' do the work of policing the non-owners; the cruel logic of property permeates so thoroughly that police enforce it and 'hard-working families' submit to it.[136] A few pages later, he repeats his description exactly when characterising the people who crucified Christ and so came to do the opposite of his bidding.

Like Strindberg (or Shakespeare or Calderón) before her, Churchill parallels the anything-goes ontology of the theatre to that of a dream, with its uncanny resemblance to and yet difference from reality. At the same time, both she and Strindberg tie on stage to off, asserting that the privations and sorrows of people in the play reflect those of the world outside the theatre doors. (Including cultural workers: 'It's nearly the end of the season and today they hear if they're going to be kept on', the Stage Door Keeper reports.[137]) The very title *A Dream Play* declares a metatheatricality which the plot reinforces when Agnes encounters the Stage Door Keeper or some 'Theatre People'. As with *Serious Money*, however, the play gained new resonances when it premiered at the National's Cottesloe Theatre on 15 February 2005 (after previews from 4 February), in a production directed by Katie Mitchell, one of Britain's most innovative directors, known for her visually stunning dismantlings of classic plays. It was the first collaboration between the two women, although Mitchell had yearned to direct *Far Away* at the Royal Court (where she was then Associate Director) some years earlier.

Mitchell began rehearsals with research and improvisation, as Stafford-Clark had done with *Serious Money*: the programme details her engagement with neuroscientific, psychological, and religious theories of dreaming and reports her reliance on writings by Sigmund Freud and Carl Jung; she asked participants to record their own dreams and used them as grist for theatrical devising.[138] Churchill took part. The play's rehearsal diary, for instance, includes an entry for 6 December 2004, which describes the playwright's own dream about visiting a doctor. But we must recall that – unlike with *Serious Money* – these rehearsal exercises took place after the text was already written. Accordingly, Mitchell's *Dream Play* very quickly deviated from the script so that, as one actor testified, 'none of us had any idea in the first weeks of rehearsal where we were headed and what the end result would be'.[139] Eventually, the director would cut almost two-thirds of Churchill's already spare text, supplementing what remained with movement devised by her and the cast. For instance, Churchill's first line – 'Look how the tower's grown', Agnes tells the Glazier[140] – occurred eighteen minutes into Mitchell's production, which transformed the line from uncanny to baffling, since she had also cut the blooming tower.

Mitchell evacuated the play of its Eastern themes entirely, cutting all of Agnes's prayers and every instance of her signal phrase: 'This is paradise. But isn't anyone happy here?'[141] In Churchill's rendering, when Agnes meets the Officer waiting for his fiancée, he tells her: 'I look at you and it's something to do with the stars and the smallest particles, you're somehow connected'.[142] Using the Western language of physics, he apprehends the interconnectedness of the universe (which Indra understands in Vedic and Strindberg in Buddhist terms): 'we are stardust, billion year old carbon', as Joni Mitchell famously put it in 'Woodstock'. And so he apprehends the otherworldliness of Agnes, Indra's emissary. The director cut this line, too. In fact, she entirely sidelined Indra's daughter, who was replaced as the play's central figure by Alfred Green, a character devised during the rehearsal process. Given how the Buddhist inflections work in *A Dream Play* (as in *Owners*), the impact of vacating them is clear. Philosophical resonances cede to financial ones. Strindberg began his dream play on a cloud; Churchill, in front of the tower with its bud. Mitchell began in an office, where Agnes seemed to work as a secretary to Alfred, a banker. The play's entire world came to be shadowed by finance: the 'Officer' was renamed 'Broker'; the Billsticker, 'Security Dealer'. And its dreamlike abandonment of time and space came to resemble *Serious Money*'s capital disorientations, with abrupt transitions, disordered timelines, simultaneous scenes, and linguistic pandemonium; actors repeatedly changed roles with the significant exception of Angus Wright, who played Alfred Green throughout.

However beautifully executed and fluidly choreographed, Mitchell's production thus utterly transformed *A Dream Play*'s meanings. First, it omitted almost all class and gender concerns. The exchange about building workers, not allowed to swim in the sea even in the sweltering heat, was removed – as indeed were the building workers. Demoting Agnes from god to secretary, Mitchell also sidelined Kristin, who in the text relentlessly pastes windows to keep draughts out but whose economising threatens to suffocate the residents. (Three of her lines – ten words – survived the cuts.) Only one working-class character remained: Lina, a maid lent an outfit by her benevolent employer. These changes were registered by the play's most astute critic, Amelia Howe Kritzer, who summarised:

> The production offers a psychological examination of the desires and frustrations of a member of England's elite rather than a survey of human suffering. Strindberg's representatives of the working class . . . are displaced by an ensemble arrayed in evening dresses, tuxedoes, business suits, ballet costumes, and lab coats. An emphasis on social embarrassment, exclusion, and personal loss replaces Strindberg's concerns with social inequality and division.[143]

Second, the production abandoned all of the play's outdoor settings, whose fantastic nature images – such as the '[s]corched earth' foregrounded against 'a beautiful seashore' – represent the vastness of the world, its sublime beauty and psychological scars.[144] Mitchell and her designer, Vicki Mortimer, used only interior settings.

Their diminishment of the play's landscape was commensurate with their diminishment of its scope. Mitchell narrowed the play's point-of-view to a single consciousness – that of a white, middle-aged, male banker – dominated by cuckold fantasies and performance anxieties. (In one of the production's most aesthetic set-pieces, he dreams of being asked to perform in *Giselle* at Covent Garden.) We find testament to Alfred's cloistered perspective in the detailed chronology of his life included in Mitchell's production diary. It begins in 1880, with the birth of Albert's father, given the name Herbert, and ends in 1950 – the production's strangely specific setting – at which point Alfred is said to be forty-two. Angus Wright described rehearsals by saying: 'What quickly became clear was that Strindberg's play (and Caryl's version of it) was full of extended dialogue . . . whereas dreams rarely seem to have much dialogue and indeed frequently feature no language at all'.[145] The play's strange happenings are indeed made intelligible through words, as Agnes reminds us when she declares that poetry is 'dreaming when you're awake'.[146] Mitchell cut this line, too. The elimination of poetry suited her solipsistic perspective, which transformed a play in the form of a dream into a representation of a dream.

Strindberg and Churchill's vision encompasses a universal consciousness in which the desires and injustices of an entire society are refracted through the prismatic logic of a dream. They enjoin the collective audience to witness the sufferings of its brothers and sisters and, like Agnes, to leave the scene acknowledging them as their own. The playwrights' shared aesthetic and political concerns fit awkwardly with the auteurist perspective brought by Mitchell and embodied by her creation, Albert Green: a dominant central figure foreign to the source text who displaces the play's original voices. The perspective prompted Nicholas de Jongh of the *Evening Standard* to ask 'Whose play is it anyway?' His review – which judged the show to be an 'amazing evocation'[147] – bridged the two camps of a polarised critical response. Critics setting their knowledge of Strindberg aside were mesmerised by Mitchell's accomplishment as a devisor: Charles Spencer described the show as 'stunning . . . theatrical brilliance'; David Benedict declared it 'extraordinary'.[148] Critics expecting something related to the script (either Strindberg's or Churchill's) were unmoved. Carole Woddis compared the show with Churchill's text and found it 'almost unrecognisable'.[149] '[A] con', declared Alistair Macaulay, estimating that 'what's being presented on stage at the Cottesloe uses less than 5 per cent of Strindberg's original'.[150] Mitchell had absented the play of its critique of private property. But the spectre of ownership returns to haunt us just like the play's revenant image of Kristin, always pasting. Recalling Peggy Ramsay's description of *Owners* as her client's property, Churchill's preface to *A Dream Play* confesses: 'I'm not sure how I'd feel if someone treated one of my plays the way I've treated Strindberg's' and 'I do feel abashed at cutting another writer's work; directors have fewer qualms'.[151] The programme describes 'a play by August Strindberg in a new version by Caryl Churchill' 'from a literal translation by Charlotte Barslund' 'with additional material by Katie Mitchell and the Company' – a billing that suggests a negotiated apportionment of credit rather than the collectivism that had animated a play such as *Light Shining in Buckinghamshire*, whose communitarian rehearsal process I discuss in the fourth chapter. And when Katie Mitchell wrote an opening-night publicity piece about *A Dream Play* for the *Evening Standard*, she didn't mention Churchill once.[152] But publicly Churchill voiced no opposition to Mitchell's whole-scale revision of the script – treated far less gingerly, of course, than Churchill had treated Strindberg's.

Whose play is it anyway? The question is never far away in the theatre industry: not when directors and actors provide the kind of creative input that Churchill allowed in *Cloud Nine*, for instance; or when the play's subjects help to determine its material, as in *Fen* or *Mad Forest*; or with an interdisciplinary collaboration among equals such as *Lives of the Great Poisoners*. But the question gains new urgency in a capitalistic industry, perhaps especially when the parties involved pull in opposite directions aesthetically and politically – as happened, for example, with Churchill's teleplay *The Legion Hall Bombing* (broadcast on 22 August 1978) from which she removed her name after her script was censored by its broadcaster, the BBC.[153] Through her limited company, the playwright owns her 'new version' of *A Dream Play*, Strindberg's being in the public domain. She licenses the performance rights: to the Source Theatre in Washington, D.C., for example, where it had its American premiere on 16 June 2007 in a production (faithful to her text) directed by Allison Arkell Stockman. Churchill might have pressed her case in 2005; many playwrights, such as Samuel Beckett or Edward Albee, have prevented changes that compromised their artistic vision, altered their property. Instead, she may have reflected on the economy of derivation – the principle of sharing – that ripples through her work, including her translations: she once described *Thyestes* as 'a collaboration with a dead writer'.[154] Churchill may have considered the financial consequences for the National Theatre – the state-subsidised producer she had teased in *Serious Money* – and its bravery in producing such a non-commercial show. She may have considered her relationship with Mitchell, strong enough that the playwright would be thanked in programme notes for Mitchell's dramatic exploration of Gertrude Stein's writing, *Say It with Flowers*, in 2013. Churchill may have weighed her and Strindberg's shared politics against Worsely's blunt point that a capitalist owner (such as a playwright) can 'do what he likes with his own'.[155] In any case, there is something quietly radical in her choice to let go of her property at precisely the moment when she might have pressed a claim of ownership. As she said at the time of *Owners*' 1993 revival in New York: 'You've got just to let them go. And by definition, plays are plays, written for other people to take away and do'.[156]

CHAPTER 3
IDENTITY AND THE BODY

In Churchill's 1968 radio play *Identical Twins*, each of the play's titular characters, Clive and Teddy, struggles to understand who he is in light of his overwhelming sameness to his brother. Even after fleeing one another, the twins repeatedly fail adequately to separate – sharing, in a pointed irony, even the illusion of successful individuation. 'Having not seen Clive/Teddy [each says the other's name] for ten years and most successfully making my own life I rarely give him a thought', they declare, their simultaneity betraying their shared delusion.[1] Such overlapping dialogue, of course, would eventually become one of Churchill's signatures. But unlike in *Three More Sleepless Nights, Fen*, or *Top Girls*, here the characters speak on top of one another while delivering the same speech, as they do repeatedly in *Identical Twins*. Not solipsistic, their existential crisis is shared – as shared, indeed, as the personal pronoun 'I' repeatedly intoned in their eerily dual voice. The only difference is a name: one says 'Clive' while the other says 'Teddy'. But this difference proves to be inconsequential. We learn that each responds to the other's name, for example, so that the confusion of others – not even the twins' parents can tell them apart – becomes something less than a misidentification. And after Clive's existential angst leads him to suicide, Teddy easily takes over his brother's identity in an unsettling expression of grief. Churchill beautifully theatricalises the twins' existential quandary (and the brothers' lack of difference) by leveraging an essential advantage of the radio play: the genre allows both parts to be played by the same actor even when the two characters share scenes or speeches. For the play's premiere production, for example – it was broadcast on BBC Radio 3 on 21 November 1968 – Kenneth Haigh portrayed both characters. Thus the audience heard Haigh (famously Jimmy Porter in the Royal Court's premiere production of *Look Back in Anger*) speak in eerie stereo as he described and made manifest the twins' stultifying similarity.

Early in the play, for example, Haigh's overdubbed voices recalled the twins being punished for a nude romp in the garden:

> **Teddy and Clive** We ran into the garden and took off our clothes. The grass was cold and the rain was wet on my back. Naughty boys. Naughty boys. Oh naughty boys. . . . It was Clive/Teddy, it was Clive/[T]eddy, I shrieked as Daddy spanked my bottom. Not me, not me.[2]

Churchill's focus on the naked bodies even as the twins disavow their identities ('not me') sketches the essential difference between stage and radio. She conjures the twins as disembodied characters who recollect in hindsight in the voice of a single, absent actor who recorded the dialogue two weeks before the broadcast. And thus the playwright underscores how radio drama works differently to secure its characters' identities. A live stage version of the same scene – as for example at the Royal Court on 1 October 2002, in a rehearsed reading of the play directed by Dominic Cooke – would require the blunt corporeality that tells against the twin's putatively identical appearance. Cooke, for example, cast brothers John and Martin Marquez, whose physical dissimilarities undermined the play's central conceit. And even if we imagine a hypothetical case with real-life twin actors (as Mark Ravenhill used in his 2009 play *Over There*, starring Luke and Harry Treadaway) differences would begin asserting themselves in and through the body, so central to identity. These differences – learned gestures, earned scars – would testify precisely to how the body is marked, altered by its own lived history. In this chapter, I take up Churchill's longstanding preoccupation with the body – and how it reveals the cultural and ideological histories written on it even as, in its own unique performance, it can modify or subvert these very histories.

Cloud Nine

Churchill turned decisively away from radio plays in the early 1970s (her last was 1973's *Perfect Happiness*). While the reasons for this turn were partly contextual – the radio play's popularity waned just as Churchill's success on the stage waxed after 1972's *Owners* – there is no doubt that live performance with physically present performers provided a richer avenue for exploring the complex relationship between identity and the body. Most obviously in *Cloud Nine*, written for Max Stafford-Clark's Joint Stock company after a three-week workshop, she turned to the question of how the body is shaped not only by self-concepts but also by the social and ideological contexts that condition its material expression: contexts that tell a boy to carry himself in this manner or a woman to sit down in that. Churchill's play theatricalises how the body expresses the weight of its historical burdens as it adapts to fit a role predetermined by ideological pressures. By working through these ideas in the theatre – precisely the genre in which actors too adapt their bodies to pre-existing scripts – Churchill addresses the forces that compel performance. She does so not only textually (in the play's themes, plot, and dialogue) but theatrically (in its stage language) and metatheatrically (insofar as the play is self-reflexive).

Famously, *Cloud Nine* is structured as a diptych. The first act unfolds in late nineteenth-century Africa and concerns Clive's role in colonising the indigenous population while disciplining his wife (Betty), son (Edward), and daughter (Victoria) into the roles prescribed to them by Victorian family structures and social mores. These attempts play out under threat from the destabilising effects of sex: the gay desire of his friend Harry Bagley for Clive's servant Joshua, Edward, and Clive himself; the lesbian desire of the governess Ellen for Betty; the straight desire of Betty for Harry and of Clive for a fellow British colonial, Mrs Saunders. Historically situating the act as she does, Churchill marries Clive's duties as colonial overseer to his duties as patriarch – a marriage succinctly suggested by the opening stage directions which juxtapose '*Flagpole with union jack*' with '*The Family*'.[3] Meanwhile, Churchill's ideas about the constraints of Victorian identity (and Britain's colonial history) on the present day, that is 1979, are enacted in the play's second half, from which Clive has been absented. Now living in London, Betty, Victoria, and Edward have aged only twenty-five years in spite of the century-long gap. The three search for personal fulfilment as they comically navigate new social constraints (loosened by feminism and gay rights) and a new set of scene partners: Gerry (Edward's boyfriend), Martin (Victoria's husband), Tommy (their son), Lin (Victoria's friend and eventual lover), and Cathy (Lin's daughter). Yet ghosts from the first act – both figurative and literal – intrude, manifesting William Faulkner's famous observation that the past is never dead and, indeed, not even past. Both acts use non-naturalistic staging devices such as cross-casting (a male actor plays Act 1's Betty, for example) and doubling (each actor plays multiple roles, actors change roles from act to act); such devices serve the metatheatrical purpose of reminding spectators that they are watching a play. And in this way the role-playing involved in everyday life (in historically determined roles of wife or father, for example) is continuously yoked to the concept of role-playing on the stage.

One moment of *Cloud Nine* might serve as synoptic of Churchill's ideas. In the first act, Edward (played by an adult female actor) is berated by his mother for playing with his sister's doll, which he refuses to return to her. 'Victoria doesn't love her. Victoria never even plays with her', he proclaims in his defence. Edward's grandmother Maud retorts that 'Victoria will learn to play with her' as his mother slaps him and he bursts into tears. Simultaneously, his governess enters and is exhorted to 'do [her] job', causing her too to cry and flee. And Maud attempts to smooth over the familial tension: 'There now, Vicky's got her baby back. Where did Vicky's naughty baby go? Shall we smack her? Just a little smack (**Maud** *smacks the doll hard.*) There, now she's a good baby. Clap hands, daddy comes, with his pockets full of plums. All for Vicky's baby. When I was a child we honoured our parents'.[4] In a clear analogue to the colonial project, Maud's smacking of the doll, like Betty's smacking of Edward and upbraiding of Ellen, represents a disciplinary force that presents itself as necessary and benign ('[j]ust a little smack') even against the material evidence of its actual impact ('*smacks the doll hard*'). Teaching Edward and Victoria (who will 'learn'), Maud serves as a surrogate for Ellen, whose role as governess makes plain her disciplinary function. But Maud ultimately surrogates the larger ideological force, patriarchy, that has forbidden Edward to play with the doll in the first place. For Edward's indoctrination into 'manliness' clearly prepares him to one day inherit Clive's patriarchal and, relatedly, colonial duties. Family, in other words, is the irreducible unit at the centre of a large structure of power relations, just as the disciplinary specialist Pierre teaches the reformatory boys in *Softcops*, written immediately before *Cloud Nine* despite its belated premiere (at the Barbican Pit on 2 January 1984, in a production directed by Howard Davies). 'Here you will live in a group called family', Pierre instructs.[5] And thus *Cloud Nine* too invokes the spectre of daddy, coming, pockets full of plums, to provide the reward for everyone's eventual conformity to prescribed roles.

Feminist theory tells us that such conformity works precisely to procure patriarchal succession: a sex/gender system organises persons into, and assigns roles according to, a neat binary pair (male/female) while privileging the former of these terms; homosexuality is condemned because it confuses the heteronormative compulsion to pair one term with its other.[6] Following Michel Foucault, the feminist theorist Judith Butler formulates it thus: the demands of sexuality produce our understanding of sex, 'an artificial concept which effectively extends and disguises the power relations responsible for its genesis'.[7] Such a system makes it inappropriate for Edward to play with the doll, who is instead meant for Victoria; she, as it happens, is played by another doll, in a potent image of her lack of agency under nineteenth-century patriarchy. Moreover, although the ostensible transgressor is Edward, Maud metes out discipline to Victoria's 'naughty baby': the punishment is visited upon the least powerful player in the familial structure. Pointedly, Churchill stresses that neither the roles nor the disciplinary actions that police them originate with Maud; rather, they are embedded in a history reaching back much farther than 'when [Maud] was a child'. Bearing the burden of history, Maud does the work of its ideological baggage, teaching Edward how discipline begets compliance: 'There, now she's a good baby'.

It is no accident that Churchill presents this moment while, just off stage, Clive is flogging some native Africans, stable boys to be given 'justice'.[8] The playwright connects onstage representation and offstage reality as surely as she entwines patriarchy and Empire. Thus, when

Clive enters immediately after the doll has been punished, Edward swiftly confesses his transgression, and Clive responds: 'You should always respect and love me, Edward, not for myself, I may not deserve it, but as I respected and loved my own father, because he was my father. Through our father we love our Queen and our God, Edward. Do you understand? It is something men understand'.[9] He too highlights the role of tradition in upholding patriarchal and colonial ideologies, expanding this tradition to include religion, in whose name these ideologies frequently act. (We see Joshua made to perform a Christmas carol in the play's second scene.) And thus Churchill provides a theoretical foundation for the mock-orgy scene in Act 2, when Edward, Victoria, and Lin will try to expiate the effects of Christianity as they condemn male domination and celebrate alternative sexualities.

An interest in class, gender, and race appears early in Churchill's work. For example, her 1963 play *Lee* dramatises the destructive privilege exercised by the titular character over the working class Edwards (whom Lee beats), Edwards's daughter Jane (whom Lee seduces), and Lee's black associate, Vin (who is held responsible for the suicide of Jane's sister, Sara). The BBC deemed the play too contrived to fit its political message, and it remains unpublished and unproduced. But Churchill's theoretical reading in the ensuing years enriched her sense that race, sex, class, and gender are messy ideological business. *Cloud Nine* in particular bears the influence of her reading of the seventies, which included writing by Frantz Fanon, Jean Genet, and Michel Foucault. It is no surprise to find that Max Stafford-Clark's journal's first mention of the project calls it 'Politiques Sexuelles'.[10] These Francophone thinkers helped Churchill understand how various ideological structures (family, class, nation, religion) could institute binaries of power in which white was preferred over black, rich over poor, man over woman, straight over gay, and in which the preferred term worked to construct and devalue its opposite.

Fanon's *Les Damnés de la terre* (1961) had inspired *The Hospital at the Time of the Revolution*, Churchill's critically admired 1972 play. (It made its belated professional debut only on 31 March 2013, when it was premiered at London's Finborough Theatre in a production directed by James Russell.) It was Fanon, too, who inspired *Cloud Nine*'s Joshua, a native African whose appearance – he is played by a white actor – recalls Fanon's 1952 book *Peau noir, masques blancs* and suggests the disciplinary force of a colonial racism that instils the merits of a putatively essential, and putatively more civilised, whiteness. As the colonised subject is made to feel inferior, Fanon teaches us, he comes to revere and parrot the codes of his oppressors as if to overcome the Otherness to which he has unwittingly acceded. Genet provided Churchill with the linchpin image of 'the colonial or feminine mentality of interiorised repression', which also informs his *Les Noirs* (1958) and *Les Paravents* (1964).[11] Moreover, an existentialist play such as *Le Balcon* (1956) demonstrates, as Joshua does, that the performance of ideological codes may trump any chromosomal fact. Like Foucault's writings – especially *Surveiller et punir* (1975), the basis for *Softcops* – Churchill stresses the power of the forces that determine such codes in the first place. And thus, as we see Joshua, who is racially cross-cast, so we see Betty, who is played by a man, since, as she herself puts it, 'I am a man's creation as you see, / And what men want is what I want to be'.[12]

In his later work, Foucault would characterise these ideological forces as 'governmentality'. But the failure of Ellen, the governess, to do her disciplinary work suggests the possibility of resistance. Such resistance may explain the cross-casting of Edward, who appears in the body of the female actor who plays him. Academic criticism would later take the play to task for apparently conflating Edward's homosexuality with femininity, criticising Churchill for reinforcing a stereotype of gay men as feminine. In a carefully argued article, for example, James M. Harding alleges that 'since casting a woman as Edward reproduces (and thus affirms rather than alienates) the stereotypical idea that to be a male homosexual is to be like a woman, one could comfortably view the play as a spoof that derives its humor at the expense of those who depart from the heterosexual norm'.[13] Two caveats to this caution should be offered. First, Churchill was self-consciously enacting the ideas of Genet, for whom the receptive gay partner was ideologically scripted as feminine and who sought to reclaim the image of the feminine from opprobrium. As Genet would see, Edward's body in Act 1 (unlike in Act 2, when he is played by a man) testifies to the absence of any other discourse through which he might be recognised as gay in the nineteenth century. Churchill saw this acutely: a pre-publication typescript had contained a single use of the word 'homosexual' in Act 1, when the subversive Mrs Saunders had declared 'I can't marry a homosexual' to Harry Bagley, but the playwright excised this word before the play's premiere and publication.[14] Second, we must appreciate how differently Edward's cross-casting works compared to Joshua's and Betty's. They appear in the image preferred by Clive and valorised by racial and sexual binaries: white for Joshua, male for Betty. Edward, who is being disciplined into manhood by Clive, appears to us as unruly. Despite the forces of family, class, nation, and religion that produce and govern subjects (such as docile servants and wives), Edward's apparently essential homosexuality, signified as his 'female' body, can never be policed into Clive's ideal. Edward's success and succession as a patriarch by the end of Act 1 – conflating familial and colonial politics, he asserts his authority and derides Joshua as his 'boy'[15] – is undermined by his physical body, which always tells against him. In what might be seen as a political victory, the body visually asserts his non-normative identity whatever his actions. If the play sets out to demonstrate how bodies are compelled to follow scripts, as Fanon, Foucault, and Genet all theorise, Edward's un-masculine body on stage always testifies to his productive resistance. He unsettles the stark binary opposition that Clive, in an early typescript of the play, had baldly formulated as '[w]omen are the enemy of man'.[16]

Harding has criticised Churchill's divergent explanations of the play's various cross-castings. But it may be that what he sees as conceptual murkiness testifies to how entangled but finally separate ideological discourses produce contradictions in lived experience. A series of exchanges in the play's opening scene succinctly traces this entanglement. Clive forces Joshua to apologise to Betty for an unkind remark but immediately undermines his apology's force by '*wink*[*ing*] *at* **Joshua**, *unseen by* **Betty**'.[17] Ellen's query 'Shall I bring the children?' is rephrased by Betty to Clive, who answers for her.[18] Clive commands

Edward to pass Victoria's doll to the governess: 'Ellen minds Victoria, let Ellen mind the doll'.[19] And finally, there is this dialogue:

> **Clive** There Betty, take Victoria now. I must go and welcome Harry.
>
> (**Clive** *tosses* **Victoria** *to* **Betty**, *who gives her to* **Ellen**)
>
> **Edward** Can I come, papa?
>
> **Betty** Is he warm enough?
>
> **Edward** Am I warm enough?
>
> **Clive** Never mind the women, Ned. Come and meet Harry.[20]

In only a few seconds of stage time, Churchill taxonomises and prioritises the competing hierarchies. While Betty ostensibly rules over Joshua, a servant, his gender seems to trump her race. Her class privilege does give her power over Ellen, who of course rules over the children. But the male child finds his power over the women secure by virtue of his sex and, of course, his deference to his father, here comically exaggerated. Despite the consonance between discourses of class, colonialism, and patriarchy, their coexistence creates competing pressures. Thus Joshua repudiates his father in deference to Clive: he chooses race over family. And thus Betty, belittled by Clive, testifies to her complicity in the colonial project ('If I lack society', she tells him, 'that is my form of service'[21]) and is oblivious to her class privilege.

The clarity with which Churchill theatricalises *Cloud Nine*'s theoretical ideas becomes apparent when comparing its published versions with its 1979 rehearsal typescript. For example, Act 1's Betty was originally wheedling in her approach to Harry. She complains that '[y]ou never try to make love to me' and alleges that it is 'the only reason you care forme [*sic*]' when Harry mentions he hasn't 'seen a white woman for six months'.[22] But Churchill's deletions and rewriting during the final rehearsals serve not only to make Betty more sympathetic but also to clarify the competing pressures of ideological discourses. A scene between Ellen and Betty was revised to excise

Betty's maudlin and self-centred complaining. In the typescript, Betty whines to the governess that 'You don't know what I suffer. You don't know what love is. . . . I can't kill myself because think of the poor children'.[23] But consider the tender scene that emerged from rewriting:

Betty Ellen, can you keep a secret?

Ellen Oh yes, yes please.

Betty I love Harry Bagley. I want to go away with him. There, I've said it, it's true.

Ellen How do you know you love him?

Betty I kissed him.

Ellen Betty.

Betty He held my hand like this. Oh I want him to do it again. I want him to stroke my hair.

Ellen Your lovely hair. Like this, Betty?

Betty I want him to put his arm around my waist.

Ellen Like this, Betty?

Betty Yes, oh I want him to kiss me again.

Ellen Like this Betty?

(**Ellen** *kisses* **Betty**.)[24]

Tellingly, Ellen can only express her attraction to Betty in a scene in which they re-enact Betty's encounter with Harry; Ellen, playing the man, uses the heterosexual role available to give expression to lesbian desire. In the original typescript, Ellen's passionate appeals hit their mark, and Betty eventually responds to Ellen's declaration that 'I'm in love with you' by saying, 'I didn't think that was possible. Yes, I think you will have to leave'.[25] But Churchill deleted these lines so that, in the final version, Ellen's proclamation of love is barely apprehended as lesbian; the category is not yet conceivable in the historical context.

('It's the loneliness here and the climate is very confusing' is Betty's understanding.[26]) These historical limitations are also semiotically encoded: Betty is played by a man, and the invisibility of lesbian desire is thus made materially plain.[27] Through her various cross-castings, Churchill shows *Cloud Nine*'s equally various identity dispositions – of race, gender, class, nationality, sexuality – as heterogeneous, sometimes disharmonious, always marked by historical limitations.

There is hope. By juxtaposing Joshua's docile white body with Edward's unruly girlish body, Churchill limns the tension between social determinism and agency that ripple through Fanon's, Foucault's, and Genet's work. Despite powerful forces of ideology, Churchill shows, people are not reducible to the social contexts that form them. And from within any pre-set role, the unpredictability of performance may assert itself. Two characters in particular offer escape from the stifling scripts of ideology. The first is Harry Bagley, the 'black sheep' of the 'one big family' of Empire.[28] Clive sees the native population in startlingly racist and essentialist terms, telling Betty, 'You can tame a wild animal only so far. They revert to their true nature and savage your hand'.[29] Harry, by contrast, disavows the colonial mantle, saying simply: 'Very beautiful people many of them'.[30] It is relevant that he is able to see Africans as beautiful, but his 'many' is even more politically productive: Harry sees Africans not as essentially homogeneous but as individuals. He is of course conditioned by historically determined mores, and he will bluntly answer Betty's request that they spend time alone by reminding her 'You are a mother. And a daughter. And a wife'.[31] But so too will he ask sincerely, when no one else does, whether Betty is happy and encourage her to assert her agency. 'That's up to you', he remarks when she complains of lacking adventure.[32] The attenuated power that Harry represents is similarly captured in the first scene's final punchline, when he asks Joshua: 'Shall we go in a barn and fuck?' Mindful as most characters are not of historically determined power imbalances, he immediately notes: 'It's not an order'.[33]

Mrs Saunders, too, represents an attenuated accomplishment. Maud, a rigorous upholder of social values, chastises Mrs Saunders for her disapproval of the servants' flogging, reminding her that '[t]he men will do it in the proper way, whatever it is. We have our own part to play'.[34] And she instructs Betty to take Mrs Saunders as a warning, since she is 'alone in the world'.[35] But Mrs Saunders disrupts the patriarchal narrative precisely by not acceding to the role of wife or helpless woman. When Clive pursues her into the symbolically loaded 'open space' away from the house, she frankly notes that 'I didn't want you to come after me. I wanted to be alone'.[36] Churchill subtly connects her two 'unwomanly' (as Clive sees them) desires: to be alone and to have sexual satisfaction. (Ironically, Betty will confirm Maud's point *and* heed Mrs Saunders's lesson in Act 2, when she finds sexual satisfaction on her own, discovering the joys of masturbation in one of the play's best-known speeches.) Note how differently Clive – who sees Mrs Saunders as 'an unusual woman' who 'does not require protection in the same way'[37] – talks to her than to his wife. Mrs Saunders pushes him to the limits of his assigned role precisely by refusing to play any of those available to her, including mistress. When she bluntly answers Clive's demand for sex with the observation that 'I answered yes once. Sometimes I want to say no', she outlines the promising politics of being untethered to a conventional script.[38] In Churchill's typescript for the play, Mrs Saunders planned to return to England and, rather banally, stay with her nurse sister. But Churchill replaced this detail with Mrs Saunders's (historically radical) proposal that she 'go to England and buy a farm there'.[39]

For both Harry and Mrs Saunders, the socially determinative forces of Victorian values prove too much. Harry ends the act unhappily married off to Ellen, and Mrs Saunders must acknowledge the limits of her historical situation ('I can't see any way out except to leave'; 'There's no place for me here'.[40]) But the political value of resisting roles – of saying yes only sometimes – stands behind the fact that, in Act 2, Churchill's characters 'change a little for the better'.[41] While the complete absence of social regulation is inconceivable and undesirable – a fact adumbrated in Harry's pedophiliac relationship with Edward – the second act stages the possibility of sometimes saying no to social roles or at least experimenting with different ones. Edward, his sexuality now kept secret only from his employer, defends his right to play the 'injured wife' when his aloof boyfriend demands, '[j]ust be yourself'.[42] He rousingly protests: 'Everyone's always tried to stop me being feminine and now you are too. . . . I like doing the cooking. I like being fucked'.[43] (Edward's additional claim, in the typescript, that he is 'monogamous by nature, it's feminine instinct to be monogamous' was excised, muddying the water as it does by tying Edward's political choices to an essential nature.[44]) Churchill relates the positive change in Edward to the second act's 'looser structure' in which 'more energy comes from the women and the gays'.[45] And fittingly the 'open space' of Mrs Saunders's encounter with Clive grows into the public space where Act 2 will be entirely set – a park that Amelia Howe Kritzer has smartly described as a 'world devoid of the stable centre provided by Clive'.[46] With less rigid gender roles, as suggested by Edward and Lin, heterosexuality seems to be less compulsory; various sexual groupings are conceivable and tried. Sexual practices become disentangled from sexual identities. Even Act 2's familial patriarch, Victoria's husband Martin – sometimes maddeningly condescending but not unsympathetic – inhabits his role differently than Clive had, having read *The Hite Report on Female Sexuality* and endeavouring to write (in one of Churchill's most satiric barbs) 'a novel about women from the women's point of view'.[47]

Thus we are provided with a theory of both performance and history. Playing roles differently, agents (and actors) begin to change the contours of these roles. In Joseph Roach's book *Cities of the Dead*, he teaches that history proceeds by a process of surrogation: each act (such as Maud's smacking of Edward) carries with it the history of its previous performances and thus reiterates and reinforces, even if it may subtly change, the meanings of this act in the present.[48] An actor inheriting a role – as, for example, when Jeffrey Jones played Clive in the first New York production after Antony Sher had originated the part in London – carries historical baggage not dissimilar to that carried by Edward, who is meant to succeed his father. Such a view is essential to *Cloud Nine*'s thematic and metatheatrical meanings. After all, the play begins in mock-celebration of England's colonial history (as the company sings of Empire) and swiftly demonstrates that history is constituted by the aggregated performances of individual agents (like Clive's flogging of the servants) whose scripts they have inherited.

This revelation is one clue to the play's temporal structure, the asynchronous gap between its two acts. Elaine Aston explains this structure well when she contrasts the 'continuity of linear history' with the deeply entrenched 'historical memory of sexual politics'. Echoing Roach, she sees that 'the past is physically marked in and on the body of the performer, present'.[49] Like a dancer whose body serves as a repository of choreography, each of us carries the ideologies that have shaped us and whose influence we reveal in our actions. But unlike dancers, we are typically unaware of these predecessor performances, a phenomenon that Roach evocatively describes as history 'forgotten but not gone'.[50]

Historical vestiges of nineteenth-century attitudes and practices remain, then, as made clear by the ghostly reappearance of first-act characters at pivotal moments in Act 2. Betty's understanding of Lin's lesbianism ('It's very nice for a girl to have a friend'[51]) specifically recalls her misapprehension of Ellen's. Lin's parenting is curiously marked by the disciplinary force of patriarchy: 'The man's going to get you', she tells Cathy, defending herself by noting, 'My mother said it'.[52] Moreover, the second act reminds us how these historical vestiges are carried in the body. Churchill effects this reminder through doubling, since the onstage bodies of Act 1 recur (in different roles) in Act 2. As spectators, we are visited by our own memories of the previous act, forcefully and perpetually reminded of Clive, despite his absence, when we see the actor who played him in a new role. In the British premiere production, for example, Sher's Clive would have haunted his portrayal of Cathy in Act 2. In the first American production, the haunting would have been even more pointed, with Jones's Clive shadowing his portrayal of Edward, Clive's successor, in the second half. When Churchill introduces literal ghosts from Act 1, she reiterates what her doubling has already effected. And she again ties the characters' personal histories to the longer histories of patriarchy and colonialism. Lin, Victoria, and Edward incant: 'Goddess of many names, oldest of the old, who walked in chaos and created life, hear us calling you back through time, before Jehovah, before Christ, before men drove you out and burnt your temples, hear us, Lady, give us back what we were, give us the history we haven't had, make us the women we can't be'.[53] But their incantation produces only the ghost of Lin's brother, a British soldier killed in Belfast. They can have no history they haven't already had. And thus Churchill's first-act concern with colonialism, now shifted from Africa to Northern Ireland as the play moves forward a century, appears in an unlikely context and as a pointedly sombre note in one of the play's funniest scenes.

Theatre history is history too, of course, with its own lingering memories and ideologies. Metatheatrically, *Cloud Nine* plays with it: Joshua alludes to blackface minstrelsy, Act 1's Betty to panto camp, Act 2's Cathy (played by a male actor) to the long history of cross-dressed boy actors. The semiotic complications of Act 1 revisit those of earlier stages, which historically excluded black and biologically female bodies. On the Renaissance stage, for example, a boy actor might play *Twelfth Night*'s Viola, dressed as a woman in disguise as a man and wooed by a woman played by another boy. Recognising *Cloud Nine*'s situatedness in theatre history – of which it is now deservedly an ineradicable part – helps us to understand its own historical context. Churchill has noted that the play was inspired in part because of the limited role of women in 1970s theatre, even in a politically progressive group: 'Joint Stock at that point was such a male company. . . . It seemed the last company which you would think of doing a show like that, and of course as soon as I had said that, we realised that was a very good reason for in fact doing it'.[54]

But every era has its ideological blind-spots. Harding, for example, has illuminated the play's naivety in its representation of gays and lesbians. And Apollo Amoko has asked us to consider whether Churchill's feminist work was accomplished by participating in the very attitudes toward non-white subjects that the play condemns.[55] When Clive comments on Betty's 'dark female lust' or remarks that Mrs Saunders is 'dark like this continent. Mysterious. Treacherous', for example, he follows Freud in linking a putatively essential female sexuality to the exoticised, 'dark' Other in colonial discourse.[56] But Churchill too might be seen to use the racial Other only as an instrument to understand the sexual Other. She once told an interviewer: 'I realized that the first act of *Cloud 9* could be in a colonial situation and I could use that metaphor of colonization as a sexual matter'.[57] Churchill also noted that the cast was chosen for its 'plural sexualities and sexual experiences' – a claim Stafford-Clark corroborates in his diary when he notes that '[o]bviously the people involved in the project are drawn from an unusual section of the community as a whole'.[58] But these claims sit somewhat uncomfortably alongside the fact that there was 'no black member of the company'.[59] Indeed, Stafford-Clark's brainstorming list of possible actors for the project, made in his journal in August 1978, contains no less than 135 names, including Simon Callow and Joanna Lumley.[60] Roach and others have explained how performances (especially on stage, with their particularly intense repetitions, night after night as the curtain raises) work to reify ideological structures and intensify their power, and Amoko's probing article has questioned how the absence of black bodies from Churchill's stage reinscribes and perpetuates the historical paucity of black experience in Western representations. Victoria and Edward may 'change a little for the better' and Betty may find peace with her body and sexuality. But Joshua is absented and, unlike Betty, fails to graduate to full subjecthood.[61]

If a 2007 revival of the play at London's Almeida Theatre, directed by Thea Sharrock, was found by at least three London reviewers to be dated, this judgement may testify precisely to the play's historical thesis.[62] In my view, the play still succeeds in dramatising its relevant issues and, of course, in its exuberant theatricality. But it does not diminish *Cloud Nine* to suggest that we 'look at it in a historical perspective in terms of learnt behavior' (as Victoria suggests when Lin claims that she hates men).[63] Doing so may index historical progress: it is now almost inconceivable, at least in the UK, that Edward could be fired from his job for being gay, as he fears in the second act. Stafford-Clark himself said of a 1997 revival at the Old Vic, that:

> [T]wenty years on, Caryl's brilliant capturing of our own hippy-go-lucky self-involvement had become as quaint and distant as the sexual mores of the repressed Victorians. The first half had always been a history play, but our endeavour to articulate our own sexual confusion had become history too in the intervening twenty years.[64]

To tie *Cloud Nine*'s onstage world to that off stage, as Stafford-Clark and Amoko each does in his own way, is to honour the play's meanings: to understand the constitutive impact of 'roles' in theatre and everyday life and to apprehend Churchill's political meaning when she juxtaposes offstage flogging with onstage smacks.

Their interrelationship is embedded in the play's DNA. It was written after a workshop, but, unlike the earlier *Light Shining in Buckinghamshire*, its thematic material was determined by the lived experience of the participating actors. Churchill began compiling material early. Gerry's riotous account of time-pressured fellatio on the train to Clapham Junction, for example, was inspired by an account given at an audition.[65] And the cast were chosen explicitly to reflect the sexual identifications of its members. Miriam Margolyes, who played Maud and Victoria in the premiere, bluntly jokes that '[t]hey needed a lesbian for a play about sexual politics' but also recounts the liberating experience of 'sitting in a circle each day, one of us in the middle, telling everyone everything about our lives, our sexuality and our insecurities'.[66] It is easy to imagine how Sher's personal experiences as a wealthy gay man from colonial Africa might have directly influenced *Cloud Nine*'s eventual plot and setting.[67] Churchill explained the play's daring jump in time by recounting that 'when the company talked about their childhoods and the attitudes to sex and marriage that they had been given when they were young, everyone felt that they had received very conventional, almost Victorian expectations'.[68] The workshop gave Churchill access to the company's conscious reflections about their experience. But she could observe, too, the often unwitting ways in which their bodily actions and reactions were guided by their learned behaviours as Stafford-Clark guided the cast through improvisations that explored social conditions under shifting power dynamics.[69] A final detail might suggest the avidity with which Churchill drew on real-life experience. The play's title was provided by a woman working at the snack bar in the Tower Theatre, Canonbury, where the workshop was held. She was induced to tell of her unhappy first marriage and her discovery of sex in her second. 'We may not do it as often as you young people', she told the company, 'but when we have our organisms [*sic*], we're on Cloud Nine'.[70]

The workshop lasted three weeks in the autumn of 1978. In early December, Churchill delivered a script to Stafford-Clark and the cast for their input.[71] It was then rewritten by 19 December, including the entire second act, before rehearsals began on 2 January 1979. This day the director describes as '[a]lmost the most unsatisfactory first day's rehearsal ever'.[72] The dissatisfactions expressed by the cast members, voluminously recorded in Stafford-Clark's diary, testify to the incredible amount of input provided and demanded by *Cloud Nine*'s inaugural cast. Even casting was submitted to consensus, with Margolyes reportedly upset not to be cast as Lin, whose outspoken lesbianism presumably owed much to the actor's personal experience.[73] Further reworking occurred, Churchill thankfully overruling Sher's suggestion that the second half be entirely dropped.[74] By 4 February, Stafford-Clark wrote that he feared the show would be a 'disaster', still fretting about whether 'we h[a]v[e] a 2nd ½ . . . at all' and complaining about everyone 'becoming bad tempered'.[75] But two months of concerns over the play, and especially its much-rewritten second half, proved unfounded. The play opened as planned at Dartington College of Arts on 14 February and, after a tour, arrived at the Royal Court, where it played to mixed critical but great commercial regard. Churchill's first time on the Royal Court's main stage had been *Objections to Sex and Violence*, premiered on 2 January 1975 in a production directed by John Tydeman; it played to mostly empty houses and lost the theatre £10,000. *Cloud Nine*, by contrast, played to 92 per cent of capacity and helped to eradicate the Court's deficit.[76] It was therefore revived only a year later, with the production's direction co-credited to Les Waters and with a cast including Graeme Garden and Harriet Walter. (Critics would then be unanimous in their praise. As Stafford-Clark wrote in his diary on 5 September 1980, '[t]he fuckers hated it a year ago and today it's a marvellous play'.[77]) On 18 May 1981, a New York production directed by Tommy Tune was premiered at the Theatre de Lys to even greater box office success, running through multiple cast changes and for almost 1,000 performances and winning Churchill her first of several Best Play Obie Awards. It effectively launched her international career. Previously only *Owners* had received a New York production, quickly closed and unremembered, but by May 1983

Cloud Nine was running alongside professional productions of both *Top Girls* and *Fen*, a rare trifecta that testified to her new prominence in the New York theatre scene.

At Tune's urging, Churchill made changes in the American script, for example moving Betty's masturbation monologue later and thus foregrounding Betty's self-discovery.[78] The production more generally amplified the play's wild theatricality in myriad ways, with Tune leveraging the showmanship for which he is known. (It is worth remembering how successful he was in the era. At the time of *Cloud Nine*'s opening, he had two shows running on Broadway; by the time it had closed, he had added a third, in addition to his off-Broadway work.[79]) Churchill reported that these changes reframed the play slightly as a celebration of the seventies' looser social constraints:

> People here [i.e. in New York] have tended to say to me that it's about everything being okay and being whatever you like and whatever sexuality you are. Naturally that is part of it, but what I thought I was writing about when I was doing it was probably more than just how change happens in the social structure and how difficult freedom is. I wanted to show it as seeming like a good thing, but a difficult thing. In England it was taken as something problematic; here it is seen as something very joyful.[80]

This difference in reception testifies further to one of *Cloud Nine*'s theses: that each historical context is unique, shaped as it is by different ideological constraints and historical experiences. Meanings are historically contingent, as Churchill recognises when she allows that 'the doubling can be done in any way that seems right for any particular production'.[81]

The Theatre de Lys (now the Lucille Lortel) is on Christopher Street, then as now the heart of New York's gay scene, just southwest from where the Stonewall riots had galvanised the gay rights movement less than a decade earlier. And to a much greater extent than in London, New York's *Cloud Nine* was initially received as a gay hit – one critic lauded it as the 'cutting edge of contemporary gay theater' – before crossing over to mainstream success.[82] Sorting through the play's archival records in New York, one discovers a *Cloud Nine* night at the now-defunct gay bar Magique, for which revellers were exhorted to 'Come Cross-dressed as Your Favorite Victorian or Modern Character' for a contest to be judged by the play's cast members.[83] Despite Churchill's apparent caution about Tune's approach – she told an interviewer that 'Tommy wanted it more outgoing, more accessible. He went for the laughs'[84] – it is clear that she was seen as offering new roles for emulation, and in a manner worthy of celebration. The linkage between on stage and off in the play's American reception is as clear as that in the London workshops that produced its script. Jeffrey Jones made this connection explicit when he told a journalist that he had been warned against the play by a friend before his audition: '"It's disgusting," she said. "And if you do it, I'll never speak to you again"'.[85] Meanwhile, a reminder of what Churchill calls the difficulties of freedom was provided years later when Jones was arrested for child pornography after soliciting a boy to pose for sexually explicit photographs.[86] The play's second act is not utopic finally, and, even as it enjoins us to sometimes say no to ideological scripts, it shows a complete absence of social regulation as impossible. We might see Jones's offstage identity as a 'sex offender', inscribed in the register of his home state, as testimony both to the enduring presence of regulatory discourses and the necessity of the social constraints they police, even if these constraints are subject to historical evolution.

Icecream (with or without *Hot Fudge*)

Tommy Tune once offered a simple description of how we play out learned scripts even as we change them with our idiosyncratic performances: 'The world is choreography'.[87] *Cloud Nine* thematises the relationship between the history that choreographs us, the identities that we take on (intentionally or not) through our performances, and the role that our bodies play in registering and resisting these identities. In the decades since *Cloud Nine*, Churchill has maintained her interest in these themes. But her stress has shifted to the extent to which subjects are alienated from the histories that shape them – the 'forgotten but not gone' aspect of our ideological baggage that Roach emphasises. Sidelights from later plays, then, might help illuminate the stage that *Cloud Nine* has set for Churchill's explorations of identity and the body.

Icecream was premiered at the Royal Court on 11 April 1989 and, like *Cloud Nine*, was directed by Max Stafford-Clark and designed by Peter Hartwell. In the decade between the plays, Churchill had become a star in the contemporary theatre, having achieved further critical and commercial success with *Top Girls*, *Fen*, and especially *Serious Money*, the biggest financial success of her career and her first play to receive a Broadway production. As Stafford-Clark wrote while rehearsing *Icecream*, 'Caryl is now so clearly at the top of her profession that she can write the rulebook'.[88] These circumstances help account for the play's abiding strangeness, its compressed and elliptical form that anticipated works such as *Far Away*. (At the time Stafford-Clark questioned such form, debating in his diary whether the play was 'brilliant and economical . . . or just plain underwritten' and worrying that if 'the play is ab[ou]t weighty matters, the structure of so many successive short scenes means it . . . may seem slight'.[89]) Despite radical differences in form and tone, clear thematic continuities tie *Icecream* to *Cloud Nine*, particularly the question of how subjects are marked by ideology. Indeed, we might see *Icecream* as belatedly fulfilling Churchill's brief from Stafford-Clark in 1978. The director had initially engaged her for a play about America to be co-produced (as *Icecream* would be) by Joseph Papp's Public Theater in New York, but a shift in direction led to *Cloud Nine.*[90]

Icecream dramatises the story of Lance, an American on an existential quest to Britain, where he imagines a family history stretching back before 1066; travelling with his wife, Vera, he discovers distant cousins, Jaq and Phil, in London's East End. In the play's opening scene, Lance and Vera are seen driving in a car, their conversation interpolated with the songs they sing. But something is amiss:

> **Lance and Vera** And by something and by something and by something I will go

> And never something dadedadeda
>
> And something and dedadeda and something in my step
>
> And I'll never something something of the isles.[91]

Singing snatches of the Scottish folk song 'Road to the Isles', the couple forget the words nearly entirely; their rendition elides almost all the relevant content. After eight scrambled lines, the song is dropped in favour of three lines (also misremembered) from the traditional 'Skye Boat Song'. Then, after Vera teases Lance for being flat, she sings a snatch of 'The Heather on the Hill' from Lerner and Loewe's *Brigadoon.* With these cunning mis-citations, Churchill plunges us into the couple's existential quandary and *Icecream*'s geographic landscape, from which distinguishable places have disappeared: the Tummel and Loch Rannoch and Lochaber by which a singer orients 'The Road to the Isles' are replaced by a disorienting 'something' and 'something' and 'something'.[92] Churchill wrote that the play was about 'people generally trying to find a grid with which they can make sense of things'.[93] But lacking geographical markers, Vera and Lance are as dislocated as Lerner and Loewe's American tourists, Tommy Albright and Jeff Douglas, when they stumble across Brigadoon, the invisible town stuck two centuries in the past. It is therefore significant that none of the first-scene songs is identified by Churchill: like Lance and Vera on their quest, the spectator must struggle to orient despite a lack of context. It is not that they have '[n]o history', as Lance will soon allege.[94] Rather, like the town of Brigadoon itself, they have become unloosed from history and thus alienated from themselves.

The play is Churchill's most prototypically postmodern work, exhibiting the same features of flat characterisation, pastiche, and fragmentation that dominate fiction in the period, such as Julian Barnes's *A History of the World in 10½ Chapters*, published the same year. (It is telling that Michael Billington in the *Guardian* praised *Icecream*'s 'sharp reminder of how much playwriting is changing in the video age'.[95]) The diary Stafford-Clark kept during rehearsal suggests how strange he found the play, so unlike his previous projects and an odd fit with his methods as a director. His method involves 'actioning': for each line of the text, he requires actors to find a specific motivation, an action expressed as a transitive verb that captures the change the character wants to impose on his or her present situation. In such a method, we find explicit recognition of the way that agency connects to desire, even as it is limited by the available script. It is the lesson, in other words, of *Cloud Nine*. But early in rehearsals for *Icecream*, the director bemoaned that the '[c]haracters live in bit of a vacuum'.[96] Weeks later he still fretted that it 'feels we're scratching the surface and not grappling with [*Icecream*] in any depth. Hard to enter the world of the kids [Jaq and Phil] particularly. By nature they are elusive . . . Jaq is like a flat stone that skims across the surface of events'.[97]

In hindsight it is clear that Stafford-Clark was confronting the play's central thematic idea. For Churchill forgoes psychology entirely, choosing instead a postmodern landscape of surfaces which reflect the theme of identity but offer few insights. Lance looks to England for roots but sees only clichés: 'The green fields. The accents. The pubs'.[98] And his English cousin Phil derides American hamburgers and gun-toting cops while he celebrates not Oregon's meanings but its thrilling surface: 'the word, just the word Oregon really thrills me'.[99] Likewise *Icecream*'s characters are two-dimensional and constantly shifting, like the cinematographic images of British and American landscapes – cropped to inhibit perspective – that comprised Hartwell's set design. Characterisation is erratic. Phil's description of the unnamed man he has killed periodically changes, and Lance is shown as an ignorant American tourist one minute and discussing the demographics of Broadmoor psychiatric hospital the next.[100] Exhibiting the self-referentiality for which postmodern literature is known, Jaq will note that 'I feel I'm in a road movie and everyone I meet is these interesting characters'.[101] In the play's London production files, the stage manager's daily reports occasionally mention the cast's difficulty with corpsing: breaking character.[102] However unintentional, such breaches would seem appropriate to *Icecream*, whose characters refuse to cohere. As the quartet quests to find a 'framework of place and time', Amelia Howe Kritzer notes, they 'resist identity as strongly as they inhibit identification'.[103] In other words, the audience is as lost as they are.

Since the characters act without dramaturgical rationale or dramatic consequence, plot too fails to cohere. Each of the short play's twenty scenes is an incomplete shard – the longest is four pages – starting *in medias res* and ending without closure; what might be important plot points (Phil's death, for instance) pass offhandedly between scenes. Like Vera and Lance sampling through songs they free-associate with Scotland, Churchill pastes fragments together, deploying and abandoning dramatic tropes such as homecomings, recognition scenes, voyages of discovery, even a flirtation with incest, with a seeming arbitrariness. Les Waters, who directed the New York production that premiered 3 May 1990 at the Public Theater, described the effect as jolting and explained it to a journalist this way:

> [T]here's nothing on the surface of one scene that prepares you for the next scene. The play reflects what the characters are going through – things happen to them and they don't understand their own behavior as they're doing it. The play's a bit like Caryl's career; you never know where it's going.[104]

Indeed, *Icecream* feels like one of many exhilaratingly strange changes of direction, such as *The Skriker*, that characterise Churchill's career more generally. It is telling that Stafford-Clark, at the time Churchill's most frequent collaborator, struggled so much with *Icecream* before deciding, according to his diary, that 'I'm now convinced it is a work of genius'.[105]

In *Cloud Nine*, Churchill had explored how historical baggage from the Victorian era had shaped her characters in the play's present. In *Icecream*, the bleaker picture shows characters utterly deracinated from, even as they long for, such explanatory contexts. As Churchill explained, the play asks: 'How do you understand the things that have happened which you don't know about, the hidden things?'[106] Therefore, Lance – who asserts that '[w]hat nobody knows isn't history'[107] – seeks to understand himself better by attempting to access a forgotten past. And when he first meets Phil, the men seem to bond over the discovery of their shared ancestry:

Lance So great aunt Dora was my great /

Phil was your greatgrandfather's –

Lance grandmother's brother's daughter – mother's great / grandmother's –

Phil – mother's, right,

Lance she was my greatgrand*mother's* brother's daughter and your greatgrand / *father's*

Phil father's

Lance brother's daughter.[108]

Churchill's trademark overlapping dialogue, with the two men's words wrapping together like the ancestral roots they struggle to reveal, makes clear their folly: like their accents, which mark substantial national and class differences, the two men could not be more dissimilar. She mocks their historical project – 'I think it was Madge. Unless it was Elsie. Let's go for Madge'[109] – and its blackly comic circumstances. Lance will soon be haemorrhaging money to his newfound relations and helping them to hide a corpse in Epping Forest. It is a beautifully ironic image. Lance had come to England to explore his family tree, to uncover kin, to find roots and himself. But he ends up more lost than ever, in a forest, covering an unidentified body with dead leaves. History fails along with his quest. Another image tells. In the second act, Jaq meets a sexually aggressive professor and chucks him off a cliff. 'A professor of what?' Vera will ask, and Jaq will answer with thematic resonance: 'I don't know, I think history, something'.[110]

Churchill cautioned that 'I just hope that people don't come with an expectation that it's going to be some kind of satiric or sociological tract about America and England'.[111] But as would happen again with *Drunk Enough to Say I Love You?* in 2006, critics found the very meanings that Churchill disavowed. Michael Coveney in the *Financial Times* declared *Icecream* 'an explosive allegory of the historical transatlantic alliance' and Peter Kent in the *Independent* wrote that it 'mocks not only cultural collisions but national collusions'.[112] Showing us the rapidly shifting social relations between two pairs of characters, one American and one British, Churchill certainly seemed to reflect the altered relationship between the UK and the US in the decade following *Cloud Nine* – a change facilitated by the ideological harmony between Margaret Thatcher and Ronald Reagan (as well as his successor, George H.W. Bush). Like the relationship years later between Tony Blair and Bush *fils* – the 'special relationship' that Churchill was thought to lampoon in *Drunk Enough to Say I Love You?* – Thatcher and Reagan's bond was presented as cemented by long-term history. But in reality it was conditioned by more recent events: the global exchange of capital that narrowed the physical distance between the two countries. When Lance and Vera track down great-aunt Dora – too late, she is dead – Vera explains that 'We're not after her money. We're researching my husband's family tree'.[113] But her anxious comment reveals that their misguided search for history is shadowed, in the sense of followed but also darkened, by the spectre of money. ('Do you not like family?' Vera will ask Dora's other distant relation, Phil. Avarice answers: 'I quite fancy Americans'.[114]) A transatlantic loan cements the bond. The American-British relationship is quickly commoditised, and their interaction soon dominated by exchanges of money, most hilariously in the play's penultimate scene when Jaq extorts airfare from Lance and Vera as a reward for having returned the car that she herself stole.

Churchill's play thus cannily prefigured the thesis that David Harvey would put forth later that year in his book *The Condition of Postmodernity*. Harvey claims that experiences of space and time have become compressed as a result of the shift from a Fordist economy (i.e. one based on industrial mass production) to a less-anchored economy of global capital exchange and flexible accumulation (in which everything is a commodity priced according to exchange value instead of use value). These ideas find theatrical expression in *Icecream*, with its spatial inconsistency – as the scene ricochets across the UK and US – and especially the startling velocity of its plot. It was precisely anti-regulation policies under Thatcher and Reagan (thematised in *Serious Money*) that facilitated the global capital flows that would reconfigure international relations and (according to Harvey) dislocate our senses of history and geography. These dislocated senses, in turn, undermine stable senses of identity, as *Icecream* reflects not only in its characters' inconsistency but also in its audience's difficulty in getting interpretive traction on them. What begins as a search for meaning, either Lance's or our own, is finally tourism – an experience, like that of *Brigadoon*, unmoored from a sense of time and place.

As Harvey writes:

> It is difficult . . . to maintain any sense of historical continuity in the face of all the flux and ephemerality of flexible accumulation. The irony is that tradition is now often preserved by being commodified and marketed as such. The search for roots ends up at worst being produced and marketed as an image, as a simulacrum or pastiche (imitation communities constructed to evoke images of some folksy past, the fabric of traditional working-class communities being taken over by an urban gentry).[115]

We recognise such postmodern simulacra and pastiche in *Icecream*'s form and in the American and British views of one another's countries, entirely two-dimensional, as in Hartwell's set design for the play (or for *Serious Money*, with its echoes of pastiche architect Michael Graves). Tourism – the commodification of place – becomes the play's central motif. The quartet's travel accelerates dizzyingly, providing more characters (introduced and abandoned at will) and covering greater distances. Phil is a victim of this velocity, unceremoniously killed off by an automobile. And Jaq spends the second act in perpetual motion and in dramaturgical free fall. She ends the play sitting in the transnational space of the airport, urged by a mysterious South American woman to '[c]hange your destination'.[116]

Churchill claimed the play is apolitical.[117] But reading closely we see how *Icecream* expands some of *Cloud Nine*'s thematic concerns about identity and history by marrying them to the critique that the playwright had launched with *Serious Money*, her dramatic exploration of the newly deregulated stock market and of neoliberalism's capacity to distort social relations. These meanings are especially clear if we read *Icecream* alongside *Hot Fudge*, the equally dark curtain-raiser that Churchill wrote as accompaniment. (In London, Stafford-Clark decided that it 'distract[ed]' and 'defocus[ed]'[118] and offered only a rehearsed reading on a few nights, but in New York Waters fully staged the play as part of a diptych: *Icecream with Hot Fudge*). The play's main character is Ruby, who spends its first scene at a pub with various family members, where they discuss a cheque-cashing scheme initiated by Ruby's niece Sonia and her boyfriend, Matt. *Hot Fudge* compares Matt and Sonia's scheme – which makes money out of thin air by leveraging the delay between funds becoming available and the bank's realisation that a cheque is bad – with the past career of Charlie, Sonia's uncle and an old-fashioned bank robber. Matt and Sonia's work, like that of Marylou Baines in *Serious Money*, requires only invisible transfers and the right timing, whereas Charlie's endeavour required guns, physical exertion, and actual contact with bank tellers from whom he took actual bills. Wryly alluding to Marxist theory – the moment recalls Mac the Knife's final speech in Bertolt Brecht's *Threepenny Opera* – Charlie alleges that the younger generation of robbers are alienated from their labour. As he explains, 'I like cash in my hand. . . . And somebody might get hurt, you hoped not but somebody might, that could be one of them or one of you. You had to take more with you than a suit'.[119]

Churchill juxtaposes the first scene about family and capital with the play's final three, which concern Ruby's date with a man named Colin and her introduction to his friends and ex-wife. These scenes express the same concerns with tourism, commodification, and history that are marbled through *Icecream.* Ruby has claimed to be a high-end travel agent whose clients experience the dizzying pleasures of a world shrunken by air travel: tourists might look to Yugoslavia, Turkey, India, Thailand, China, even Gambia, for a 'long weekend' or 'luxury adventure . . . pick'n'mix'.[120] The sociologist John Urry has described the deleterious effects of such a tourist gaze in his book of that title, seeing international tourist flows as one more symptom of globalisation.[121] Colin agrees with the terms but not the analysis. He approvingly ties such travel to the allures of flexible accumulation:

'You're lucky in your chosen field because everything in the world is a potential commodity. Every lake, every town, every donkey walking by. Every single person in the world is either a potential customer or a potential commodity in so far as they are part of the ambiance'.[122]

When the pair meet Colin's friends – an American couple, Jerry and Grace, and a British man, Hugh – such pleasures of global tourism are neatly tied to a postmodern world like that which Harvey describes. Its view of history is summarised by Hugh, an estate agent who teaches that '[a]nyone who can afford one house can afford two', perhaps in Turkey where there's no tax on capital gains.[123] 'There's a development near Cadiz where you can have an individual antique door tastefully incorporated. Just that one thing completely changes the image', he instructs.[124] The postmodern space about which he enthuses compresses historical time and thus changes its meanings, here flattened to an 'image'. And the temporal compression the development suggests meets its spatial corollary in Grace's work. She coaches what she calls off-court tennis: 'no ball, you visualise the ball. And more important you visualise yourself. You visualise yourself hitting the ball . . . the important thing is to convince yourself and others that you are a winner'.[125] Thus the play recalls themes Churchill had addressed as early as 1962, when she proposed a radio play to the BBC called *The Love Salesman*. Its titular character – Churchill's treatment calls him only 'Father' – is an advertising executive who tries to market his shy son Alec to women. But Alec prefers the romance of commodities and, even after his successful seduction of his cousin Edna, withdraws again to a world of objects, 'charged with excitement by their advertisements' in Churchill's description.[126]

Unlike radio, I have said, stage plays require bodies, and the sort of dislocation that *Hot Fudge*'s Grace describes – in which the body is freed by becoming materially unmoored – is difficult to stage. As she did in *Cloud Nine*, Churchill theatricalised her theoretical concerns by means of doubling. In New York in particular, audiences watching *Icecream with Hot Fudge* would have failed to assign specific identities to specific bodies by virtue of the play's speed, compression, and large character list: Waters used only six actors to play twenty-three characters and, significantly, corrupted the play's primary axis of difference, having most actors play both American and British characters. John Pankow – a veteran of Churchill productions since his first, when he inherited the roles of Betty and Gerry from Željko Ivanek in New York's *Cloud Nine* – was cast in seven roles. When Julianne Moore's Jaq met a drunken partygoer, a hitchhiker, and her assaultive professor in three short, sharp, consecutive scenes, audiences would have seen the same person, Pankow, embody each of them.

Because the play's characters so strongly resist coherence and identification, the effect was not that earlier characters meaningfully haunted later ones, as in *Cloud Nine.* Rather, the flat characterisation had its effects intensified, as uncannily similar images from a closed sign-system circulated rapidly in front of the set design's two-dimensional images. (In New York, these were designed by Annie Smart, who so memorably put *Fen* in a field of dirt.) No meaning could adhere. It is a fitting image of postmodern globalisation which, Harvey tell us, offers a pastiche of signs deracinated from any meaningful context. When several of the play's New York reviews complained of its inconsistencies and shallowness, they apprehended Churchill's postmodern strategies without quite understanding her point. Mimi Kramer in the *New Yorker*, for instance, bemoaned the play's wilful arbitrariness and the fact that 'characters' accents change from scene to scene, sometimes from speech to speech'[127] – a phenomenon also clearly discernible in the play's 23 September 2008 staged reading at the Royal Court, directed by Wallace Shawn. This theatrical failure turns out to be richly suggestive of the play's ideas.

A Number

Icecream received mixed reviews in both London and New York, with reviewers unsure of the fit between the play's jolting theatricality and its obvious (whatever Churchill may have claimed) political resonances. Writing for the *New York Times*, for instance, Frank Rich found the play 'rich in bracing theatrical bile' even if he didn't 'swallow all of Ms. Churchill's at times knee-jerk didacticism'.[128] By contrast, *A Number*, which opened at the Royal Court on 23 September 2002, garnered the most uniformly positive reviews of her career to date, with stellar notices in every major British daily except the *Independent*.[129] Even the *Daily Telegraph*'s Charles Spencer – who once confessed that he 'never understood the regard in which Churchill is held' – raved that the play 'contains more drama, and more ideas, than most writers manage in a dozen full-length works' and called it 'magnificent', 'tremendous', 'moving, thought-provoking and dramatically thrilling'.[130] Like most reviewers, Spencer focused his praise on the play's aesthetic innovations. But if Nicholas de Jongh in the *Evening Standard* called it 'the first true play of the 21st century', John Peter in the *Sunday Times* correctly saw it as belonging to a long tradition of Churchill's innovation: he noted that *A Number* 'confirms Churchill's status as the first dramatist of the 21st century' but clarified that, for British theatre, the twenty-first century had actually begun 'in 1979, when Max Stafford-Clark's Joint Stock company first performed Caryl Churchill's *Cloud Nine*'.[131] Peter recognised that *A Number* trained Churchill's eye on questions that preoccupied her already decades earlier. Sam Shepard, who starred in the New York production two years later, saw this too, telling an interviewer that the play was not about cloning as some had claimed: 'That's not what it is about. It has to do with identity'.[132] We might expand Shepard's précis by saying that it takes concerns that flickered across the glossy surfaces of *Icecream* and incorporates them (the Latin root is *incorporare*, 'to form into a body'). It has to do with identity in an age of commodification.

The play concerns a man, Bernard, who realises that he is one of a number of clones made from a predecessor. Pressed for answers, his evasive father, Salter, confesses that he had neglected his son, the original Bernard, in the years following his wife's suicide and eventually abandoned the boy in favour of a newborn clone. Salter explains his actions in five terse scenes, each with a single scene partner: Bernard 2 (scenes 1 and 3), Bernard 1 (scenes 2 and 4), and a third clone, Michael Black (scene 5). The play is even more compressed than *Icecream*, marked by still more elliptical, more abbreviated dialogue. Whereas *Icecream* was theatrically busy – even without *Hot Fudge*, it spans seventeen settings and twelve speaking parts – *A Number* is spare: a single set and two actors. This spareness is thematically meaningful.

First, Churchill reprises an idea from *Identical Twins* by having a single actor play all three sons and thus embody the central dramatic problem: discovering that one is 'not very like but very something terrible which is exactly the same genetic person'.[133] Second, the ensuing existential crisis – 'if that's me over there who am I?' is Salter's précis[134] – reflects the absence of a grounding context for identity. The social roles that structured *Cloud Nine* are here largely absent. Bernard is only a son, this sole identification becoming undermined when he learns that he is a clone and that his mother was (as he puts it) 'already always' dead.[135] History is reduced to DNA, inherited from ancestors but inscrutable to the person it shapes. Mirroring this lack of context, Churchill provides no stage directions besides this preliminary guidance: '*The scene is the same throughout, it's where Salter lives*'.[136] As the pronoun *it* reaches back to its antecedent, *the scene*, readers are left no wiser about their location but are primed for metatheatrical insights. The comma, meanwhile, is one of hundreds in the script that splice independent clauses like genes. Form matches content.

Compared to *Cloud Nine* or *Icecream, A Number* moves into more elemental and existential territory. It asks questions of being. Each of us, like Bernard, can be considered a sum-total set of biometric data or a mappable genome, a landscape of terrifyingly common nucleic acids. Each of us is a number. Thus, in a time when genes can be bought and sold, patented and copyrighted, we are susceptible to dehumanisation and objectification. Churchill expresses these worries in the first-scene exchange between Salter and Bernard 2. Salter's first question is 'how many of these things are there?'[137] But despite Bernard's flat rebuke – 'you called them things. I think we'll find they're people' – Salter wonders if they can sue on the grounds of stolen cells. He swiftly moves to monetisation: 'a million is the least you should take, I think it's more like a half a million each person because what they've done they've damaged your uniqueness, weakened your identity, so we're looking at five million for a start'.[138] Salter is mired in the very discourse that troubles Bernard in the first place. By attempting to quantify the value of his uniqueness, Salter reduces him to exchange value and thus reiterates the hideous rationale behind the son's laboratory beginnings. It is bitterly ironic when Salter argues that the clones 'belong to you

. . . they've been stolen from you and you should get your rights', since, by Salter's logic of belongings, the beloved son 'belongs' to his discarded predecessor.[139] And when Salter consoles this predecessor with the very same language of theft and ownership, he unwittingly emphasises the sons' exchangeability. '[T]hey stole your genetic material', he tells Bernard 1: 'you and I have got common cause against the others don't forget, I'm still hoping we'll make our fortunes there. I'm going to talk to a solicitor'.[140]

However harrowing Salter's emotional journey – he is destroyed after the younger son is killed by the older, who in turn commits suicide – his logic persists. He will confess that he found the original Bernard to be 'a disgusting thing' by the time he had him cloned, and at the end of the play when he meets Michael Black, he clings to the narrative that the others are 'things'.[141] Salter conceives of the clones – as he conceived Bernard 2 – as commodities. Like Monsanto (the biotechnology corporation that has patented agricultural seed) or Harvard (America's oldest corporation, which owns the rights to a transgenic laboratory rodent called Oncomouse), he reduces life to an acquisition, just the word that Bernard 2 uses to understand his origins. In a speech that underscores the clones' fungibility, he laments that 'there were a number a number of us made somehow and you were one of the people who acquired'.[142] This description, with its definition of 'people' as those who acquire instead of being acquired, indicts Salter and links him with a long line of Churchill characters stretching back through *Cloud Nine*'s Clive, whose daughter is an objectified doll, and to *The Love Salesman*'s Father, marketing his son as a sexual product. It is a patriarchal habit, but not exclusively male. We should recall Marion in *Owners*, the black comedy that launched Churchill's professional career in England. Like her fellow estate agent Hugh in *Hot Fudge*, Marion preaches better living through acquisition, and in a pivotal plot point she acquires another woman's baby through a commercial transaction.

As *Cloud Nine*'s Victoria transforms from a doll to a breathing woman – as she walks and speaks on her own – she moves from objecthood to subjecthood. She develops consciousness. If we contemplate the difference between doll and actor, we see clearly how conscious behaviour might begin to overcome the limitations that shape us. *Cloud Nine* focused on scripts shaped by ideology and passed down through history; *A Number* focuses on a genetic code under threat of commodification. But both plays show that these influences, however fundamental, need not be deterministic, precisely because of the consciousness of the agent who expresses them. *Acting* and *agency* share an etymology. In this regard, Churchill's play is metatheatrical, drawing attention to how its script, like DNA, is brought to life only in performance. On the page a play may be a commodity, its owner a limited company: '*A Number* copyright © 2002, 2008 Caryl Churchill Ltd'.[143] But on stage, a play is animated by conscious beings and thus transcends its status as object. We can put this idea another way. As a literary creation, Salter is words. But as a theatrical character, he lives in the scene.

This idea is made powerfully clear by contemplating the independent, entirely unique productions that *A Number* has engendered. At the Royal Court, designer Ian MacNeil (who, like Churchill, won an *Evening Standard* Award for the production) devised a blank set that captured Bernard's lack of context: a rectangular platform built over the stage with no décor other than two chairs and a glass side table for Salter's ashtray. His costumes, too, provided no contextualising or semiotic help: just a suit for British acting legend Michael Gambon, who played Salter, and jeans and a T-shirt for Daniel Craig, who didn't change clothes from scene to scene or clone to clone. (By contrast, Salter added a tie to meet Michael Black.) The production's director, Stephen Daldry, testified that it was 'more powerful' to mark the change between Craig's characters only 'in behaviour, rather than notating it through outward choices of costume' – in the realm of conscious action, that is, and not of objects.[144] And thus he honoured Churchill's vision in the play, in which the basis of identity, the source of the self, may be 'a scraping cells a speck a speck' but in which the human expressions of this speck are as astonishingly varied as Daniel Craig's performances of Bernard, Bernard, and Michael Black.[145] Rumours circulated of a transfer directly to New York (as had happened, for example, with Stafford-Clark's first production of *Top Girls*) or of the production being remounted with a new cast (as had happened with Daldry's previous collaboration with Churchill, *Far Away*).[146] Instead, celebrating the play's insistence that a different environment will produce a different way of being, Churchill chose a new set of theatrical collaborators for the American premiere, which opened on 16 November 2004 at New York Theatre Workshop.

There, director James Macdonald and set designer Eugene Lee reconfigured the space into an operating theatre, with the spectators sitting on steeply raked tiers rising from a round space, harshly lit by a single instrument: an antique surgical lamp. The space contained only a couch. Macdonald and Lee represented the play's setting – the scene where Salter can live – differently than Daldry and MacNeil had, emphasising its almost clinical examination of an existential problem. And although the two productions used identical texts, in performance they could not have looked or sounded more dissimilar. Take Salter's evasive, elliptical lines. With his imposing physique and booming baritone, Gambon played the character as garrulous and self-interrupting, while Sam Shepard, with his sinewy body and whispered intensity, suggested taciturnity and a reluctance to self-incriminate. Similarly, Dallas Roberts distinguished the three clones as beautifully as Craig had in London but by different means. Craig inflected Bernard 1's and Michael's speech with Cockney and Liverpudlian touches, respectively, while Roberts focused on the clones' body language and used the same American dialect for all. Each actor stood to each of those characters as each of them stands to the others: a genetically identical person with a nonetheless different way of being. We might consider the play's other progeny in the same manner. For *A Number* continues to proliferate: in Argentina as *Copias*, in Brazil as *Um Número*, in the Czech Republic as *Řada*, in Denmark as *Kopier*, and so on through the alphabet and across the globe. These works are tied together by a shared DNA – their nature, if you will – but each is nurtured in a different environment.

Thus Bernard 2 explains his difference from his older brother when he recognises that Bernard 1's childhood has made him a 'nutter'.[147] And thus he explains why Salter could love one Bernard and monstrously neglect another:

> someone with the same genetic exactly the same but at a different time a different cultural and of course all the personal all kinds of what happened in your own life your childhood or things all kind of because suppose you'd had a brother with identical an identical twin say but separated at birth so you had entirely different early you see what I'm saying would he have done the same things who can say he might have been a very loving father and in fact of course you have that in you to be that because you were to me so it's a combination of very complicated and that's who you were so probably I shouldn't blame you.[148]

Note the absence of punctuation. Churchill leaves the text's precise signification up to its actors and to the environment – scene partners, set design, audiences – in which interpretation will occur. But Salter remains mired in the logic of genes, of text, of essential meanings. In the play's final scene, he reaches out to Michael Black, from whom he longs to hear 'something from deep inside your life'.[149] When Michael responds with an anecdote about his wife's 'disney elf' ears – 'noticing that, I mean the way I love her, felt very felt very what you said something deep inside' – Salter is dissatisfied.[150] He does not apprehend the lesson Michael offers; he cannot understand Michael's happiness, his sense of belonging. The logic of belongings possesses him still, as he betrays when he warns Michael that 'there are things that are what you are'.[151] Accordingly he misreads the diminishment he feels after the loss of both Bernards. He understands himself as missing an object whose replacement he seeks in a genetic double, just as he had done when Bernard 1 was five years old.

A Number, premiered in 2002, represents its dystopian future with greater elegance and assurance than had *Crimes*, Churchill's 1982 teleplay set in 2000 and preoccupied with the genetic engineering of its doctor, Melvin Schwartz. It will suffice to say that her formal innovations and thematic content have kept pace with, and frequently anticipated, shifts in the larger culture. *Cloud Nine* sketched a theory of identity predicated on historical and ideological forces. Steeped in the influence of Fanon, Foucault, and Genet, Churchill theatricalised the process by which history scripts narratives and shapes roles to be enacted and embodied by those who inherit them – a concern present already in plays such as *Vinegar Tom* and *Light Shining in Buckinghamshire*, both preoccupied with identity at historical crossroads. But history has become a less pressing concern for Churchill, who has not written a play with a substantial historical basis since 1991's *Lives of the Great Poisoners* – unless we consider the oblique *Drunk Enough to Say I Love You?*, which compresses decades of American atrocities in the love affair between a country, Sam, and a guy, Guy. According to Harvey, history has become less legible as our world has been remade by the torrents of capital driving globalisation and neoliberalism. If *Icecream* and *Hot Fudge* showed a world in which history was being compressed, they also suggested the compensatory role that commodification might play in identity formation. In her first major play of the twenty-first century, *A Number*, Churchill focused more acutely on the relationship between the self and the body that houses it. The play therefore feels summative of Churchill's career-long exploration into identity.

Churchill has repeatedly theatricalised how the body changes its roles through its unique performance. The second scene of *Cloud Nine* provides a telling image. In it, the characters play hide and seek, a game in which one person – the 'he' – is named the policing force and made responsible for finding others. The game limns the disciplinary workings of Empire and family, the play's central concerns. But if the game suggests the process by which Edward is conditioned into his role as 'he' – 'I've found you', he will excitedly declare to Ellen and Betty – it also suggests the possibility of simply refusing to play. 'We're not hiding Edward', they reply.[152] They adumbrate the political power of resisting the scripts that we inherit. And as it is for policed subjects, so it is for those meant to police: Harry Bagley flaunts his lack of interest in assigned roles when he is 'he', blithely offering to leave mid-game and accompany Maud back to the house. New scripts, new identifications, are possible, as Lin makes plain in her Act 2 declaration – unimaginable in Act 1 – that 'I'm a lesbian'.[153]

Churchill registers resistance to prescribed identities, I have said, through the actors' bodies and the metatheatrical force they summon, especially through doubling. In *Cloud Nine*, doubling visually disrupts the ideological forces at work; in *Icecream* and *Hot Fudge*, doubling inhibits identification and undermines any sense of stable character. In *A Number*, the doubling of Bernard, Bernard, and Michael Black works powerfully to embody Churchill's thesis about the unique value of each human being even in an age of biotechnological reproduction, when our reducibility to chromosomal patterns renders us vulnerable in a corporatised world. Churchill clearly feels the encroaching threat. In the same season that *Icecream* was produced, for example, her longstanding relationship with the Royal Court became strained over the issue of corporate sponsorship. Two years earlier British Telecom, upset by the anti-capitalist messages of *Serious Money*, had refused to provide the Court with telephones for the set design; and their declaration – '[t]his is a production with which no public company would wish to be associated' – provided a public relations opportunity when the quotation was cheekily circulated in the press.[154] But by 1989, after Thatcher had further shifted arts funding from the state to corporations, the Royal Court would become reliant on business interests for more than set dressing. Only months after *Icecream*'s premiere, Churchill would feel conflict with the Court's Council when Barclays emerged as a financial sponsor. Stafford-Clark's journal for 23 October 1989 notes Churchill's disapproval at a board meeting, where she declared it dubious that a left-wing theatre would partner with Barclays, still tainted by its scandalous investment in apartheid South Africa, another vestige of the colonialism whose longstanding damage *Cloud Nine* thematises.[155] The journal reveals that the conversation between him and Churchill – which he characterises as 'good humoured, friendly' – continued almost daily.[156] But nothing broke the impasse. A few weeks later Churchill would reiterate her position, writing to the Council's chairman that 'I can't be part of the Court's administration any more' and explaining that 'I still can't accept the Royal Court being used to launder the image of the bank'.[157]

In the decades since, corporate involvement in the arts has become a fact of theatrical life. But the power to resist, *A Number* tells us, inheres in the particular ontology of performance, the subject of my fifth chapter. On the page, a play is not ontologically distinct from a sculpture, an art-object to be bought. But on stage, a play offers itself to consumers only as Michael Black offers himself to Salter: not as an object with exchange value but as an occasion for encounter. *A Number* thus enacts a theory of being. An identity may be shaped by scripts, written by genetic or ideological forces. But it is not reducible to them; both a play and a person constitute themselves through performance in a process that unfolds moment by moment in the present. This fact explains how we evolve: the changes in Betty as *Cloud Nine* progresses, for example. It explains the peculiar joy of seeing *Top Girls* for the fifth and yet the first time. And it explains the enduring appeal of characters – from Oedipus to Hamlet to Bernard, to name three examples – who grapple on stage with the elusive mystery of being. Bernard 2 articulates this mystery thus:

> it feels it always it feels doesn't it inside that's just how we feel what we are and we don't know all these complicated we can't know what we're it's too complicated to disentangle all the causes and we feel this is me I freely and of course it's true who you are does freely not forced by someone else but who you are who you are itself forces or you'd be someone else wouldn't you?[158]

We cannot know – it's too complicated, as *Icecream*'s Lance learns – why we are who we are, even as we know that our identities are expressed in our actions ('who you are does') and touch on wellsprings interior and yet inaccessible to us. We feel the opposition between our agency and the forces that script us; we feel too that these forces may be internalised ('who you are itself forces'). We recognise how substantially these feelings – this affective dimension – determine the self ('how we feel what we are'). And we recognise the peculiar tension between our unique subjectivity and our epistemological certainty that everyone else feels this unique subjectivity, too. We feel, *this is me*. Michael Black celebrates the fact that he shares his genetic material with a number of others and contextualises this fact for his biological father: 'We've got ninety-nine per cent the same genes as any other person. We've got ninety per cent the same as a chimpanzee. We've got thirty percent [*sic*] the same as a lettuce. Does that cheer you up at all? I love about the lettuce. It makes me feel I belong'.[159] His genetic similarity to others does not overwhelm him as it had Teddy and Clive in *Identical Twins.* And thus, in performance, he can resist the script that Salter pushes, just as Harry, Mrs Saunders, and eventually even Betty resist the scripts thrust upon them. Refuting the existential dread that crippled the Bernards, he plainly asserts his free will when Churchill gives him the last line:

> **Salter** And you're happy you say are you? you like your life?
>
> **Michael** I do yes, sorry.[160]

CHAPTER 4
THE AESTHETICS AND POLITICS OF COLLABORATION

Elaine Aston has noted that Churchill's 'reputation for working with practitioners from theatre and other arts-related media is second to none among contemporary British dramatists' – a claim which Aston supports with a rich survey of Churchill's collaborations with other theatre-makers, with composers such as Orlando Gough and Judith Weir, and with choreographers such as Siobhan Davies and Ian Spink.[1] These relationships have produced work that pushes against the borders of theatre in more ways than one. In *Lives of the Great Poisoners* – which premiered on tour at Bristol's Arnolfini on 13 February 1991 – the three stories of Medea, Mme de Brinvilliers, and Hawley Crippen are made to intersect not only through the magic of doubling (since nine performers play twenty-seven roles) but also through the weaving of narrative arts: the story is told partly in dramatic dialogue, partly in operatic singing, partly in choreographed movement. Churchill devised the text; Gough, the music; Spink, the dance. The whole comes together not as a Wagnerian *Gesamtkunstwerk* but as a hybrid whose elements work sometimes in harmony and sometimes in dissonance – like the characters themselves, with their here congenial and there fractious interactions. Such a fit between form and content marks all of Churchill's work, of course, but it marks her collaborations uniquely – especially since the 'watershed' of 1976 (her word), when she first worked with the Joint Stock and Monstrous Regiment troupes.[2] Ever since, the plays borne of her collaborations have exposed both their method of construction and the politics that governed their making. These politics, meanwhile, challenge the borders of theatre in another way. By linking the world of the play with the world of its production, Churchill ties the characters' action to the actors' agency. She thus offers challenges and rebukes to the politics of the world off stage, suggesting different models for social cooperation.

Light Shining in Buckinghamshire

Light Shining in Buckinghamshire dramatises 'the amazed excitement of people taking hold of their own lives' during the English civil war – a time when, as Churchill writes in her preface, 'anything seemed possible'.[3] But it also dramatises considerable discord. For a community united in its anti-Royalist desire came to express radically different visions for England's future after the execution of Charles I and the exile of Charles II. In the Putney Debates of 1647 (the public fora whose extant transcripts provided Churchill with a key scene), members of the Parliamentarian New Model Army debated a new constitution for England and the ideal workings of the franchise: the demand for greater suffrage, pressed by some parties, chafed against the rights of property, asserted by others. Debaters like Thomas Rainborough, Edward Sexby, and John Wildman represented the Levellers, who argued for every man's right to vote; Oliver Cromwell and Henry Ireton sought to limit enfranchisement to landowners as in the pre-revolutionary Parliament. Beyond Putney, a breakaway sect of True Levellers or Diggers agitated for shared property and established communes like that at St George's Hill, Weybridge, where Gerrard Winstanley's collective built shelters and shared both labour and fruits of its agrarian project. And a more radical sect known as Ranters advocated pantheism and a philosophy of economic and sexual freedom. Proto-communist like the Diggers, the Ranters exhorted followers to 'give up your houses, horses, goods, gold, Lands, give up, account nothing your own, have ALL THINGS common', in the words of the preacher Abiezer Coppe or Cobbe.[4] Fiercely anti-clerical, they prepared for Christ's return to a heaven on earth, expressing an 'ecstatic and anarchic belief' that Churchill characterises as 'the last desperate burst of revolutionary feeling before the restoration'.[5] The play thus demonstrates how the united, sometimes utopian politics of those sympathetic to or fighting alongside Cromwell fractured into a 'revolt within the Revolution' and eventually collapsed into disunity and despair.[6] The Levellers were crushed by Cromwell's army at Burford in 1649, a few weeks after the execution of Robert Lockyer, whose funeral is described in Churchill's second act. The Diggers' dream of universal liberty predicated on the establishment of a universal community went unrealised. And the Ranters, misunderstood and persecuted, died out: Christ never came. The Parliament's new and ostensibly expanded liberties did not embrace a common people. Instead, even as feudalism was challenged (and eventually abolished), political power became re-concentrated among the propertied. A period catalysed by utopian hope instead came to enshrine the logic of ownership whose potential corrosiveness I explored in the second chapter.

Light Shining in Buckinghamshire depicts this history in twenty-one scenes populated sometimes by historical figures such as Cobbe or Cromwell but more often by fictional players such as Margaret Brotherton, a vagrant driven from parish to parish by a heartless judiciary, or Jone Hoskins, a Ranter preacher. It is history largely told by those on the ground, those usually omitted from the archival record and its fictional treatments. In both form and content, then, the play is Churchill's most indebted to Bertolt Brecht, whose work she first encountered as an undergraduate at Oxford, where she acted in *The Caucasian Chalk Circle*.[7] Like Brecht, Churchill forgoes a central hero, instead interrogating how behaviours express the socioeconomic conditions of their context; she showcases the development of a class consciousness rather than individual psychologies. Too, Churchill resists an overarching dramatic arc in favour of the style that Brecht, following Aristotle, called 'epic'. A smooth narrative is replaced by jaggedly juxtaposed vignettes and multiple points of view: 'like small chips of film, black and white stills, grainy', as Churchill wrote in her notebooks at the time.[8]

Conjuring 'history' not as a coherent narrative centred on a hero but as an accumulation of heterogeneous actions and actors, Churchill also mimics the unsettled tone of the time she represents – most obviously in a scene involving Thomas Briggs (a man drafted into the revolutionary forces) and Laurence Claxton (whom Churchill based on a real-life figure). When Briggs and Claxton's conversation unfolds simultaneously with the recruiting speech of the preacher Star, we see Churchill's signature device in the overlapping dialogue, which in fact began earlier than 1980's *Three More Sleepless Nights.* (Indeed, we see it foreshadowed already in *Having a Wonderful Time*, whose amateur production at the Questors Theatre, Ealing, opened on 5 August 1960. Its opening attempts to capture the casual cacophony and interruptions of a number of people in voluble conversation.) *Light Shining in Buckinghamshire*'s polyvocality becomes literalised in performance, as the voices mingle and threaten to obscure one another. In the text, Churchill honoured this polyvocality with her method of construction: the script agglomerates historical documents along with imagined dialogues, weaving a tapestry whose strands go back to the Bible (the play's opening words are from Isaiah) and texts from the period (such as the Digger pamphlet from 1649, *More Light Shining in Buckinghamshire*, that furnishes her title). Meanwhile, some anachronistic verse by Walt Whitman – sung by the whole company – creates the critical distance Brecht called *Verfremdung*. Drawing on an assortment of public material, Churchill makes use of communal property as the agrarian workers at St George's Hill did. Her text becomes a collective creation, with real-life figures such as Cobbe or Winstanley drawn into service as assuredly as the actors themselves. In Brechtian fashion, these actors sometimes appear as themselves, but they are pointedly anonymised to stress not the individual but rather his or her role in the acting collective: a representative speech prefix reads 'One of the Actors'.[9] The linkage between form and context – and between the world represented by the play and the world of the play's production – is tight. When 'Winstanley' asserts, in the play's twelfth scene, that '[t]here can be no universal liberty till this universal community be established', Churchill uses his actual words. He is pointedly followed not by a seventeenth-century character but by a '1st Actor'.[10]

Highlighting the presence of the actors as actors, Churchill reveals her second authorial conceit. The play was made with Joint Stock – Churchill's first of several collaborations with the group – so that the communal politics of the play's Levellers and Diggers were honoured in its process of creation. Director Max Stafford-Clark's 1976 diaries show that this process was initiated on 26 April, when a meeting was held with Churchill and Colin Bennett, who had written Joint Stock's *Fourth Day Like Four Long Months of Absence* two years earlier. Periodic meetings ensued, with Churchill's early enthusiasms coalescing around Quakerism. But the focus shifted. By June, Bennett had left the project and a group of eight actors had joined; general subjects – the Revolution, the Ranters, millennial thinking, utopianism – had been established.[11] Together, the group read history: Churchill's reading included Norman Cohn's *The Pursuit of the Millennium*, A. L. Morton's *The World of the Ranters*, and Christopher Hill's *The World Turned Upside Down*.[12] And the group explored ideas through improvisation and exercises for three weeks in June. One exercise explored the breaching of social conventions, with actors improvising degrees of idiosyncrasy determined by playing cards.[13] In another, they visited a manor house in character as peasants.[14] This work provided Churchill with grist for a script that would be refined through additional workshops over five weeks beginning on 3 August, with a revised company of actors.[15] The result was 'something much more open, a much less *private* way of working' as Churchill put it: a script produced by a '*common* imagination'.[16] Private gives way to common. The possibility of greater freedom or 'something much more open' results. The 'I' of individual ownership gives way to an enlightening and expansive 'we'. And the play's politics thus resonate more clearly 'than when you just sit down and write a play by yourself' as, for example, Churchill had tried to do with 1962's abandoned project *The Demonstration*, concerned with the eponymous political action that attracts and repels its main character, Andrew.[17]

We must nonetheless recognise Churchill as the dominant creative force behind *Light Shining in Buckinghamshire* as a dramatic script. In a writing process that she would later characterise as more difficult than working alone, Churchill marshalled the collective's creative energies, as she marshalled her source materials, into a text of her own devising.[18] For example, she has explained that 'I wrote the description of a battle and Claxton going over the hill after improvisations by Nigel [Terry] and Will [Knightley], the first time I'd known the pleasure of giving an actor back a speech in that way, and the only time I remember working quite like that'.[19] We see the central importance of her contribution, too, when we compare the extant transcript of the Putney Debates with the scene that emerged from her condensation (well established by critics) and rewriting (largely unrecognised). Churchill reduced the thirty-one speakers recorded in the transcript to six. She radically compressed the speeches: for instance, the Leveller John Wildman's twenty-word claim that '[t]hey believe that if an obligation is not just, then it is an act of honesty not to keep it' took ninety-four words to make, historically.[20] She regularised the characters' use of the term 'vote' and omitted words with unhelpful historical specificity, such as 'burgesses'.[21]

An expert dramaturgical hand steers the diction, as when vocabulary changes made the debates speak forcefully to a contemporary audience, and the structure, as when a speech of Rainborough was re-crafted as a dialogue between him and Wildman, or when an oppositional interjection by Ireton ('I will tell you –') was inserted into one of Rainborough's speeches.[22] Moreover, the Brechtian open-endedness of the Putney Debates, including their relevance for 1970s England, is underscored by Churchill's cliffhanger ending for the scene: 'I move for a committee', Cromwell says.[23] In reality, the debate had days and thousands of words to go. The scene demonstrates Churchill's use of documentary theatre techniques, such as those of Brecht or, nearer her time, Peter Weiss. The scene demonstrates Churchill's sure hand with dramatic adaptation, which she had first exercised in an early, unpublished play *The Finnsburg Fragment*, based on the Old English poem, and which she had honed since, as in her unproduced television adaptation *The Brown Bride*, based on the traditional folk ballet 'Lord Thomas and Fair Annet'.[24] Most significantly, the scene demonstrates the extent to which compression and minor changes can shape the source material, as the playwright would prove again in 1978 when she edited the transcript of an in-camera 'Diplock trial' from Northern Ireland to create her BBC teleplay *The Legion Hall Bombing*, which came under considerable fire for political editorialising.[25]

Light Shining in Buckinghamshire's most radical formal feature – and the one tied most closely to the play's content – emerged organically during rehearsal on 9 August, when it was decided that actors would not own but instead share their parts: the dialogue, woven from collective improvisation and public-domain sources, became a commons in another sense.[26] Typically at the theatre an actor assumes a role, and this relationship is encoded in a play's programme and dramatis personae page, which equate each actor to a character and align them in parallel columns. Reaching back to the Renaissance and classical theatres, Brecht sought to disrupt this identification by encouraging doubling and a presentational acting style that would remind viewers of both actor and character at any given moment. In *Light Shining in Buckinghamshire*, Churchill goes farther. In lieu of a character list, she lists 'Scenes' alongside 'Parts played by'.[27] The actors take primacy, not only sharing roles but also appearing as themselves, as clarified in many of the speech prefixes. Emphasis is laid on the performers who engage in a revolutionary act of theatre rather than disappear into fatalistic roles. These actors become itinerant like the Ranters, roaming from scene to scene and from character to character: here they play Levellers like Rainborough; there, one of the forces that would silence the Levellers at Burford. Dispossessed of individual property, they find the basis for greater liberty. Their shifts in actions and motivations highlight (and encourage) their political potential, reminding us that 'acting' and 'agency' share an etymological link: *agere*, to do. And we are returned to the significance of Stafford-Clark's signature directing method – 'actioning' – in which each beat of the script reveals a particular motivation and transitive verb to be played by the actor. Onstage actions, in turn, suggest models for off stage; in consort with others, any might make a revolution. In the play, Will Knightley as Claxton explained that 'My body knew I was doing something amazing. I knew I was in the midst of something, I was doing it, not standing still worrying about it, I was simply walking over the hill to another preacher' – a speech, we should recall, that originated in Knightley's rehearsal improvisations.[28]

The decision to share roles among the company resonates on two levels. First, it honours Churchill's understanding of history as discordant, heterogeneous, offering potential chaos instead of clear arcs. It encompasses many points of view and is lived by many players, not merely the singular heroes emphasised by history and its dramatisation, such as Robert Bolt's *A Man for All Seasons*. As Churchill has written, the audience confusions that resulted from *Light Shining in Buckinghamshire* were deliberate, reflecting better the reality of events such as war and revolution.[29] She and Stafford-Clark did not provide star vehicles to compensate for a lack of heroes; rather, the communal politics of her seventeenth-century subjects were respected. Second, the sharing of roles respects the process of their creation. As Michelene Wandor once said about the Joint Stock method, '[t]he individual roles of writer, director and performer are deliberately blurred to maximize participation; everyone is free to suggest and initiate areas of work, books to read, ideas to discuss'.[30] Here, a similar solidarity becomes encoded in the fabric of the text, woven in like the strands of historical sources: any 'One of the Actors' might appear. When, in the play's first act, Claxton and his wife provide care to Hoskins (who has been beaten by Calvinist worshippers), their act of sharing is neatly tied to the sharing of the central role. In the inaugural production, Linda Goddard played Hoskins confronting the Calvinist preacher, but the role was assumed in the next scene by Janet Chappell or, later in the run, Carole Hayman. Goddard, in turn, took over the role of Claxton's unnamed wife.

The play opened at the Edinburgh Fringe, where it won an award from *The Scotsman*. Three weeks later, after a week of previews, it opened in London on 27 September 1976, when Michael Billington would praise its form for 'precisely match[ing] its subject'.[31] But if the play's fit between form and content was noticed by its early critics, they did not all approve. On BBC Radio 4's 'Kaleidoscope' with Michael Oliver, broadcast on 28 September, playwright John Griffith Bowen derided the play's lack of 'a unified tone of voice' and 'narrative' in favour of a 'mosaic, not of a straight line, not of a story'; he compared the play unfavourably with *A Man for All Seasons* and Arthur Miller's *The Crucible*, two plays with an undisturbed narrative arc and a male hero. '[T]he single voice . . . the single eye, has been taken over by a kind of committee,' he lamented, while criticising the tonal difference between the dialogue from historical sources and contemporary invention.[32] Similarly criticising the play on BBC Radio 3's 'Critics'

Forum' on 2 October, historian John Weightman condemned Churchill's anachronisms and lack of objectivity. Both he and Bowen recognised – and ironically validated – the play's Brechtian political potential. By mixing historical and modern texts and diction, Weightman complained, '[i]magination is free to do whatever it likes with the material' and the objectifying glance of 'history' is compromised in favour of a subjective understanding.[33] Such subjective understanding, of course, works as Brecht theorised: it reveals the play's relevance to modern times. 'Even if we felt obliged to do something for a work like *Antigone*', he famously wrote of his adaptation of Sophocles' play, 'we could only do so by letting the play do something for us'.[34]

It was precisely the play's relevance to modern times that had attracted Churchill, who commented that '[t]he revolutionary hopes of the late sixties and early seventies were near enough that we could still share them, but we could relate too to the disillusion of the restoration and the idea of a revolution that hadn't happened'.[35] *Light Shining in Buckinghamshire*, we recall, was inaugurated during unsettled Parliamentary times: after a nail-biting leadership race, James Callaghan had taken over premiership of Harold Wilson's fragile Labour government only three weeks before Joint Stock's first meeting with Churchill. (The absurdities of the Parliamentary stalemate Callaghan inherited, which lasted until the Conservatives' 1979 victory under Margaret Thatcher, are lampooned in James Graham's 2012 play *This House*.) If Parliament was stuck in seemingly intractable deadlock, the larger culture was equally unsettled – suspended, in Siân Adiseshiah's assessment, at a crossroads of optimism and cynicism.[36] British playwriting, meanwhile, preoccupied itself with the theme of class that had thrived during (and in response to) Conservative Edward Heath's tenure as Prime Minister. Plays such as John McGrath's *The Cheviot, the Stag, and the Black Black Oil*, catalysed by socialist conviction, reflected the increasing militancy and yet worsening impotence of Britain's Left – especially its trade unions, under perennial legislative attack. Central to this period, of course, was *Fanshen*: Joint Stock's 1975 documentary drama based on William Hinton's book, which examines the civil war whose aftermath saw the establishment of the People's Republic of China in 1949. Prior to *Fanshen*, Joint Stock co-founder Bill Gaskill has clarified, 'we were not a politically committed ensemble'.[37] But inspired by their subject matter, the company began operating as a cooperative, with all decisions made collectively – even if theatre scholarship now tends to emphasise the show's directors, Stafford-Clark and Gaskill, or its writer, David Hare, another founding member of the company.

A year later, then, *Light Shining in Buckinghamshire* – with its shared focus on revolution and its epic scale – could find an easy thematic fit with, and a working political structure in, the Joint Stock company. At the same time, there can be little doubt that Churchill's experience brought something new. Her own previous collaborations had been with other women: *Strange Days*, her 1975 Young People's Theatre Project co-written with Joan Mills,[38] and *Save It for the Minister*, her 1975 teleplay co-written with Mary O'Malley and Cherry Potter.[39] By contrast, Joint Stock had been run exclusively by men, a perspective whose limitations have been questioned.[40] As *Light Shining in Buckinghamshire* cast member and Joint Stock actor Carole Hayman once attested: 'women were very peripheral . . . the workshops tended to be organized on a ratio of three men to one woman roughly, and the parts usually came out on a ratio of ten men to one woman, if you were lucky'.[41] Elsewhere, Hayman complained that the Joint Stock board was deaf to calls for more projects by and about women. She claims to have been told that 'women had nothing to write about – they hadn't *done* anything in the world' and, after complaining about the lack of women's roles in *Fanshen*, that 'men ran the revolution'.[42] (It may be useful to remember, as most critics have not, that Hayman's comments may be coloured by her offstage role as Stafford-Clark's ex-partner. As *Cloud Nine* has taught us, family relations and larger social relations are imbricated. In a different context, Stafford-Clark would characterise Hayman as 'reconstructing history in public according to feminist doctrine'.[43])

In *Light Shining in Buckinghamshire* – Joint Stock's first show written by a woman – we see the first promising expansion of the company's point-of-view. Men and women contributed to the workshop in equal numbers, even if the ratio of parts in the finalised script was three to one. And the theme of women's oppression and invisibility from historical discourse is explicitly foregrounded. In Hoskins, Churchill gives us a woman who can speak back to a Calvinist preacher, even if her refusal to be silent gets her beaten and ejected from church. To Hoskins, Churchill gives the play's funniest line, when the character engages with another Ranter in a disagreement that culminates in laughter and their shared conferral of communion on Brotherton:

Claxton St Paul to Timothy, 'Let the woman learn in silence'.

Hoskins Jone Hoskins to St Paul, fuck off you silly old bugger.[44]

The scene underscores the emancipatory potential of Ranter thought when Brotherton obsesses about the sinfulness of her adultery and forced infanticide and is reassured by Claxton. Most powerfully, Churchill provides a first-act scene in which two peasant women look at themselves in a broken mirror, which has been looted from an abandoned feudal manor. 'That's you and me', one tells the other, who struggles to recognise herself as she struggles to accept the mirror's provenance: 'That's stealing', she worries.[45] The moment's political potential is captured in the Brechtian *Gestus* of looking in the mirror, an act which brings the women self-awareness and a dawning consciousness of their collective power: 'They must know what they look like all the time. And now we do'.[46]

Note the communal 'we'. It ties the communal politics of the Diggers to the proto-feminism of the women, on the brink of seizing control of their destinies. It effects Churchill's signature manoeuvre, tying the struggle against class oppression to the struggle against patriarchy. Churchill famously declared that 'socialism and feminism aren't synonymous, but I feel strongly about both and wouldn't be interested in a form of one that didn't include the other'.[47] And we might see her as bringing a feminist voice to the socialist Joint Stock – a voice that would flourish, especially two years later in their work on *Cloud Nine*. (Hayman would be the first woman to direct the troupe with 1984's explicitly feminist *The Great Celestial Cow*, written by a woman [Sue Townsend], about women of colour, and starring a cast, including a young Meera Syal, in which women outnumbered men two to one.) If *Light Shining in Buckinghamshire* reflects the seventeenth-century's sexism in its themes and dialogues, this sexism is tempered by its 1976 presentation. In 1647, not even the most progressive Leveller debaters spoke of expanded rights for women. But in 1976, the roles and dialogue sometimes cut across gender lines. When a female actor (Linda Goddard) played Nathaniel Rich in the Putney Debates that end the first act, the Brechtian potential of the play was realised: a woman was introduced into a public discourse that had excluded her in 1647. (The play's revivals, too, have tended to follow Stafford-Clark's cross-gender apportionment of dialogue: a National Theatre touring production that opened in Canterbury on 7 November 1996 and landed at the Cottesloe starting 9 January 1997, directed by Mark Wing-Davey, for instance; or Mark Ravenhill's 2008 rehearsed reading at the Royal Court; or Polly Findlay's 2010 production at London's Arcola Theatre.)

There can be little doubt that Churchill's feminist voice was encouraged and amplified by Monstrous Regiment, a theatre troupe formed precisely in response to the industry's male bias and in order to explore 'socialist-feminist ideas and politics in theatrical practice'.[48] Churchill had spent 1976 moving between the two companies. The feminist company – including Gillian Hanna, later to perform, too, in Churchill's *Icecream* – had met the playwright during a political march earlier that year. Monstrous Regiment then commissioned a play, originally called *Witches*, and Churchill found herself 'happy and stimulated by the discovery of shared ideas and the enormous energy and feeling of possibilities in the still new company'.[49] After historical research into women's prosecution in Tudor and Stuart England, Churchill produced a draft of *Vinegar Tom* before beginning workshops for *Light Shining in Buckinghamshire* in June. When Joint Stock rehearsals finished in August, she returned to Monstrous Regiment to rehearse and refine her other play with Pam Brighton, its director. It is no surprise, then, to see explicit linkages between the two works. In *Vinegar Tom*, for example, Alice expresses her wish to hear London's Ranter preachers, about whom she learns from an unnamed sexual partner. He might be describing Cobbe and Hoskins: 'There's some in

London say there's no sin. Each man has his own religion nearby, or none at all, and there's women speak out too. They smoke and curse in the tavern and they say flesh is no sin for they are God themselves and can't sin'.[50] Moreover, when Monstrous Regiment added a musician (Josefina Cupido) to the company during their September rehearsals, Churchill had to integrate a new character into *Vinegar Tom* quickly. So she wrote an additional role: Betty, whose primary scene shows her being bled by a doctor. Churchill had in fact cut this moment and dialogue from *Light Shining in Buckinghamshire*, where it was intended to dramatise a moment of Hoskins's life.[51]

The two plays, then, share a historical timeframe and underwent entwined processes of rehearsal and production: *Light Shining in Buckinghamshire*, workshopped, written, and rehearsed in summer, opened in September; *Vinegar Tom*, written in the spring and rehearsed in September, opened at the Humberside Theatre, Hull, on 12 October. Certainly the experiences must have informed one another. It was Monstrous Regiment – the name taken from John Knox's misogynistic pamphlet of 1558 – who encouraged Churchill to share her ideas instead of working primarily in solitude. (The playwright would return to the troupe for *Floorshow*, a cabaret show collaboratively written with David Bradford, Bryony Lavery, and Michelene Wandor that premiered on 18 January 1978 at the Theatre Royal, Stratford East.) And these learned lessons benefited Joint Stock, with its more radically communitarian workshop process. The two scripts represent Churchill's first excursions into a Brechtian dramaturgy: *Vinegar Tom*, too, features songs and wilful anachronisms, grafting an Edwardian music hall aesthetic onto its seventeenth-century plot, and it features Churchill's first sustained use of cross-gender casting, so successfully deployed in *Cloud Nine*. Feminist themes are present in early Churchill works, including 1960's *Having a Wonderful Time* (in which a man trifles with the affections of a vacationing woman) or 1971's *Abortive* (which hinges on a husband and wife's differing understandings of her sexual encounter with their handyman).[52] But such themes appear less obscured after *Vinegar Tom*. No doubt influenced by her collaboration with Monstrous Regiment, feminism wends its way into *Light Shining in Buckinghamshire*, produced by the male-dominated Joint Stock.

Collectively the two plays focused Churchill's concerns, altered her methods, and changed the course of her career. As she told an interviewer, 'my attitude to myself, my work and others had been basically and permanently changed'.[53]

In a scene between Claxton and his wife, he explains that England has grown toxic to people like him:

> How we live is like the sea. We can't breathe. Our squire, he's like a fish. Looks like a fish too, if you saw him. And parson. Parson can breathe. He swims about, waggles his tail. Bitter water and he lives in it. Bailiff. Justices, Hangman. Lawyer. Mayor. All the gentry. Swimming about. We can't live in it. We drown.[54]

The environment, Claxton argues, determines what organisms will be able to sustain themselves, and the Putney Debates, like the larger debate happening around them, determined that England would be an environment governed by laws of property. 'I am a drowned man', Claxton concludes.[55] We might see Joint Stock, with its socialist principles, as trying to create a communal micro-environment with their working practices. But we must recognise, too, that the larger environment was inimical. Churchill shows Briggs entering the communitarian army but shows too his difficulty relinquishing titles, which mark a still-hierarchical society outside: 'Yes sir. I mean, yes, I do', he says to Star, the corn merchant turned Digger leader against whose authority Briggs will eventually chafe.[56] And Star will subsequently undermine the values he holds dear, lending credence to Briggs's pointed accusation: 'Shall I tell you why the Levellers have been shot? Because now the officers have all the power, the army is as great a tyrant as the king was'.[57] Star becomes a private landholder when Parliament sells confiscated land; he learns that his benign plan to 'send for [the tenants] all to drink my health and I'll drink theirs' is 'the custom with the new squire'.[58] As Star and the vicar come to understand, the discourse of collectivism sits ill in an endeavour framed by notions of individual responsibility and governed by private ownership. We might see analogies to the theatre: Gaskill characterised Stafford-Clark's agreement to shared decision-making as made '[r]ather grudgingly'.[59] And despite ostensibly communal politics, Joint Stock actors sometimes complained of their lack of power.[60] Rehearsing *Light Shining in Buckinghamshire*, Stafford-Clark could complain in his diary that 'there's only me and I bear the whole weight'.[61]

Hierarchy lingers. And it brings consequences in a capitalist world governed by laws of property. One instructive case: years after *Vinegar Tom*, Pam Brighton would find herself in a protracted legal battle with Marie Jones over *Stones in His Pockets*, a production of their shared company DubbelJoint whose commercial success in the West End and on Broadway made it a valuable asset. A High Court judge, guided by a common law enshrined during the seventeenth century, determined an owner: Jones, who was not obliged to share its proceeds.[62] In the case of *Light Shining in Buckinghamshire*, the legal owner is also the playwright, whose script Jean E. Howard has beautifully described as 'the hardened shell of property'.[63] But the work itself renounces claims of private ownership. As Howard explains, the text 'casts an ironic light upon any claims to "own" either the script, the performances that spring from it, or the past it both creates and recreates'.[64] Through its borrowings, through its inclusion of the actors in its speech prefixes, through its themes, it declares itself a work of many hands. It may be significant that, unlike *Stones in His Pockets*, *Light Shining in the Buckinghamshire* has been produced only in the not-for-profit sector of the theatre industry: in 1991, at New York Theatre Workshop, for instance (in an award-winning production directed by Lisa Peterson and featuring Bill Camp and Cherry Jones) or in Wing-Davey's 1996 revival, which ended with the actors breaking down the set before the audience had left. With their own bodies, the company honoured the play and its politics by showing that theatre is not only a collective joy and a collective responsibility but also a collective labour.

Fen

This lesson recurs in Churchill's play *Fen*, in whose first scene a Japanese businessman provides a history of eastern England's agricultural fenlands, as well as a reminder of property's prerogatives:

> Mr Takai, Tokyo Company, welcomes you to the fen. Most expensive earth in England. Two thousand pounds acre. Long time ago, under water. Fishes and eels swimming here. Not true people had webbed feet but did walk on stilts. Wild people, fen tigers. In 1630 rich lords planned to drain fen, change swamp into grazing land, far thinking men, brave investors. Fen people wanted to keep fishes and eels to live on, no vision. Refuse work on drainage, smash dykes, broke sluices. Many problems. But in the end we have this beautiful earth.[65]

As the speech adumbrates, the play returns to some of *Light Shining in Buckinghamshire*'s motifs: land and its value, both monetary and emotional; contested ownership; peasants' resistance. (Indeed, a pre-rehearsal typescript pointedly specified that 'Fen people supported Cromwell . . . but now Cromwell wants to drain fens', thus tying the play directly to its revolutionary predecessor.[66]) Again Churchill connects the present to a historical past: the seventeenth century with Mr Takai's speech or a surreal stilt-walking scene; the nineteenth century with the tattered crow-scaring boy who opens the play or the labourer ghost who visits Mr Tewson, a present-day landowner. 'You bloody farmers could not live if it was not for the poor', she tells him.[67] The ghost associates Tewson with his landowning ancestor – perhaps the 'great great grandfather' he invokes in *Fen*'s tenth scene or the 'old Tewson' that Ivy remembers in the sixteenth, when her ninetieth birthday is celebrated.[68] One owner changes to another and, as in the French epigram, the more things stay the same. It is the same lesson the new squire Star learns in *Light Shining in Buckinghamshire*, which had connected the dashed dreams of the 1640s with those of the 1970s.

The new wrinkle is globalisation, driven in the play as in real life by the policies of Margaret Thatcher, whose first term as Prime Minister was winding down as *Fen* debuted, and whose second electoral victory came in May 1983, as the play continued its initial run. As I detailed in my second chapter, Thatcher's policies intensified acquisition and enlarged its scale after she opened the English economy to foreign investment. *Serious Money* dramatises the effect on the Frosbys and

Grimeses of London's City, old-boy brokers rendered obsolete in the new order. *Fen* shows us farm owners like Tewson becoming tenants themselves: crippled by property taxes and forced to sell to multinationals represented by Mr Takai or Miss Cade, a young City dealer. The early typescript is particularly explicit, with Tewson bemoaning 'EEC regulations' and 'common market city slickers buying up all the farms'.[69] The previous continuity of ownership – with land passing to an heir upon each owner's death – cedes to a different kind of successive ownership, unthreatened by mortality: the corporation. As Tewson tells Cade even in the play's published version: 'I need to be bloody immortal. Then I'd never pay tax'.[70] Thus the fen now belongs, as Takai teaches us, to 'Baxter Nolesford Ltd, which belongs to Reindorp Smith Farm Land trust, which belongs 65 per cent to our company. We now among many illustrious landowners, Esso, Gallagher, Imperial Tobacco, Equitable Life'.[71] So we see *Fen*'s workers picking potatoes for faraway owners or grading onions for faraway supermarkets. Nature itself is privatised: the bitter meaning of Mr Takai's line 'in the end we have this beautiful earth'. The earth is owned by faceless corporations (the antecedent-free 'we') who repackage it as alimentary or touristic commodities, often out of reach of the rest of us. The theme revisits Churchill's dystopian *Not Not Not Not Not Enough Oxygen*, first directed for radio by John Tydeman and broadcast on BBC Radio 3 on 31 March 1971. That play had dramatised a then-distant future – 2010 – in which London's parks have been converted to for-profit amusements, their depleted oxygen supply sold in canisters.[72]

Like *Light Shining in Buckinghamshire*, *Fen* was a Joint Stock production, directed by Stafford-Clark's then-protégé Les Waters. (He had previously staged *Three More Sleepless Nights* at Soho Poly and co-directed the first *Cloud Nine* revival at the Royal Court, both in 1980.) Stafford-Clark first mentions the project in his November 1981 diaries and during meetings with Churchill and Waters in December he recorded a cluster of ideas all ultimately integral to the play: Mary Chamberlain's book *Fenwomen*, an oral women's history of the region; historical prison records; Waters's own fen-based family; dream sequences. Stafford-Clark compared the proposed show to the National

Theatre's adaptations of Flora Thompson's *Lark Rise to Candleford* novels, but he also noted that, in light of Churchill's intellect, 'I'm sure it won't get nostalgic'.[73] This judgement seems considerably understated in retrospect. Eventually *Fen* would resemble Lark Rise much less than *Fanshen*'s Long Bow, the agrarian village whose land ownership provided a microcosmic instance of a larger economic phenomenon. But whereas the Chinese peasants provoke an arduous but hopeful *fanshen* or restructuring, *Fen*'s workers end where they begin, mired in a centuries-old economic problem exacerbated by Thatcherite politics.

The workshop was more immersive than *Light Shining in Buckinghamshire*'s had been. In September 1982, Churchill, Waters, and six actors – Linda Bassett, Amelda Brown, Cecily Hobbs, Tricia Kelly, Jennie Stoller, and Bernard Strother – relocated for two weeks to a cottage in the fen village of Upwell. (They were joined for part of the time by Annie Smart, the show's designer and Waters's wife.) Living in modest quarters – cooking, eating, cleaning together – the company would separate in the mornings to wander the village, gathering impressions and talking to people they met in public or while knocking on doors. Upon reuniting in the afternoons, Churchill, Smart, and Waters would describe their days, and the actors would report in character as those they had met, prompted into improvisation as the others asked questions. Four of them worked as day labourers picking fruit, living (however briefly) the back-straining work of their farming subjects. Returning to London for a third week of workshops, the actors did improvisational work based on people they had met and themes that had emerged in Upwell.[74] As Churchill later described, these included 'anger and violence, caused by hard conditions of work, turned inward to self-mutilation or deflected onto people who weren't responsible for it'.[75]

The three-week workshop left Churchill with 'a lot of notes and quotes and things different people had said', drawn from Upwell residents and the participants themselves.[76] Waters's own mother inspired a character, May, whose dreams of a singing career were dashed and who now refuses to sing at all.[77] A story of a woman murdered by her lover inspired another of *Fen*'s key elements. Relayed as it was by someone 'who had been the secretary of the agricultural union', the story suggests the play's pivotal linkage of personal and economic struggles in the fens, with their long history of domestic violence and class tension.[78] Over a nine-week writing gap that began in October, the playwright used her notes and quotes to shape a story of people living in the then-present day: Val, a woman torn between a lover and children whose care she cannot afford; her disapproving mother, May, and senile grandmother, Ivy; her sometimes supportive and sometimes judgemental fellow workers; their gangmaster and landowner. Churchill also portrayed characters more remote to Val (such as a co-worker's husband, a teenaged boy doing day labour, an abused girl, a trio at a Baptist women's meeting); remote to the area (such as Mr Takai and Miss Cade); or remote to the time period (such as the crow-scaring boy and the ghost). Without basing characters on any particular people, Churchill made liberal use of others' words. So the disjointedness of Ivy's birthday monologue reflects its status as a composite of real shards of quotations,[79] and so the play begins with five epigraphs from Upwell residents. The fatalistic lyrics to 'Girls Song' – in which three girls blithely sing of their constrained career options – were stitched together from the words of several real girls, aged six to ten, documented in *Fenwomen*.[80] (Another song, its lyrics taken from the first of Rainer Maria Rilke's *Duino Elegies*, was meant to sit between the play's fifteenth and sixteenth scenes but was cut in rehearsal.[81]) The resulting play Churchill has called her 'most documentary', acknowledging that it contains 'more direct quotes of things people said . . . than any other I've written'.[82]

Borne of collaboration like *Light Shining in Buckinghamshire*, *Fen* resembles the earlier play superficially. Each has twenty-one short scenes whose dialogue weaves documentary material together with invented dialogue; each is written for six actors performing multiple roles; each focuses on the social conditions of a milieu rather than the psychology of an individual, however much *Fen* foregrounds the character of Val. But the plays differ substantially in tone. *Light Shining in Buckinghamshire* juxtaposes its disparate scenes in epic style, whereas *Fen* unfolds continuously, morphing one scene into the next: Churchill describes '*one set which doesn't change*' with '*all furniture and props on stage throughout*'.[83] The resulting tableau is less a Brechtian pastiche than an ever-fluctuating dreamscape. Doubling erodes the boundaries that separate characters. When Val's lover Frank imagines a conversation with his boss, he plays both roles to the speech's climax: '**Frank** *hits* **Mr Tewson**, *that is he hits himself across the face*'.[84] But the scene's potentially straightforward explanation (and comedy) is transformed when the same actor reappears *as* Tewson several scenes later. The effect unsettles. When the actor playing Val appears to Tewson as the nineteenth-century ghost – '*as real as the other women workers*'[85] – bodies we recognise as lovers share space in a radically different context. 'I live in your house. I watch television with you', she warns him.[86] Time, like subjectivity, is shown to be fluid. When the actor who plays the fifteen-year-old Becky plays the ninety-year-old Ivy, or when an actor (Cecily Hobbs in the premiere) plays a character of a different race and sex (Mr Takai), spectators are estranged in a different way than in *Light Shining in Buckinghamshire.* We are primed for *Fen*'s hallucinatory final scene in which all distinctions between places, times, and ontologies collapse. Past and present events co-exist with Becky's dream, which Val enters and describes after she reappears on stage, moments after Frank has killed her. 'There's so much happening', she reports. 'There's so many of them all at once'.[87] The moment foreshadows *The Skriker*, in which Churchill (and Waters) would even more radically distort space and time.

However bleak its ending, *Light Shining in Buckinghamshire* had emphasised the agency of those who make history, and it tied this agency to that of its real-world actors, on stage as themselves. In *Fen*, agency is enervated. Val tries to seize a grim destiny in suicide but, pointedly, fails to use her own hand. Her co-worker Angela, longing for a happier life, flirts with Frank at a pub – 'You wouldn't consider running away with me?' – as if imagining the same escape that Val had imagined earlier in the play, to a London where she wouldn't be a 'freak'.[88] She fails, and her attendant self-hatred manifests in a horrifying moment when she punishes Becky, her stepdaughter, for having capitulated to her abuse:

> **Angela** Now why not say sorry and we'll have a biscuit and see what's on telly. You needn't say mummy, you can say, 'Sorry,

> Angela, I'm bad all through'. I don't want you driving me into a mood.
>
> **Becky** Sorry, Angela, bad all through.
>
> **Angela** *strokes* **Becky***'s hair then yanks it.*
>
> **Angela** No stamina, have you? 'Sorry Angela'. What you made of, girl?[89]

Becky in fact betrays a family resemblance: she, like Angela, is finally beaten by her cruel environment. When we see her working in the fields alongside her stepmother, we see a future as limited as those in 'Girls Song', sung by the mean but pitiable girls who torment Nell. 'I don't think I'll leave the village when I grow up', they trill. 'Nasty, nasty children', Nell diagnoses, before confirming the play's assessment of their future: 'What will you grow up like? Nasty'.[90]

Nasty in the past, nasty in the present, nasty in the future. History seems static, with little resolution or progress, its motifs blurring and recurring like the characters themselves. A small detail from a long-ago story – 'he told my grandfather his missus had been having an affair with the chap from the next smallholding', Nell recounts[91] – ties this historical infidelity to Val, who like Nell's protagonist imagines a life elsewhere. When Val meets Margaret at a Baptist women's meeting, the latter woman reports: 'I've been unhappy as long as I can remember. My mother and father were unhappy too. I think my grandparents were unhappy'.[92] And this timeless unhappiness seems yoked to a superstitious fatalism, expressed in a story about finding Jesus in some jam: signs made into wonders, as with the fairy stories that proliferate in the fens and threaten to justify their hardships. Geoffrey, the husband of Val's co-worker Shirley, takes a no less fatalistic view, telling Val of her failed marriage that

> I don't hold you personally responsible, Val. You're a symptom of the times. Everything's changing, everything's going down. Strikes, militants, I see the Russians behind it. All the boys want to do

> today . . . is drive their bikes and waste petrol. When we went to school we got beaten and when we got home we got beaten again. They don't want to work today.[93]

On one hand, Geoffrey's conservatism is laughable, with its mix of paranoia, xenophobia, and absurd nostalgia for bygone days that offered only beatings: on the evidence, the present offers plenty of its own. On the other hand, he, like Churchill, shifts our attention to the oblique links between a small local unhappiness (such as that of May with her refusal to sing) and the larger forces that buffet those who work the fens. We see the sinews of such a link in Frank's 'poor old brother', helped by the Tewsons at a critical juncture. Now a disciplinary force used to retain Frank's underpaid labour, he is therefore implicated in the sorrow that shadows Frank's relationship with Val. 'We're like family', Frank-as-Tewson supposes.[94]

Indeed, *Fen* repeatedly shows the family as an instance of its larger cosmology. Angela, as much oppressed as oppressing, proves analogous to Tewson, out of touch with his workers and menaced by the forces of international capital embodied by Miss Cade. None is a villain, as clarified by the doubling: Angela appears to us, too, as the minister's wife, Mrs Finch; Tewson as the teen labourer Wilson; Miss Cade as Shirley, etc. Consider, too, Val's argument with her mother and daughters, with its shifting allegiances and competing righteous claims. In Churchill's signature overlapping dialogue, the characters reveal their interdependence even as slashes mimic the aggressions cutting through their straitened relationships:

> **Deb** Shut up.
>
> **Val** Don't speak to your nan like that.
>
> **Deb** You shut up, / none of your business.
>
> **May** Don't speak to your mum like that. She's getting dreadful, Val. / You've only yourself to blame.
>
> **Deb** I'm not. You are. You're getting dreadful.
>
> **May** You see what I mean . . .

Val Don't start on me. Just because you had nothing.

May Don't speak to me like that, / my girl, or it's out you go.

Deb Don't speak to my mum.

Val I've not been here / five minutes.

Deb Don't speak to my nan.

Val Shut up, Deb.

May Don't speak to the child like that.[95]

The scene serves as yet another example of how Churchill edited incisively during rehearsal: the scene was originally longer, with mother criticising daughter for abandoning her children – May calls Val a 'monster'[96] – and daughter condemning mother as sexless and trapped in an unhappy marriage. With her revisions, Churchill better highlighted the women's unacknowledged similarity, defined by the play's most frequent imperative: don't speak. Self-expression is shut up, potential escape barred. Frank in fact won't ask Tewson for a raise; Becky promises Angela to never write again after she is upbraided for writing poetry. And, as Deb and May and Val make clear, the forced silence and violence of the fens affect women disproportionately, as reflected in the composition of the play's cast (five to one) and in one of its working titles (*Rural Women*, as announced in a Joint Stock press release on 6 July 1982).[97]

Sheila Rabillard has offered an explanation in her 1994 article '*Fen* and the Production of a Feminist Ecotheater', still the finest scholarly consideration of the play. For Rabillard, *Fen* exposes the ideological structure of privatised agriculture, which since the seventeenth century has aligned the process of 'development' with sexist imperatives and eradicated traditionally feminine ways of speaking to and through the earth. Women have been divorced from the land insofar as its resources have been removed from their control, yet they remain bound to it: land provides their subsistence, however meagre. Female labour still preponderates. Another of Churchill's provisional titles was *Strong Girls Always Hoeing*, taken from an 1842 agricultural report advising employers that '[s]trong girls who are always hoeing can do the work better than men' at a fraction of the cost.[98] Research in Upwell confirmed this historical insight, which the play grants to Tewson when he admires women for being '[b]etter workers than men'. He, like an Upwell gangmaster whom Joint Stock met during the workshop, reports that 'I've seen women working in my fields with icicles on their faces'.[99] Therefore, the play shows us women never free of the dirt whose potatoes they unearth: Annie Smart's brilliant set planted its vegetables and its furniture in a field which, in one revealing moment, Shirley irons. Farm labour is tied to domestic labour, as when the always hoeing Nell works in her garden or when Shirley, immediately after packing onions in the fields, is seen ironing, mending, babysitting. Linda Bassett, in the first of her many collaborations with Churchill, found the scene's timing her biggest challenge: playing Shirley, she had to perform all of her domestic tasks while preparing soup to coincide with Geoffrey's entrance, after which she had to coordinate not only her domestic labours but also the carefully overlapped dialogue she shared with her stage husband, played (like Tewson and Frank) by Bernard Strother.[100]

The scene emerged from a workshop exercise in which a set of tasks – ironing, sweeping, peeling potatoes, serving tea – had to be accomplished in a set time.[101] And this fact, like Bassett's nightly challenge getting it right in front of an audience, reminds us that actors, too, are workers. If Rabillard related communal and capitalist models of agriculture to 'feminine and masculine principles in human relations', we might extend this observation to the theatre, its usual hierarchies challenged by Joint Stock's socialist organisation and Churchill's feminist commitment.[102] Not that 'masculine' and 'feminine' are coextensive with 'male' and 'female', of course – as we are alerted by the gangmaster Mrs Hassett when she berates Wilson, or indeed by Waters himself, one of the five men who have comprised Churchill's closest collaborators. He once told the *New York Times* that 'most of the writers [I direct] are feminists. . . . The world must change and they're changing it'.[103] Change begins in the politics of everyday interaction, which prove microcosmic of a larger system. We are returned to Joint Stock principles, with all members of the *Fen* collective sharing the same cottage, using a single bathroom, some sleeping on the floor.

If the offstage world sometimes seems determined by forces beyond our control, in other words, the theatre can offer other possibilities. It is no accident that in the final scene – after the play casts off the cloak of realism it has worn only loosely – *Fen*'s theatricality amplifies. Possibilities expand. When Val re-emerges on the stage (after Frank has put her corpse into a wardrobe), the play undercuts the apparent fatalism of her death. In the words of Elin Diamond, she appears to us not as a ghost but as a 'consciousness that instantiates a new theater space'.[104] In this space, Val can speak from beyond the grave to reassure the lover who killed her: 'It's what I wanted'.[105] She can see the entire unhappy history which haunts the fens but which may not doom the future. Angela can find an insight previously denied her and connect her own pain with the pain she inflicts on her stepdaughter. May can sing. Meanwhile, Nell appears on stilts. She has always been the play's likeliest Jone Hoskins: nonconformist ('I just can't think like they do'[106]) and equally quick with a politically charged one-liner. (Learning of a landowner's suicide, she remarks: 'Best hope if they all top themselves. Start with the queen and work down and I'll tell them when to stop'.[107]) In an earlier version of the script, Nell had recounted to Frank how she fought both an employer, Acton's, and her own union in order to get what she was owed after the company was bought by 'international capital'.[108] But Churchill's revisions left Nell's speech (in the play's eighteenth scene) more ambiguous. As she stilt-walks across the stage in the play's final moments, Nell seems to realise her political potential less prosaically: 'I was walking out on the fen. The sun spoke to me. It said, "Turn back, turn back". I said, "I won't turn back for you or anyone"'.[109] Like the Baptist Margaret, the sun has preached acceptance and retreat. But Nell answers with defiance. Far from having her actions determined by forces beyond her control – the sun or anyone – Nell knows that something else is possible, as, in a line vibrating with its doubled meaning, she 'walks out on the fen'. The play transcends the deterministic view of history that has shadowed it and offers hope instead: Nell's stilt-walking not only pulls her out of the dirt but also re-animates the resistance that their ancestors had expressed in smashed dykes and broken sluices.

Fen began with a tour that opened on 20 January 1983 at the University of Essex and reached London on 16 February, where the Almeida Theatre's inadequate heating system augmented the play's environmental resonances: audiences were plunged into a cold that, for some, mirrored the labourers' privation.[110] Critical praise was near-unanimous, with all of London's major reviewers – Michael Billington, Michael Coveney, Robert Cushman, Benedict Nightingale, and Irving Wardle – lodging only minor complaints, mostly about the disorienting doubling.[111] The Almeida run sold out; more tour dates commenced. The success must have surprised Churchill's agent, Peggy Ramsay, who had written to Joseph Papp of the Public Theater on the day of the Essex opening and expressed her worry that Joint Stock was not 'good enough' and that Waters (whose work she generally disliked) was not up to the task of directing.[112] Undeterred by Ramsay's concern that the play would be 'too alien for America'[113] – and with *Cloud Nine* and *Top Girls* still running in New York – Papp plotted to bring *Fen* to the Public at the earliest opportunity, programming it as part of the 'New York Salutes Britain' festival that June. There, *Fen* met more sellout crowds and even more enthusiastic reviews: '[e]very aspect of this production is brilliant' was one assessment.[114] Papp immediately began planning a new American production, scheduled in the Public's regular 1983–84 season.

Looking through the play's production records – Joint Stock's in London and the Public's in New York – one is struck by how *Fen*'s circles of collaborators repeatedly widened. Behind the scenes, workers in London prepared extensive costume and lighting plots for use by those in New York, who recorded a warning about Churchill's dreamscape. 'The flow of this production relies heavily upon backstage costume changes most of which need to be fast. Ideally the costumes or simulations should be available for rehearsal at least two or three days before any other technical aspect is added, otherwise technical rehearsals will be a nightmare', one memo reads.[115] (The Public would ultimately hire three dressers for its six-member cast to help manage the scores of quick changes.) Ironies strike, too. The theatre remains the rare American industry still well protected by union agreements, so that the British cast could only be brought to New York through an arduously negotiated exchange agreement between actors' equity associations. The American branch had to agree to each of Papp's short extensions, which could finally stretch the run only to six weeks (during the height of summer, when the air conditioning at the Public's LuEsther Hall offered inadequate cooling and a stark contrast to the frigid Almeida). With no further extensions possible, the cast departed for London at the end of July, where the show immediately took up residence at the Royal Court for a return engagement brokered by Stafford-Clark. It ran for the rest of the summer.

Papp's American remount also exposes ironies relating to the production of socialist theatre in a world governed by capitalist principles. When Papp mounted his first Churchill play, *Top Girls*, he was dealing with a text properly considered the writer's individual property, and accordingly his contract negotiations concerned only her and the Royal Court, the play's first producer and its director's artistic home.[116] For *Fen*, the picture was more complicated. Legally the play's rights were (and are) held by Churchill, who could licence them to the Public, which in turn promptly hired Waters and Smart as director and designer. But the other six Joint Stock members were also integral to *Fen*. Prevented from performing in New York by union regulations, they had no remunerable role and no claim of ownership; they were tenants on a property that they had helped to build, not unlike Pam Brighton when she was jettisoned from *Stones in His Pockets*. Churchill immediately saw the irony and dispatched her agent, who wrote to the Public's manager:

> The Joint Stock Company devised this play with Caryl over a number of weeks, and they provided a great deal of the background of the play which was included in Caryl's final script. . . . Caryl is extremely anxious that the negotiations we make with you for Joint Stock, when they are not performing the play themselves, should be higher than what you would pay the Royal Court, which is merely a theatre.[117]

And after a remarkably quick negotiation – a contrast to those governing *Serious Money* a few years later – a percentage of the Public's profits was allocated directly to Joint Stock.

Churchill makes theatre, and does its business, differently. One detail of the arrangement speaks to her desire to restructure social relations too often deranged by capitalism: the playwright matched the Public's share, voluntarily reducing her own royalties. If the play had manifested its politics in its communal workshop and enacted them in the tight-knit ensemble work of its performance, it pressured the capitalist model of ownership behind the scenes, too. We find further evidence for Rabillard's understanding of *Fen* as 'Churchill's own self-conscious attempt to enact an alternative to the capitalist model of the production and ownership of aesthetic goods – an effort to construct in the aesthetic realm not simply a critique of the capitalist economy but a commons that somehow escapes it'.[118] Because of Churchill's intervention, Joint Stock continued to be paid for the American production even as the original performers ceded to a new cast that included Pamela Reed, David Strathairn, and Concetta Tomei, who had played Edward and Victoria in Tommy Tune's *Cloud Nine*. (Urged by Churchill, Papp sought without success to involve Linda Hunt, who had just finished her celebrated run as Pope Joan in the recast *Top Girls*.) Another round of enthusiastic notices followed: for example, Clive Barnes returned to praise the 'astonishingly, wonderfully dense and complex' play for the *New York Post*.[119] And even before *Fen* had officially re-opened on 23 February 1984, Churchill would return to New York to receive the Susan Smith Blackburn Prize, her first but not last.

A flurry of regional productions followed in the next few years: for example, at the Empty Space in Seattle; at Center Theater in Chicago; at Eureka Theatre in San Francisco (Churchill's most important West Coast collaborators) in a production directed by Tony Taccone and featuring Sigrid Wurschmidt as Val. Yet the play surprisingly received no further professional revivals for almost two decades. In the UK, Alex Cox directed a production in June 2004 at the Studio Theatre in Sheffield, where Churchill was given a career-honouring season (and where *Fen* was paired with *Far Away*). And in March 2011, Ria Parry directed the play's first London revival at the tiny but estimable Finborough Theatre. Parry's designer, James Button, again put *Fen* in a field of dirt, the source of its owners' abundance and its labourers' hardship. ('[B]rilliant but which I can't claim as part of the play as I wrote it', Churchill has said of the set, acknowledging Smart's indelible contribution.[120]) Sinking into this earth and also rising from it, *Fen*'s timeless characters appeared again in the forms of Alex Beckett, Katharine Burford, Elicia Daly, Nicola Harrison, Wendy Nottingham, Rosie Thomson. Sometimes ghosts but always fully embodied, they warned us anew about a globalised economy that can make resistance seem futile. They enacted the straits on the fen-workers' agency – straits that seem to doom them to perennial unhappiness – even as they urged us beyond fatalistic thinking. Parry handled the play's considerable demands masterfully, situating the audience, too, in a fully realised social and physical environment: a wooden bridge, deftly used to keep Mr Takai or Miss Cade above the muck, joined the two sides of her traverse staging. Bridging audience to audience, bridging audience to set, bridging the fens to London, the staging unearthed the continued relevance of *Fen*, surely one of Churchill's finest plays.

Mad Forest: A Play From Romania

Churchill, Smart, and Waters (as well as actor Amelda Brown) would collaborate again, together with choreographer Ian Spink and playwright David Lan, for Joint Stock's workshop-based *A Mouthful of Birds*. But it was not her last use of the company's signature method. In early 1990, Mark Wing-Davey – later to direct *Fen*'s Amelda Brown in his revival of *Light Shining in Buckinghamshire* – convinced Churchill to collaborate with him and his students at London's Central School of Speech and Drama to devise a play about the recent revolution in Romania. There, the harassment of an ethnic-Hungarian priest, László Tőkés, had spurred a protest in Timişoara on 16 December 1989, which intensified and spread into a mass insurgency that crested when the military defected on 22 December. The country's President, Nicolae Ceauşescu, and his wife, Deputy Prime Minister

Elena Ceaușescu, were promptly arrested, tried, and executed on 25 December, ending their decades-long authoritarian rule. Churchill and Wing-Davey had met years before through their shared involvement with Joint Stock, on whose steering committee both served in the late 1970s. (He was acting in Stephen Lowe's *The Ragged Trousered Philanthropists*, directed by Bill Gaskill, while she and Stafford-Clark were conducting their workshops for *Cloud Nine*.) And having met in a context informed by socialist views, both were no doubt gripped by the cascading political events in the Eastern Bloc, where the revolution in Romania capped a year of upheavals immortalised in the fall of the Berlin Wall.

Churchill had two concerns. First, 'she felt it was important to go and see what was happening for herself', as Wing-Davey noted.[121] Second, she insisted that no funding come from corporate sources, since she had recently resigned from the Royal Court's board over its sponsorship by Barclays Bank.[122] Armed with grants from the British and Camden arts councils, Churchill and Wing-Davey spent 3 to 7 March touring Romania, where they returned on 31 March with thirteen others, including students from the Central School, designer Antony McDonald, and lighting designer Nigel Morgan. Their circle of collaborators widened to include students from the Caragiale Institute of Theatre and Cinema, some of whose families billeted the British students and provided insider views of quotidian life in Bucharest. The workshop mixed acting exercises, on-the-street interviews, and ethnographic observation as *Fen*'s had. Actors would portray their interview subjects or re-enact vignettes they had witnessed, for example, improvising in character as others posed questions and Churchill took notes. Other exercises examined differences between British and Romanian culture. Given playing cards – that classic prop of Joint Stock rehearsals – actors would confess or invent a secret designed to correspond with a card's number (from least to most shameful) and colour (with red and black representing true and false). Through this exercise, Wing-Davey and Churchill explored cultural understandings of shame and gauged their actors' facility with dissemblance.[123] After the workshop, Churchill was needed in New York City, where Les Waters's production of *Icecream with Hot Fudge* was set to open on 3 May. On her return to London, with *Mad Forest*'s rehearsals already scheduled to begin, she wrote the play in only three weeks. Thus she conjured the febrile intensity and unvarnished chaos of revolutionary times, giving her play an 'unfinished feel' that would be celebrated by critics as consonant with its themes.[124]

Mad Forest has a tripartite structure. In its first and third parts, the play contrasts the lives of two families, the working-class Vladus and the middle-class Antonescus. Part One is set before the revolution: Lucia Vladu's betrothal to an American, Wayne, has aroused the suspicion of the secret service, the Securitate, whose harassment her family suffers; Florina Vladu's relationship with Radu Antonescu has been forbidden by his parents, Mihai and Flavia. Borrowing the inciting action of comedies such as Shakespeare's *A Midsummer Night's Dream* or Goldoni's *The Servant of Two Masters* (each with its intertwined sets of lovers), Churchill ends Part One with Lucia and Wayne's wedding. But as in Beaumarchais's *The Marriage of Figaro* – the comedy, banned by Louis XVI, that catalysed the French Revolution – this wedding resolves neither personal conflicts nor the political issues with which they are imbricated. (For a start, Lucia is also involved with Ianoș, whose Hungarian ethnicity arouses other prejudices.) Part Three traces the families' fortunes after the revolution, in which Lucia and Florina's brother Gabriel has been injured. The impediments to Radu's and Florina's relationship are lifted; the play ends with their wedding. But Churchill again subverts this tension-dissipating trope of comedy. Class, ethnic, and familial tensions erupt. Brawls ensue. Reaching an unparalleled complexity with her overlapping dialogue, the playwright has up to eleven people speak at once.

Between 'Lucia's Wedding' and 'Florina's Wedding' sits 'December'. Abandoning the Vladu and Antonescu families, this section introduces eleven new characters – one for each of *Mad Forest*'s cast – who in unconnected but intertwined monologues describe their doings during the December days of revolution. The fictional narratives of Parts One and Three, in other words, frame a documentary-style Part Two, with its on-the-ground dispatches from eleven Romanians, derived from the actors' interviews: a housepainter, Margareta Antoniu;

a flower-seller, Cornelia Dediliuc; a translator, Dimitru Constantinescu; etc. Unlike the Vladus and Antonescus, whom we imagine to be speaking Romanian as they talk to one another in unaccented English, these characters speak compromised English with Romanian accents as they address the audience directly: the first speech begins, 'My name is Valentin Bărbat. I am a painter'.[125] Their reports are signalled as verbatim accounts of December's extraordinary insurrection, whose status as documentary truth is thrown into relief by what precedes and follows. At the same time, these accounts are threaded with details that tie them to the Vladus and Antonescus' experiences, as if Churchill were modelling the process by which she embroidered fiction with fact.

For example, the prejudice against Hungarians exposed in the fictional experience of Ianoş reflects the real-life bias that motivated the army initially to attack protestors. ('They say Hungarians come from Hungary into Romania', reports the soldier Gheorghe Marin, who might remind us, too, that the state's persecution of Tőkés took cover from pervasive anti-Hungarian prejudice.[126]) The codes of the Vladus – who elude the listening secret service by communicating in pantomime, whispers, or under the blare of radios – reflect the testimony of a doctor, Ileana Chiriţa, who reveals her mother's code-word for Radio Free Europe. And the situation of a bulldozer driver, Ilie Barbu, whose work on Ceauşescu's People's Palace ends with the revolution, reflects the reality of the fictional Mihai Antonescu, whose first-act allusions to his architecture practice – 'We will make an improvement to the spacing of the columns'[127] – are clarified in Part Three, when work on the palace is suspended. Radu's Part One gibe at this work ('So is that the third time he's made you change it?') foreshadows the character's next appearance, when he queues for meat and loudly whispers 'Down with Ceauşescu'.[128] Thus Churchill ties familial politics to a larger macropolitics again: Cobbe chafes against his father; Becky against her stepmother; the Vladu and Antonescu children against their parents and the self-proclaimed Father of Romania, Ceauşescu.[129] Thus, too, Churchill reminds us that Romania's youth incited its revolution. They are represented in the various students providing testimony in 'December', one of whom notes that 'it was 99 per cent young people in the square'.[130] Indeed, Churchill explained her interest in the Central School project by noting that she wanted to work 'with students of the same age as the people who made the revolution'.[131] She draws a connection between the actors' agency and that of those who excite offstage change, as she had in *Light Shining in Buckinghamshire*.

Churchill herself connected the plays, telling a journalist that *Mad Forest* is 'not that different in structure to a play I wrote . . . about the English revolution that didn't work out the way people thought'.[132] In a familiar pattern, the time immediately after revolution teems with possibility. Divisions dissolve: the doctor attests in her Part Two testimonial that '[t]he doctors and the orderlies were equal'.[133] Visiting the hospital where Gabriel convalesces in Part Three, the Antonescu parents bridge differences between families and generations. Flavia will concede that the 'young show us the way'; Mihai will explain that '[w]e have to put the past behind us and go forward on a new basis'.[134] The words invoke what the Chinese called *fanshen* or the Soviets *perestroika*: the restructuring of relations. But old narratives fill the vacuum left by revolution, and disillusionment again taints victory. Romanian elections would bring to power a party, the National Salvation Front, closely associated with the old regime. As Radu rues at his wedding, 'I don't care what they're called, it's the same people'.[135] He will malign the workers and peasants whom he holds responsible. 'I don't mean your family in particular', he tells Florina, in a passive-aggressive formulation that fails to exclude them.[136] And after her brother mocks Hungarians, Lucia will note: 'This is what we used to say before. Don't we say something different?'[137] The moment recalls the fraught, second-act scene between Briggs and Starr in *Light Shining in Buckinghamshire*, in which the comrades find disagreement over Cromwell's conquest of Ireland. As Briggs sees, this conquest re-instantiates hierarchical structures that revolution was meant to eradicate.

Mad Forest contrasts other British plays inspired by the recent history of the Eastern Bloc. Three months after *Mad Forest*, in September 1990, the Royal Shakespeare Company debuted Howard Brenton and Tariq Ali's *Moscow Gold*, whose theatrical reflection on *glasnost* and *perestroika* includes among its characters Gorbachev, Yeltsin, and Lenin himself (during the 1917 revolution, in a funeral scene, and later from beyond the grave, when his ghost counsels Gorbachev). And in November, the National Theatre premiered David Edgar's *The Shape of the Table*, the playwright's first of a trilogy of plays about the region; it examines the fall of a Communist government in a fictionalised Eastern European country resembling Czechoslovakia. Despite their radical differences in tone – Edgar's play is realistic, Brenton and Ali's a wild pageant styled after Vsevolod Meyerhold – both shows represent powerful men making history. The striking difference of *Mad Forest* relates to Churchill's discomfort with seeing Eastern Europe from a position of Western privilege or cultural authority or from the perspective of 'cultural tourism', as she explained to a journalist. In a clear reference to *Moscow Gold* and *The Shape of the Table*, she noted that she 'wouldn't have agreed if the RSC or the National had asked me'. Interested instead in 'working away from the mainstream' (as she put it), Churchill connects the collaboration that spawned *Mad Forest* to its aesthetic shape.[138] Her collaborators were students instead of professionals; her play's characters originate on the margins of power. A Securitate officer, Claudiu Brad, is the closest we get to the Ceaușescus, who are represented only obliquely in a dream of Florina's or the role-play of some drinking friends. The playwright revisits the polyvocal method – the mosaic of everyday events, the grainy 'chips of film' – with which she had theatricalised the English revolution and its *mise-en-abyme* revolts. She again shows how 'fractured and dissonant this apparently collective experience' of revolution was for those who made it, in the astute assessment of Alison Light, for '[a] historical record which can offer no account of subjectivity . . . is no history at all'.[139]

Mad Forest reflects the subjectivity not only of its characters but also of its makers. The title derives from a research source: it identifies the plain where Bucharest now stands ('Teleorman' or 'Mad Forest'), which 'could only be crossed on foot and was impenetrable for the foreigner who did not know the paths'.[140] Accordingly, the foreigners proceeded gingerly. 'When we arrived, the Romanians said, "What is your program?"', Wing-Davey explained, 'and we said, "We don't know. It depends on what we discover in the course of the week". We'd work, and in the evening Caryl and I would discuss the day's work, and say, "What are the questions that we have?"'[141] Rather than explain impenetrable elements of the culture, the workshop explored the cultural difference that produced these feelings. And along with details from Romanian life – the ubiquitous queuing, cigarette smoke, and power outages – the play reveals this ethnographic perspective. Every scene begins with '*one of the company reading from a phrasebook as if an English tourist, first in Romanian, then in English, and again in Romanian*'.[142] For instance, the first scene's caption – '**Lucia are patru ouă. Lucia has four eggs**' – summarises one of its key events: Lucia arrives with eggs procured through her American fiancé. But the caption also adumbrates the simplistic grasp a British audience might have on such an event. After all, the scene begins with an argument between Lucia's parents, Bogdan and Irina, conducted under the '*very loud*' radio so that '[*w*]*e can't hear anything they say*'.[143] With the radio on, dialogue is unintelligible; with the radio off, it may overlap to the point of incomprehensibility or lapse into untranslated Romanian. The play is not about Romania but *A Play from Romania*, as its subtitle declares. It foregrounds the experience of not understanding.

Exacerbating this difficulty, Churchill shoots *Mad Forest* through with *Fen*'s surrealism. A priest chats nonchalantly with an angel. The ghost of a dead revolutionary appears to Florina, warning her that '[i]t's lonely when you're dead' and expressing the same desire for companionship as the play's talking dog, which licks the blood in the streets and searches for someone to dominate him.[144] 'You could talk to me. I could talk to you. I'm your dog', he tells the play's vampire, who has been drawn to the square by the promise of easy kills.[145] The dog's pitiful desires may reflect those of a long-subjugated people voting in a new leader, Ion Iliescu, whose resemblance to Ceaușescu startles: as Charles ceded to Cromwell and the Tewsons to the multinationals, a new master awaits. But any symbolic resonances remain murky and inexact. The vampire might represent Romania's Vlad the Impaler or capitalism come to feed or any other charming tyranny. The ghost of Flavia's grandmother confesses to welcoming the Nazis, then the Russians, then the Communists. 'I had no principles', she tells her granddaughter, whom we have seen placidly indoctrinating students with Ceaușescu propaganda.[146] When the revolution rouses Flavia's own longing for a new master – 'Let them give me a new book, I'll teach that'[147] – we find ourselves some distance from 'the amazed excitement of people taking hold of their own lives', as Churchill had dramatised in *Light Shining in Buckinghamshire*.[148] The last words of *Mad Forest* emphasise a futile cycle over actual change: 'Incepi sa vrei sînge. Membrele ted dor, capul îți arde. Trebuie să ti miști din ce în ce mai repede'.[149] An English audience, like the workshop participants, finds comprehension precluded, since the vampire's words go untranslated. Romanian viewers recognise only that he circles back to an insight from several scenes earlier: 'You begin to want blood. Your limbs ache, your head burns, you have to keep moving faster and faster'.[150]

Brecht, too, resisted closure: both his *Caucasian Chalk Circle* and his *Sophocles' Antigone* begin with framing narratives to which they never return. As Louis Althusser remarked in *For Marx*, the playwright 'wanted to make the spectator into an actor who would complete the unfinished play, but in real life'.[151] *Mad Forest* reveals Brecht's influence when it refuses to reconcile real with surreal or to integrate its disparate sections. The documentary-style 'December' sits interposed in the play's middle, and divergences between its own dispatches remain unresolved, since none of its characters speaks to the others. Gaps between them provoke questions about reality and representation, as do gaps between scenes juxtaposed in epic style. (They are not run together: 'time has clearly passed'.[152]) But *Mad Forest* blunts Brecht's faith in the special mirror that art might hold up to life. In the play's third act, Gabriel, Rodica, Radu, Florina, Lucia, and Ianoș engage in a play-within-a-play that seems to test theatre's ability to untrouble history. As they parodically re-enact the trial and execution of the Ceaușescus, their pretend taunts of '[g]ypsy' and '[w]e've all fucked your wife' encourage barely latent hostilities.[153] At the end of their role-play, Gabriel will attack Ianoș after he hugs Lucia: 'Get your filthy Hungarian hands off her'. His immediate disclaimer – '[j]ust joking'[154] – no more expiates his sentiment than their little play has expiated the casual racism and misogyny that it expresses. The concept of representation is put under stress. In the play's documentary section, the violence he witnesses traumatises the painter, who notes that 'I didn't want to paint for a long time then'.[155] The translator has a radically different experience of the revolution but reaches much the same conclusion. Of his emotion that December, he declares: 'There were no words in Romanian or English'.[156]

Self-consciously failing to represent the revolution, Churchill leaves her audience equally unsettled. In the play's most startling *coup de théâtre*, we find ourselves inside Florina's nightmare, just as *Fen*'s Val was plunged into Becky's dream. Florina appears as Elena Ceaușescu, abandoned by her soldiers and menaced by a matchbox that holds the revolting crowd, whose chants she hears when she opens it. When dream logic turns the matchbox into a pill, she swallows it:

> *A* **Soldier** *comes in and searches, kicking at anything in the way.*
>
> *He goes to her and opens her mouth.*
>
> *'Ole ole ole ole' chanted by huge crowd.*
>
> *He opens and closes her mouth several times, the chant continues each time.*[157]

Florina-as-Elena incorporates the revolution, which she nonetheless cannot contain. Inside and outside collapse, just like the differences between one character and another in the play's rampant doubling and just like the differences between ghosts and people – or between fiction and reality – in the play's woozy ontology. In McDonald's set design, the audience was funnelled through a back door and into a distressed gymnasium with its cinder-block set, filled with cigarette smoke and dimly lit by bare bulbs. Programmes were in Romanian. Amelia Howe Kritzer has argued that the effect was to 'immerse the audience in the play's events, almost as if some power had transported them and set them down in a foreign country'.[158] But we must remember that Churchill sought to convey not only the foreignness of Romania but also the hallucinatory fever of its revolution, whose reality seems uncertain even to those who lived it. Lucia is assured since she saw it on television from America, but Radu and the others are unconvinced. 'It was all a show', he will assert, joining Florina and Gabriel in asking the same questions posed by the mentally disturbed patient who stalks the hospital and challenges his audience: 'Did we have a revolution or a putsch?'[159]

Mad Forest, which eventually replaced one of its workshop participants with Gordon Anderson and Philip Glenister, debuted on 25 June 1990 at the Central School's Embassy Theatre, where its four scheduled performances were extended to eleven. After it opened to strong reviews – it would eventually win a London Fringe Award for Best Ensemble – the company opted to keep the show running: they established a cooperative called Quick Change, rented space from the Central School, and shared running costs and profits through the summer. In September, they returned to Romania at the invitation of Andrei Serban (then the artistic director of the country's National Theatre), their trip funded by patrons including Peggy Ashcroft, Julie Christie, and Cameron Mackintosh, as well as Churchill herself.[160] Unlike *Fen*, which could not be staged in Upwell for want of an appropriate venue, a play from Romania returned to the population that inspired it.[161] Again Churchill witnessed the myriad perspectives of an ostensibly collective experience. In a diary she kept for the *Guardian*, for example, she described the reaction to Florina's saving a broken egg scraped from the floor. In a post-show discussion, one woman confessed to having done so herself, while another claimed that a Romanian would feel too much shame: a powerful cultural force, as the workshop had explored.[162] The Bucharest run sold out its four nights, then three more, playing to almost 3,000 people. And then *Mad Forest* returned to London, where it took up residence Downstairs at the Royal Court for a valedictory run that started on 9 October.

Attempting to bring the show to New York, Joseph Papp met interference from Actors' Equity, and, perhaps burdened with a tepid reception for *Icecream with Hot Fudge*, he could not raise sufficient capital. But James Nicola of New York Theatre Workshop – who was preparing the New York premiere of *Light Shining in Buckinghamshire* as *Mad Forest* was winding down in London – commissioned a new production with Wing-Davey as its director. Like Waters remounting *Fen*, Wing-Davey could no longer rely on the firsthand experience of the workshop participants. But he sought compensatory experiences for his young cast, which included Calista Flockhart and Tim Blake Nelson, and engaged the city's Romanian community to help. He found a masterful designer in the expatriate Marina Draghici, who imported hundreds of Romanian cigarettes.[163] Improving on McDonald's work, Draghici built a more fully realised environment at the Perry Street Theatre, including mismatched seating that encroached on the set's rubble, collapsing the border between stage and audience as the play collapsed the border between Parts One and Two: the first interval was cut. *Mad Forest* had its North American premiere on 22 November 1991. Mel Gussow judged it stronger than the London production.[164] Frank Rich declared it to have sharpened as its historical events receded.[165] Even John Simon, infamous for the poisonous pans he has liberally bestowed for decades, praised Churchill.[166] (He later took it back.[167]) Scheduled to close at the end of December, *Mad Forest* extended twice, to 2 February 1992. Wing-Davey and Draghici (who would re-team for *The Skriker*) won Obie Awards. And less than eight months later, their production was remounted by Manhattan Theatre Club with a single casting change, where it again ran through several extensions.[168] Production records note that attendance never dropped below ninety-seven per cent of capacity. And they identify some of those who attended and whose names attest to Churchill's status in the contemporary theatre: Edward Albee, Ariel Dorfman, Arthur Miller.

A 'Diary of Events' in the New York programmes helps audiences navigate the sometimes impenetrable *Mad Forest.* The Timișoara demonstration in support of Tőkés (later one of the European Parliament's several vice-presidents) appears, as do Ceaușescu's execution and Iliescu's election. Alongside them, the timeline situates the playwright's trips to Romania, *Mad Forest*'s debut, its Bucharest run. In other words, it writes Churchill and her play directly into Romania's extraordinary history. We might see proof of the theory *Light Shining in Buckinghamshire* had offered: the actions of onstage agents tie to the offstage world, whose improvement can be imagined, enacted, and, with enough collaborative effort, secured. The earlier play, after all, had matched its form with its means of production as it offered a model for socialist cooperation. In the rehearsal room for *Mad Forest*, Churchill again promoted this egalitarian way of making theatre, which she had subsequently refined with *Cloud Nine*, *Fen*, *A Mouthful of Birds*, and *Serious Money*. And again these politics manifested on stage, in the cast's dedicated ensemble work, as well as off stage. For the London run, Quick Change self-produced and shared profits – remarkable considering that most of its members were newly graduated students while another was one of Britain's most celebrated playwrights. At Manhattan Theatre Club, after actor Rocco Sisto injured himself during a performance on 28 October, the company redistributed roles so that he could continue performing with fewer physical demands. From each according to his ability, to each according to his need.

The process for *Mad Forest* may have unfolded according to the principles of Joint Stock, the great socialist company that disbanded (in a remarkable irony) in 1989, just as Bulgaria, Czechoslovakia, East Germany, Hungary, and Poland, too, took their uncertain steps into an uncertain future. But the play – situated at the end of a socialist experiment begun in 1917 and curdled into tyranny – seems less sure of the theatre's ability to change the world. It self-consciously subverts the Brechtian aesthetics so central to *Light Shining in Buckinghamshire* and doubts their political certainties; it rewrites the earlier play's positivist view of history in a more nebulous tone. After *Mad Forest*, Churchill changed the nature of her political writing. The text of *This Is a Chair* – premiered in the same year, 1997, that the Conservatives finally lost power in the UK, to be replaced by a market-friendly New Labour – would have a scene captioned '**The Impact of Capitalism on the Former Soviet Union**' that leaves the page completely blank.[169] I do not suggest that she has abandoned collaborative politics or its aesthetic rewards. After all, different kinds of collaboration awaited: Churchill wrote the text 'she bit her tongue' for use in choreographer Siobhan Davies's work *Plants and Ghosts*, for instance, and the libretti for Orlando Gough's operas *We Turned on the Light*, discussed in my first chapter, and *A Ring a Lamp a Thing*, premiered at the Royal Opera House, London on 18 June 2010.

But the shift to an emancipatory theatricality seen at the end of *Fen* – one that sets itself apart from the inimical world off stage – has become much more pronounced. 'In the theatre anything's possible', she once told an interviewer, leaving a contrast to the so-called real world implicit.[170] The shift marks her written texts, too, all of which Churchill now writes solo, with neither workshops nor documentary sources. (The sole exception is her 2003 play *Iraq.doc*, a found-text collage of chatroom transcripts.) When the playwright specifies in *Mad Forest* that '[*t*]*he following conversations take place, sometimes overlapping or simultaneously*' – before providing sixteen pages of dialogue with little other guidance for how to arrange it – she signals a different understanding of collaboration, in which the writer predetermines less and less and turns more and more to the rehearsal room, a political haven.[171] James Macdonald, who directed *Lives of the Great Poisoners* and would later become her primary collaborator, described it as Churchill's move toward a 'much freer shape . . . where it's really up to the director to excavate the right rhythm for the text'.[172] She engages the designers and actors, too, in determining the play's meaning, and thus she uncovers a new freedom and a redemptive power in performance. Its political – even utopian – power is the subject of the next chapter.

CHAPTER 5
PERFORMANCE AND/AS THEATRE

Performance has animated every text of Churchill's career. It is central to a play such as *Far Away*, with its nonverbal parade of hatted prisoners, or *Mad Forest*, with its reliance on foreign text most spectators cannot understand. It makes possible the meanings of *Cloud Nine*, whose pointed cross-castings and doublings can only signify once the roles are embodied. And it manifests the politics of *Light Shining in Buckinghamshire*, as individual actors collectively share the play's written characters. Performances – by which I mean bodily practices that produce meaning – take centre stage in this chapter. For Churchill's career has traced the disparate facets of performance as a concept as well as its relationship to the genre it animates. Performance sometimes appears as theatre's antonym, as when it distinguishes real behaviours from theatrical pretences. This distinction comes to the fore, for example, in Churchill's collaboration with David Lan, *A Mouthful of Birds*. In that show – premiered on 2 September 1986 (after previews from 29 August) at Birmingham Repertory Theatre – actors sometimes pretended to be others as they gave voice to a pre-scripted text: Vivienne Rochester played the role of 'Yvonne', for instance. Other times, performed actions erased the line between actor and role, as when Rochester inserted acupuncture needles into other bodies or when the cast members engaged in dances that reached back to the ritual origins of *The Bacchae*, Churchill and Lan's source text.

Especially since 1997, when her plays turned markedly spare, Churchill has highlighted another aspect of performance: its necessary role in bringing meaning to a written script. Consider *Hotel* – premiered at the Schauspielhaus in Hanover, Germany on 15 April 1997 – for which Churchill provided 'no complete sentences, just little chunks of what was said or thought, that could be absorbed first time round or in a repeat or even never'.[1] Or consider *Drunk Enough to Say I Love You?*, shorn of punctuation and stage directions and written in partial lines that await the significations bestowed by actors:

Guy I

Sam if you want

Guy of course I

Sam so you'll

Guy so no I can't possibly

Sam of course not[.][2]

The meanings of such dialogue inhere less in Churchill's words than in the non-linguistic supplements that performers provide. And these supplements were different when Scott Cohen and Samuel West performed the text in New York (at the Public Theater's Newman auditorium, starting on 5 March 2008) from when Ty Burrell and Stephen Dillane performed it in London (at the Royal Court Downstairs, starting on 10 November 2006) – even though James Macdonald directed both shows on the same set, a levitating couch designed by Eugene Lee.

Churchill has lately veered further into minimalism, producing text whose lack of stage directions, identified speakers, and even plot forces us to find its dramatic meaning elsewhere: in the interaction between the script (given different shape in each production by actors and directors) and spectators (made to perform, too, as they generate meaning). We see such a form in *Seven Jewish Children*, for example, which premiered at the Royal Court on 6 February 2009 in a production directed by Dominic Cooke. The Board of Deputies of British Jews denounced the play as blood libel: as perpetrating the horrific lie that Jews ritually slaughter non-Jewish children. But in declaring the play 'beyond the boundaries of reasonable political discourse', the board's spokesman betrayed (in ways he surely did not intend) just what makes *Seven Jewish Children* so unsettling.[3] Its radical indeterminacy does seem strangely unreasonable for an apparently issue-driven play subtitled *A Play for Gaza*; and the seven-page drama no doubt attracted opprobrium less for its content than because Churchill offered it free to any theatre producing it for the benefit of Medical Aid for Palestinians. For without characters, plot, speech prefixes, or stage directions, the play is an inkblot. It guarantees only that disparate meanings will emerge in the imagination of those who apprehend it.

Traps

Churchill's most rigorous exploration of a performance modality occurs in *Traps*, which she wrote in early 1976 but set aside for her two collaborative projects of that year, *Light Shining in Buckinghamshire* and *Vinegar Tom*. *Traps* would finally open on 27 January 1977 at the Royal Court's Theatre Upstairs, in a production directed by John Ashford. The play concerns six people in their twenties and early thirties whose communal living only partly explains their complicated entanglements: the dramatis personae reveals that '**Jack** *is* **Christie***'s younger brother, and* **Reg** *is her husband*', but evidence emerges of romance between Syl and Jack, Syl and Albert; Albert and Jack, Albert and Del; Del and Christie, Del and Jack.[4] The six characters inhabit a communal space which the setting never leaves and in which various disharmonies crest and recede: Del demands money from the others, for instance, and Reg brings Christie chocolates in apology. We hear too of offstage events ranging from banal to shocking: Reg speaks of social engagements with professional colleagues; Del describes raping and killing a woman. Thus the play's relationships and plot points proliferate – improbably and with remarkable tonal variety – because the characters are 'living many of their possibilities at once', as Churchill's prefatory note puts it. For the play is 'an impossible object, or a painting by Escher, where the objects can exist like that on paper, but would be impossible in life. . . . There is no flashback, no fantasy, everything that happens is as real and solid as everything else within the play'.[5]

The play thus mirrors a many-worlds theory of quantum mechanics such as that pioneered by the physicist Hugh Everett, in which every possible permutation of events exists and reality is an infinitely proliferating set of alternatives. Such a theory answers the thought experiment of physicist Erwin Schrödinger by conceiving of his famous cat as dead in one world and alive in another. Overcoming Schrödinger's common-sense objections, the cat both lives and doesn't, simultaneously, with no contradiction. (We see the inverse of Schrödinger's cat in Syl's foetus, which she claims 'isn't either sex until it's born'.[6]) In representing such a many-worlds reality, however, *Traps* does not conceive of each realisation in its own ontologically secure world, as Everett's and related physics theories do. Neither does it enact its plot permutations sequentially as happens in similarly themed plays, such as John Mighton's *Possible Worlds* (1990) or Nick Payne's *Constellations* (2012), which surprised insiders when it won the *Evening Standard* Award for Best Play over Churchill's *Love and Information.* Rather, Churchill collapses the spatial and temporal barriers that keep possibilities distinct; she resists the boundaries that encompass each of Everett's many worlds. Or, indeed, almost all plays. In a dramatic representation as in life, a time and space typically provide ontological grounding. ''Tis now struck twelve', Bernardo announces at the beginning of *Hamlet.* 'This is Illyria, lady', the Captain instructs in *Twelfth Night*. *Traps*, by contrast, scrambles time: 'I've gone', Jack announces before he has left; Syl speculates whether she'll have a child in the next five years only minutes after she has put her baby down to sleep; 'Come to tell you bastards what I think of you', Del declares as he enters the commune, in a moment that replays itself, identically, twice.[7] Similarly space is ruptured: although the set never changes, it is sometimes in the city, sometimes in the country. Albert says that the King's Head (the Islington pub in whose theatre Churchill first staged *Schreber's Nervous Illness*) is on the corner, before talk of chickens and crops re-situates us elsewhere.

Churchill has been shifting the ground under her characters' feet for decades, disrupting the theatrical conventions of space and time throughout her career. In *Easy Death* – premiered at Oxford University Experimental Theatre Club on 9 March 1962, when the playwright was twenty-three – one plot takes place in a single day while a parallel plot unspools over several years. In *Moving Clocks Go Slow* – which Ashford had staged in a single-night performance Upstairs at the Royal Court on 15 June 1975 – aliens introduce a new notion of time, circular rather than linear, in which a character can meet herself as a young girl and in which wormholes produce identically repeated dialogue, as in *Traps*. In *The Skriker*, space shifts with filmic speed from place to place – including, most spectacularly, the Underworld, where time passes at an entirely different rate. Most famously, the opening scene of *Top Girls* brings women from various locations (thirteenth-century Japan, nineteenth-century England, etc.) together in one space, and the play's remaining acts unspool in an upset chronology that moves forward and back. But nowhere in her work is the ontology fractured as decisively as in *Traps*, or with such significant dramaturgical consequences. As I demonstrated in the third chapter, a stable time and place is necessary for a stable identity. In *Traps*, absent such stability, the characters' actions negate one another: Syl is both a mother and childless; Albert both dead from suicide and still furtively eating biscuits in the communal living space. '[M]otives and relationships cannot all be reconciled', Churchill writes.[8] As a result, characters do not cohere, and audiences struggle for interpretive traction. Each bit of character-defining action or dialogue sets a trap, an expectation that will be upended when an irreconcilable moment presents itself. Inducing the play's spectators to false beliefs, these traps inevitably unsettle. Viewers and readers come to inhabit the same anxious state that the play evokes with its recurrent references to paranoia and schizophrenia. 'Who was this Del character you talked about?' asks Del. 'I never met him'.[9]

These traps draw attention to our normalised practice of watching a play, to our own performance of meaning-making. As Aristotle formulated in the *Poetics*, 'all men take pleasure in imitative representations . . . they enjoy the sight of images because they learn as they look'.[10] Onstage actions lead one to another and collectively constitute the plot; witnessing, audiences come to understand the characters whose personalities and decisions these actions reveal. Moreover, we gauge what we witness by analogy to the world outside the theatre – a logic of probability or necessity, in Aristotle's terms – even when the play departs from this world, as in the surreal opening of *Top Girls*. When the beginning of *Traps* shows Syl soothing a baby as Jack rests in a chair, these actions provide a context within which these characters might be legible. We might imagine them as a couple, the room as their home. When Albert interrupts the scene moments later, we might adjust these expectations by imagining a love triangle or a lodger – two readings probable in reality and reinforced by our previous experience of representations such as John Osborne's *Look Back in Anger*, the iconic Royal Court production whose opening tableau Churchill slyly mimics. But her radical dramaturgy stymies this interpretive process quickly. Within moments, strange goings-on upend all expectations. Consider Syl's bizarre *non sequitur*: 'Did you know a little baby is three times the size of a human being?'[11] Watching a science-fiction play such as Churchill's 1971 *Not Not Not Not Not Enough Oxygen*, we might adjust to a new set of conventions forged in a world different from our own. But in *Traps* there is no logical relationship between events, no coherent plot or character at all. Forcing us to apprehend these failures, Churchill reminds us of the mechanisms by which plays construct a secure dramatic world and a coherent narrative onto which psychological motivations and causal logics can be projected.

Traps thus exposes how plays and their reception work, as various critics have seen: Philip Roberts, for instance, declares it 'an analysis of the mechanics of theatre'.[12] But this analysis yields troubling results. Instead of making a case for theatrical representation – as metatheatrical plays such as Calderón de la Barca's *Life Is a Dream* or Pierre Corneille's *The Theatrical Illusion* do – *Traps* returns us repeatedly to theatre's false pretences. We might worry about Christie's disturbing bruises, apparently the result of an abusive relationship with Reg; we might fret about Albert's suicide. But when Albert returns to the stage (and his unruffled friends) or when Christie's bruises disappear, the author's hand is shown dictating the characters' fate and the audience's experience. Putatively spontaneous lines are revealed as predetermined: Jack can predict that Christie 'will be' 'here' not because of clairvoyance but because the script guarantees her entrance two lines later.[13]

Churchill offers an analogy in the play's multiply performed card trick, whose magic is undermined by her note explaining its workings just as it is undermined by the characters themselves: 'I know this trick', Syl declares, even as Del keeps doing it.[14] A script similarly stacks the deck. Its pretences usually secure a pleasing emotional investment on the part of its audiences, as a play sucks them into a stable fictional world. But Churchill keeps exposing the fictiveness and rupturing the ontological boundaries, as if to chastise the audience for being duped.

Philosophically minded readers will recognise a Platonic strain. *Traps* seems to worry about theatre's capacity to mislead, just as Plato does in Book 10 of the *Republic*, which bans poetry and its inherent falseness. The philosopher declared that representations move us away from truth. Recall his discussion of the painter's table, a representation removed one degree from the carpenter's (with its compensatory utility for eating or working at) and two degrees from God's, whose table expresses its original, truthful form. Churchill, like Plato before her, offers an antidote to such falseness: performance. Plato had opposed misleading representations, such as dramatic poetry, to aesthetic bodily activity, such as dance; so his *Republic* implicitly allows non-representational artistic pursuits, and so his later *Laws* more explicitly praises them. Similarly, Churchill frustrates our attempts to understand *Traps* as a representation even as she highlights the coherence provided by the play's few unchanging elements: a puzzle on the floor, periodically worked on by actors and progressing seamlessly toward completion; an onstage clock, telling real time throughout. The actor playing Syl may feign having a child (or not), but she actually does the jigsaw; she either finds a fitting piece or doesn't. An actor may pretend to be hurt, as Christie does with her ersatz bruises, but she actually tears a real leaf from an onstage plant. Such non-imitative actions – that is, those which cannot be faked – ripple through the play. A bowl is broken and glued back together. Clothes are ironed.

It is telling that none of these actions involves words with their slippery meanings – each referring to another in an endless trap of metaphorical exchange. Indeed, these actions direct us away from language, away from the writer-dominated text, and toward the bodies of the performers, whether embracing one another or preparing a meal to be consumed in the play's final scene. In it, the actors bring a tub on stage and, carefully mixing hot and cold water from saucepans, prepare a bath. One by one, they cleanse themselves, as the others wash backs and dispense towels. Note that I write 'actors' and not 'characters'. For the play has left aside its anxious and incoherent characters and found concinnity in the ontologically stable actors who played them. As in performance art, the metaphors of drama and theatre are rejected in favour of the actual living body, a metonym for the subject it houses. Churchill's teleplay *Turkish Delight*, discussed in my preface, explores this particular power of nakedness when the Fiancée removes her sexually objectifying harem-girl outfit. Initially she imagines a new costume, Lady Godiva. But she realises that there is more delight – and more subversive power – in foregoing representation altogether and re-entering the party as 'just me with no clothes on. . . . Yes, that's what I'll be'.[15] Similarly, in *Traps*' debut performance, audiences watched Nigel Terry in the bath as much or more than they watched Jack, the character Terry played.

Elin Diamond first detailed Churchill's opposition of theatre to performance in the landmark book *Unmaking Mimesis*, where Diamond found in *Traps* a clever revision of Luigi Pirandello's *Six Characters in Search of an Author*.[16] In that play, he had opposed the world of illusion, represented by his characters in search of an author, to the world of reality, including its actors and directors. In *Traps*, Churchill opposes the world of theatre, with its pre-scripted lines and make-believe, to the world of performance, with its non-imitative doings. Pirandello's play ends with the Child drowned in the fountain, night after night, and thus he demonstrates the theatre's fatalism. So too does he reveal its falsity: no one really dies, and the child actor re-emerges for the curtain call. Churchill's play, by contrast, ends with the actors themselves in the tub, sloshing around and threatening to soak the audience, as they might do wittingly or unwittingly on any given night. As the bath ritual quells the disharmonies among the six characters, it celebrates the performances of its six actors no longer in need of an author. We recognise that the bodies of these actors render their onstage actions coherent, however incoherent they may have seemed from the perspective of character. And thus the bathing scene also resolves the play's fractured ontology, its insecure setting and its puzzling atemporality. The latter gives way to the real time marked by the onstage clock, visible throughout the show and signifying what performance theorist Richard Schechner calls 'event time'.[17] Imitative time (''Tis now struck twelve') is suspended. The performance begins when the houselights dim (say, 7:37 p.m.) and ends after the final body is clean and the actor playing Reg '*starts to smile*' and '*laughs*'.[18] Everyone is pulled into temporal correlation. Instead of perseverating on a fraught past or fretting about an uncertain future, they enjoy the present moment just as Henry does at the end of Churchill's 1972 radio play *Henry's Past*: 'now . . . is the present moment', he declares, finally pleased.[19] 'Here you are not experiencing a time that pretends to be another time', as Peter Handke's *Offending the Audience* had put it.[20] Meanwhile, the unstable country house or city flat cedes to the material reality of the stage-as-stage with its pleasing ontological stability: the commune turns out to be a theatre. Representing nothing, it is simply itself, as in Handke's *Kaspar*, in which '[t]he audience does not see the stage as a representation of a room that exists somewhere, but as a representation of a stage. The stage represents the stage'.[21]

As a scripted work of literature, *Traps* teases us with clues to its dramatic meanings: the play borrows its first line from Trevor Griffith's *Comedians* and two of its character names from *Christie in Love*, Howard Brenton's play about the murderer Reg Christie.[22] But these clues too are traps, we learn, as words give way to smiles and laughter; Reg and Christie, to those who play them. Finally, 'the actors are and play themselves at one and the same time' – a stage direction from Handke's *The Ride Across Lake Constance* that could as easily apply to *Traps*' final scene.[23] Churchill acknowledged that she had written her play after *The Ride Across Lake Constance* – which she undoubtedly saw in its English premiere, starring Nigel Hawthorne, an unlikely commercial success in 1973. She remembers: 'the thing I liked about it was that whatever happened on stage was purely that – what was happening on stage. The character's actions didn't have any other reality'.[24] Ultimately her play owes much less to her countrymen Griffiths and Brenton than it does to her more philosophically radical brethren such as Handke and Samuel Beckett, whose influence she also acknowledged.[25] Both have been tied to a long line of anti-representational playwrights who strive to make work that, not about something, is the something itself (to paraphrase Beckett's famous assessment of *Finnegans Wake*).[26] *Traps* is Churchill in her most radical push toward the something itself of performance.

While it takes different guises, the opposition between real and pretend pervades the philosophy of art. It starts perhaps with the ancient Greek distinction between *mimesis* (with its emphasis on the imitative artist and the passively receptive audience) and *methexis* (with its emphasis on participation); it continues in contemporary critical cognates such as *absorption* and *theatricality*, the titular terms of Michael Fried's influential 1980 book. Throughout the history of theatrical practice, too, the opposition finds expression. Consider the basis for *A Mouthful of Birds*. In *The Bacchae*'s original performance context in 405 BCE, the onstage thymele would have *represented* Semele's grave in the opening prologue (spoken by an actor playing Dionysus) and simultaneously *was* the altar of the namesake god whose worship the play celebrates. But the opposition of the methectic (or absorptive) to the mimetic (or theatrical) gained particular traction in the late 1960s and 1970s, with the era's proliferating alternative theatre: the fringe in Britain, for example, or happenings in the United States. A year after *Traps*, a play such as *Buried Child* could similarly ground its plot in a staged liveness, in the peeling of vegetables or the smashing of bottles: '*the actual smashing of bottles and not tape sound*', Sam Shepard instructs.[27] (Churchill's work, we know, would later coax Shepard out of his retirement from stage acting, when he embodied Salter in *A Number*.)

Plays such as *The Ride Across Lake Constance* or *Traps* or *Buried Child* testify to a larger theatrical culture galvanised by the era's performance art and marked by a turn toward the sort of environmental, participatory event that Reg invokes when he complains that 'I've no time for these religious performances'.[28] To name only one example of an abundance, a play such as the Living Theatre's *Paradise Now* could erode the fourth wall and bind its actors to its audience with methectic action. Such theatre aligned easily with the political and social agitations of the time: *Paradise Now* encouraging non-violent revolutionary action to secure the state its title names, for instance. Churchill herself wrote about the revolutionary hopes of the sixties and seventies, and we see parallels in her work of the period.[29] In the last chapter, I addressed the collaborative politics that engendered *Vinegar Tom* and *Light Shining in Buckinghamshire*, each marked by a Brechtian faith in the theatre's political potential. Indeed, it is instructive that Churchill came to make *Vinegar Tom* with the socialist-feminist collective Monstrous Regiment after the women met in Hyde Park, following a march for the National Abortion Campaign.[30] The period's political progress may manifest in the fact that gay desire – expressed in Albert and Jack's kissing, or Albert and Del's – is among the characters' many possibilities. But the play strongly registers the limitations of its era, too. Several years after Ruskin College hosted Britain's first Women's Liberation Conference, Christie and Syl's possibilities seem startlingly limited, as Albert bluntly reminds Syl when he ridicules her suggestion that she become the more substantial breadwinner. 'I'm not saying it's fair', he says. 'Just a fact'.[31]

Traps is beloved by Churchill's most philosophically astute critics, such as Elin Diamond and Daniel Jernigan, but is also among her least-performed major works. Indeed, the play has had no major British revivals since its 1977 debut, when it was lambasted by a bewildered critical community. (An exemplary response: Michael Billington wrote in the *Guardian* that 'I could feel the energy draining out of me'.[32]) In the United States, the play was given a 1983 production at the now-defunct Remains Theatre in Chicago, with William Petersen directing Gary Cole and Amy Morton, before all three joined the legendary Steppenwolf Ensemble. *Traps* had a smaller-scale production in New York, directed by John Stix and opening on 22 March 1988 at St John's in the Village. (An accomplished director and a professor at Juilliard, Stix had done a workshop production a year earlier, in April 1987, at the Samuel Beckett Theatre on New York's Theatre Row. Churchill attended, having already given her blessing to Stix's slightly Americanised script.[33]) Its highest-profile American production opened in March 1993 at New York Theatre Workshop, where Lisa Peterson's production shared a cast and a space with Mark Wing-Davey's simultaneous production of *Owners*. In this iteration, *Traps* was well received, praised by Mel Gussow in the *New*

York Times and Clive Barnes in the *New York Post*; it eventually shared with *Owners* the Lucille Lortel Award for Outstanding Revival. That this production succeeded where its British premiere apparently failed may testify to the theatrical gifts of its director: Peterson had honed her touch with Churchill's work two seasons earlier, when she won an Obie Award for directing *Light Shining in Buckinghamshire* at the same theatre, and she may have grasped the play's resemblance to performance art better than Ashford had. (He would later direct the performance piece *Midday Sun* in 1984, which Churchill made in collaboration with other artists.) Or it may testify to the performance of J. Smith-Cameron, repeatedly singled out by critics for her portrayal of Christie.

But the production gained, too, from showing its audiences Smith-Cameron in another role – *Owners*' Marion – on alternating nights. The repertory method, I would argue, served to intensify the power of *Traps*' conceit: the theatre's pretence and scriptedness were made even more apparent as the 'many possibilities' of *Traps* expanded to accommodate an entirely different play and its nine other characters. Five members of *Traps*' six-member cast appeared in the other play, one of them in multiple roles: Melinda Mullins, a veteran of Broadway's *Serious Money* several years earlier, played Mrs Arlington and one of Clegg's customers in *Owners*; she played Syl in *Traps*. Audience members attending both shows would have witnessed the actor embodying Del (Tim Hopper) live a whole other set of possibilities on alternate evenings, when he embodied *Owners*' Buddhism-inspired Alec; they would have seen *Owners*' Clegg as Albert (John Curless), *Owners*' Worsely as Reg (Robert Stanton).[34] The roles – like *Owners* and *Traps* themselves – are radically different. But performance, we have seen, unites antimonies. It grounds both actors and audience in the properly communal space of the theatre: the stage at New York Theatre Workshop, in this instance, which served as *Traps*' commune and portrayed *Owners*' eight different settings. Anchoring these disparate representations, the stage augmented the work of the actors' bodies, eventually on view without even the theatrical disguise of clothing.

Churchill told an interviewer that her play is 'about attempting to live communally'.[35] And its political intervention is to propose performance as itself pregnant with utopic possibility. In its plot, *Traps* might work as a many-world theory does in quantum physics: it might remind us of the unmet promises of the 1970s and its galvanic politics; it might gesture toward as-yet-unrealised alternatives to our compromised present-day world. But in its performance, *Traps* resides in the stage-as-itself realm that Churchill privileges, a realm agreeably suspended from a flawed and unjust real life. Handke had called *The Ride Across Lake Constance* a 'Utopian comedy' since his play is 'free from explanation and the necessity to prove' that limit our own reality.[36] In *Traps*, Del reminds us that '[u]topia means nowhere'.[37] Only in performance can the play foment harmony among parties by proposing a here-and-now nowhere in which all can be '*increasingly happy*', to quote Churchill's final stage directions.[38] Only in performance can the theatre model a paradise now, a true community in the 'live, present-tense relationship between performers and spectators'.[39] I quote from theorist Jill Dolan's *Utopia in Performance*, whose understanding of performance's utopic potential we see clearly in *Traps*' final moments. We too might join Reg as he laughs and smiles, experiencing (as Dolan experiences) 'feelings of possibility, hope, and political agency' even as the performance ends, as harmony dissolves, and as we are reminded of the implication of Del's definition of utopia: no one lives nowhere.[40]

Blue Heart

Because they renounce representation, Peter Handke's theatre pieces have often been called 'anti-plays'. In an apposite coincidence, Churchill used the same term twenty years after *Traps* to describe her 'Heart's Desire' and 'Blue Kettle', two one-act plays paired under the portmanteau title *Blue Heart* when they were directed by Max Stafford-Clark in 1997. In the eight years since collaborating on *Icecream*, Churchill and Stafford-Clark had experienced tensions: first over the Royal Court's acceptance of a sponsorship from Barclays (which compelled her to resign from the theatre's administration) and then over *The Skriker*, after the director declined to stage it. Future discord awaited, when Churchill chose Stephen Daldry to direct *Far Away* in 2000. *Blue Heart* would therefore be Stafford-Clark's last work on a Churchill premiere. But like many before it, the show would prove to be a remarkable collaboration between the two artists.

Blue Heart was produced cooperatively between Out of Joint, the company Stafford-Clark founded after leaving the artistic directorship of the Royal Court, and the Court itself, since 1992 under Daldry's leadership. After rehearsals in London, the co-production premiered at the Theatre Royal in Bury St Edmunds on 14 August 1997 and moved to the Traverse Theatre for the Edinburgh Festival, where it opened on 19 August; it then returned to London and the Court, where it began previews on 17 September and opened a week later. (With the Sloane Square site under renovation, the show was housed in the Court's temporary home at the Duke of York's Theatre, where earlier that year Daldry had staged Churchill's gnomic *This Is a Chair*.) The next year, the production underwent some casting changes before an international tour with stops in Denmark, Estonia, Finland, Germany, Portugal, and Russia, as well as Brazil, Canada, and Israel. This tour included a three-week engagement at New York's Brooklyn Academy of Music, where it opened on 27 January 1999. In each of these venues the play met near-universal acclaim: 'ingenious', pronounced London's *Telegraph*; 'one of the season's happier successes', declared the *New York Times*.[41] Terrifically directed and beautifully played by its cast, *Blue Heart* became Churchill's first unqualified critical and commercial success since *Mad Forest* in 1990.

Critics have understood the work's anti-play qualities using different metaphors. Ben Brantley called its two parts 'self-sabotaging'; Gerard Raymond adjudged that 'each carries the seed of its destruction within it'.[42] Stafford-Clark himself likened 'Heart's Desire' to a 'naughty play that doesn't behave' and to a 'frisky pony', and he understood 'Blue Kettle' as infected with a 'language virus'.[43] Each of these images emphasises the play's wilful independence – 'the play itself becomes a character', declared Stafford-Clark[44] – as if the text's agency extended beyond its cast and writer (or rider, in the director's pony image). It is bent on its own anarchic path, disruptive to the usual workings of drama. These disruptions manifest differently in the two halves. In 'Heart's Desire', the action begins benignly, with three elderly people preparing for a homecoming, setting cutlery and restlessly waiting: 'She's taking her time', Brian says to his wife, Alice.[45] But after only two lines, the play resets to its beginning, and an element is changed – Brian's red sweater replaced by a tweed jacket – before the play begins again. Such reboots continue, prompted by increasingly strange twists of dialogue and plot: in one iteration, '[*t*]*wo* **Gunmen** *burst in and kill them all*' before we again '[*r*]*eset to top*'.[46] Sometimes the dialogue accelerates to unintelligible speed; sometimes lines are only partially spoken ('She's taking') or absurdly compressed ('It's not occasion occasion deliberately ruin it forty years stupid nasty').[47] Successive iterations proceed further into a linear plot – about a woman named Susy's return from Australia and to her parents, aunt Maisie, and troublesome brother Lewis. But the play cannot get past its final hiccup, Brian's strange declaration to his homecoming daughter that '[y]ou are my heart's desire'.[48] Denying closure, the first half ends where it begins: 'She's taking her time'.[49]

After an intermission, 'Blue Kettle' introduces new roles and a new plot, in which a man named Derek attempts to con each of four elderly women – Mrs Plant, Mrs Oliver, Mrs Vane, Miss Clarence – into believing he is the biological son she had given up for adoption decades before. His plan meets disapproval from his girlfriend, Enid, but none from his senile and uncomprehending mother. The 'language virus' starts manifesting in the second scene, when the words 'blue' and 'kettle' displace more semantically appropriate words: 'You don't have to blue anything up', Derek tells Enid in the first such instance.[50] Such substitutions occur with greater and greater frequency, so that by the seventh scene meaning is compromised. Eventually speech disintegrates further. The play ends with Derek and one of his false mothers behaving normally but speaking unintelligibly:

Mrs Plant T b k k k k l?

Derek B. K.

End.[51]

Thus the play reduces language to its foundations: on the page, graphemes such as <b> and <k>; on stage, phonemes such as the plosive /b/ and /k/. Isolating them, the playwright accentuates these smallest units of language, of meaning – the importance of whose correct ordering is foreshadowed in 'Heart's Desire' when a misplaced letter causes one of the resets: Alice's declaration that 'You don't sleem peased' sends the play scrambling, for the tenth time, back to its beginning.[52] Language, Churchill shows, is the DNA of any script. (It is surely no accident that 'Heart's Desire' features twenty-six resets, an entire alphabet of dramatic possibilities.) But she shows too this DNA's potential to mutate, to imperil its own functioning, to self-destruct. The 'self-sabotage' of the play's second half is anticipated in a moment from its first, in which Brian describes his misdirected hunger. 'I have this terrible urge to eat myself', he tells Alice and Maisie, as he describes a vivid self-cannibalism. 'I've swallowed my whole self up I'm all mouth can my mouth swallow my mouth yes yes my mouth's taking a big bite ahh'.[53]

Blue Heart revisits several ideas from *Traps* including its many-worlds ontology, which finds expression in its successor's both halves. In 'Heart's Desire', the play's iterations represent different theatrical possibilities, here presented sequentially as they are in Payne's *Constellations.* (Accepting his *Evening Standard* Award in 2012, a humble Payne reminded the audience of Churchill's influence, citing *Blue Heart* as an inspiration.) In 'Blue Kettle', the divergent possibilities are suggested more obliquely, in Derek's multiplying narratives as well as in a crucial citation: Enid takes her name from Enid Blyton, whose *Faraway Tree* books hinge on the proliferation of worlds – some delightful, some terrifying – that the child protagonists find in the eponymous tree. Churchill herself highlights the intertextual relationship between her book and Blyton's when she has Derek report on his childhood reading: 'I liked the one where there was a tree and every blue you climbed up it there was a different country'.[54] His description adumbrates the structure of 'Blue Kettle'. It shifts among many mothers as Blyton shifts among many worlds: the Land of Dame Slap, the Land of Birthdays, the Land of Take-What-You-Want. Derek shares his reminiscence with his biological mother, whose senile lack of memory recalls Blyton's Mr Watzisname and raises its own ontological and epistemological conundrums. 'If you didn't have any [memories]', Derek has explained, 'you wouldn't know who you were would you'.[55]

As in *Traps*, the strange happenings of *Blue Heart* direct us to the workings of the genre. And the latter play borrows from the former not only its modus operandi but also its opening trap. *Blue Heart*'s initial tableau – especially in Stafford-Clark's production, set-designed by Julian McGowan – presents an image of domestic realism such as that pioneered by Osborne: fridge, stove, table, and (of course) kitchen sink. Moreover, its earliest resets seem like fine-tunings, as if the play were refining this very image. When Brian replaces his red sweater with a tweed jacket and then an old cardigan, for example, he marks himself more effectively as 'father' and thus better establishes his relationship to the woman invoked in the play's opening line. Consequently we expect domestic drama: recall Aristotle's dictum that we learn as we look, with its emphasis on our past experience. Simultaneously we are made self-conscious about these expectations, especially when the wilful plot begins dispatching the play to foreign territory: to the murder mystery of Agatha Christie (when Alice and Brian and Maisie discuss the body in their garden); to the Ibsenite problem play (when a Young Woman who seems to be Susy's lesbian lover turns up instead); to absurd farce in the key of Ionesco (when, for example, a ten-foot-tall bird enters). The many possibilities of *Traps* unfolded simultaneously, but the possibilities of 'Heart's Desire' are rigorously teleological. Each time the play resets, it returns to an earlier moment whose repetition reinforces the impression that it is stable, unaffected by the frisky refusals of the rearing play. When a deviation is met, a rewind forced, our conditioned apprehension of a 'correct' plot effects Churchill's metatheatrical trick: she draws attention to the playgoing practices, the dramatic and theatrical conventions, with which we navigate and understand onstage happenings.[56]

Blue Heart is more thorough-going than *Traps* in exploring the genre's DNA, the dramaturgical analogues to language's graphemes and phonemes. The most basic is conflict. In its content, 'Heart's Desire' demonstrates the near-infinite variety and yet structural similarity of its various *agones*: whether between Maisie and Alice, Brian and Lewis, or the family and a jostling man in uniform who roughly demands to see their documentation. (Indeed, it is telling that the most atypical and therefore arresting interruption occurs when Susy first arrives and derails the plot with her frankly undramatic opening line, so lacking in agonistic grist: 'Mummy. Daddy. How wonderful to be home'.[57]) In its form, meanwhile, the play recalls the constitutive process that stands behind all finished theatrical products. Its stop-and-start unspooling mimics the rehearsal room and its absurd repetitions: sometimes ludicrously fast (as in a speed-through or Italian rehearsal), other times using incomplete lines (as in a blocking rehearsal). This emphasis on the dramaturgical bases of playmaking recurs in 'Blue Kettle', one of whose scenes unfolds as a metadramatic *mise-en-abyme*. Mrs Vane and Derek plot a dinner with their partners, but Mrs Vane wants her husband kept ignorant of Derek's putative identity; and thus she directs Derek in a lie (that he works at the hospital where she volunteers) just as he has directed his girlfriend (who knows that Mrs Vane is being conned). Conflict arrives when the wary Enid threatens to derail their script by informing Mr Vane of Derek's fraud: 'He's not her son at all'.[58] But Derek reframes her words with a canny improvisation. He reassures his pretend mother with a dramatically plausible scenario: 'She might be a bit jealous because ever since I found you I've blue a blue preoccupied and . . . I have to kettle her that just because I've found my mother doesn't blue I don't still love you Enid'.[59] Derek's representation – probable, in Aristotle's terms – compels theatrically. The proof comes when no one believes Enid.

Audiences watch this performance unfold with a particularly rich dramatic irony. None of the characters possesses the same information, and yet Churchill's spectators believe they know the 'truth'. Scare quotes are apt. Derek's stories vary constantly: he tells Mrs Oliver that he discovered his adoption by mistake at age sixteen; he tells Mrs Vane that his adoptive parents informed him in childhood. In the final scene, Derek explains to Mrs Plant that he had met her abandoned son while travelling – that he had hatched his cuckoo plan and resumed this man's search for a biological mother upon his death. But even in this apparently revelatory dénouement Derek lies, telling Mrs Plant that his own mother is dead: 'Tle died ket I ket a child'.[60] Derek's yarn-spinning, in other words, never ceases. And thus it recalls us to another fundament of theatre, which by design involves people misrepresenting themselves. When we see Ibsen's *Ghosts*, for instance, the actors we understand as Helen and Oswald Alving are no more biologically related than Derek and Miss Clarence. Another example can be found in Churchill's dramatis personae, which asserts that Derek is forty years old. He may fib to Mr Vane in the seventh scene, in other words, when he gives his age as forty-one. But the actor who originated the role engaged in a mathematically greater deception: Jason Watkins was barely thirty-five when the play opened in Bury St Edmunds. On stage, people such as Watkins pretend to be other than they are just as Derek does, because a script has compelled them to do so. And in this sense, the inanimate play – a 'character itself' – is in fact endowed with an agency exceeding that of the agents who bring it to onstage life. The idea is dramatised, too, by Churchill's contemporary Tom Stoppard, whose *Rosencrantz and Guildenstern Are Dead* shows its titular characters doomed to their fate by Shakespeare's *Hamlet*. The author is revealed to be stacking the deck and controlling the audience's experience. For behind the faltering plot of *Blue Heart*'s first half and the faltering language of its second stands Churchill herself. '[O]f course, it's an unsuccessful anti-play', she told Stafford-Clark. 'If I'd really wanted it to be successful, I'd have gone on for another two scenes in "Blue Kettle". That would have really driven the audience out'.[61]

Performance provides potential for subversion, however. Stoppard opposes his passive courtiers to the Player, who urges them to resist their fate through the freewheeling power of play; against their gloomy acquiescence, he sets contingency and chance. 'Tonight we play to the court. Or the night after. Or to the tavern. Or not', he reports.[62] *Blue Heart* similarly celebrates performance and its capacity to resist dramatic scripts, with their sometimes duplicity and sometimes fatalism; it understands *Traps*' bathtub message. For instance, the opening line of 'Blue Kettle' puts script and performance into productive tension. The text reads:

Mrs Plant I can't speak.[63]

The actor playing Mrs Plant – Valerie Lilley in the premiere – in fact speaks this precise line, and thus the semantic content of the on-page representation is playfully negated by its onstage performance. At the same time, the script pushes back. Consider the claim of 'Heart's Desire' that Susy will 'never come home from Australia again'.[64] With this line, Brian seems to summarise the central premise of almost all performance theory, articulated best in Peggy Phelan's book *Unmarked.* A live performance, Phelan tells us, is ephemeral, always receding into an irrecuperable past; it can never be exactly repeated. Churchill slyly mocks this idea, and Susy will arrive into the scene thrice, on each occasion apparently for the first time. Moreover, the playwright compels Brian to repeat his claim fully five times – seven if we include his two partial utterances ('She'll never' in the thirteenth repeat; 'again' in the seventeenth).[65] Of course, despite the actor's best efforts – Bernard Gallagher in the premiere, for instance, or Ewan Hooper on tour – the line will be never be precisely the same from one avowal to another, not only because of the impossibility of exact replication but also because the context of each linguistic occasion changes its exact meanings – the insight, we might say, of 'sleem peased' and its stray phoneme. Churchill would later explore this insight in greater depth in *Ding Dong the Wicked*, discussed in my epilogue. In that play, the same dialogue is used in each of the play's two halves, but the text's shuffled arrangement, new speakers, and different context render the familiar words eerily unfamiliar.

Traps had celebrated the realm of performance whenever its actors shelled peas or removed toenail clippings, two of Jack's onstage activities. 'Heart's Desire' repeats this anti-representational trick when a '*horde of small children rush in, round the room and out again*'.[66] In a spectacular moment I shall never forget, kids overtook the stage like maddened bees, swarming the characters and breaching the set's every barrier, climbing even through the kitchen cabinets. Only with some effort could the three elderly actors chase them off stage. The local children who participated (in full voice!) did not play characters or imitate something so much as they gleefully performed their feral childhood selves: an internal Royal Court memo about the offstage 'corralling of the children' is instructive.[67] The effect was similar to that proposed by the enormous bird that occasions a later restart. Like the dog in Francesco Cangiullo's 1915 performance *Non c'è un cane*, a bird cannot know it is acting or be precisely scripted. It appears in the unselfconscious mode preferred by Futurist performance artists such as Cangiullo and called 'absorption' by Michael Fried. (Stafford-Clark, more pragmatic, opted for a theatrical imitation: an actor in an ostrich costume.)

But if *Traps* opposed theatre to performance with Platonic rigour, *Blue Heart* is less troubled by imitation's inherent duplicity. Indeed, Derek's false-pretences relationship with Mrs Plant seems a boon to both; a relationship of mutual benefit is glimpsed in the play's final scene. Performance in *Blue Heart* appears instead as the necessary supplement to theatre, with its predetermined but always partial scripts. A line such as 'Bl bl ket b b b excuse?' may look meaningless on the page, but each person on the stage – both as an actor (say, Lilley) and as a character (Mrs Plant) – knows exactly what her or his scene partners say.[68] Each in turn behaves accordingly. If Charles Isherwood, reviewing the show in New York, could declare that the language virus causes 'scant loss in power or meaning', it is because virtuosic performers such as Lilley imbued each of their lines with precise significations – a further testament to Stafford-Clark's 'actioning' method.[69] Another fact might suggest the power of performance to supplement a script. However surprising it may seem in retrospect, the two parts of *Blue Heart* were not written as a diptych. Only at her director's urging did Churchill decide that they 'suited each other well enough to be shown together'.[70]

In other words, the bodily work of actors literally fleshes out the text, whether the lopped lines of 'Heart's Desire' or the deliquescent dialogue of 'Blue Kettle'. This work is extra-textual, outside what Churchill wrote. But it unifies the fragmentary script just as Haydn did in Stafford-Clark's production, in which the same piece of music signalled the beginning of all twenty-six scenes in 'Heart's Desire' and then recurred, appropriately de-composed, in 'Blue Heart'. (The expert sound was by Paul Arditti, a frequent Churchill collaborator. He also designed *Thyestes*; *This Is a Chair*; *Far Away*; *A Ring a Lamp a Thing*, her opera with Orlando Gough; and Wallace Shawn's *Our Late Night*, which she directed at the Royal Court in 1999.[71]) Through the power of doubling, bodies continued this work of unifying *Blue Heart*'s constituent parts: Brian reappeared as Mr Vane, Alice as Mrs Plant, Maisie as Mrs Oliver, tying one half of the play to another. Such doubling demonstrates at the most basic level the performer's capacity to supplement the text's meanings, as a final example will illustrate. 'Heart's Desire' introduces the threat of incest in its title, in the father's repeated utterance of a weirdly intimate line, and in Lewis's aggression on his father ('Where's my big sister? I want to give her a kiss. . . . Dad knows where she is, don't you Dad? Daddy always knows where Susy is'[72]). In performance, the actor I saw playing Susy in New York (Sally Rogers) amplified this hint of incest with her (nonverbal) response to her father's declaration. But she amplified it still further with the simple material of her body, when she and Lewis (Pearce Quigley) reappeared after intermission as a couple, Derek and Enid.

Incest ripples through the canon since Oedipus and Jocasta, whose story pairs incest with death as the ur-themes of Western drama. And in repetition after repetition, 'Heart's Desire' reveals death as the one fate that cannot be avoided. In one iteration, Susy's train meets an accident, for instance, and of course there are those gunmen, killing them all in a spray of bullets. 'Do you ever wake up in the middle of the night and be frightened of dying?' Maisie asks her brother-in-law.[73] The question finds a different poignancy in 'Blue Kettle', with its expanded cast of geriatric actors. Watching them, we may feel more urgently the reminder that Herbert Blau presses in his book *Blooded Thought*:

> [I]t is the actor's mortality which is the acted subject, for he is right there dying in front of your eyes. . . . Whatever he represents in the play, in the order of time he is representing nobody but himself. How could he? that's his body, doing time.[74]

Against this unsettling fact we can again set the utopic promise of performance – perpetually unfolding in the present tense, frantically fending off the final curtain, offering us *Traps*' life-giving tub instead of Pirandello's deadly fountain. Stoppard too had opposed the script of *Hamlet* to the subversive thrum of performance. 'Do you know what happens to old actors?' the Player asks Rosencrantz and Guildenstern, before answering: 'Nothing. They're still acting'.[75] Similarly, even as mortality haunted *Blue Heart*, it gave us too the timeless virtuosity of its performers: Gabrielle Blunt or Mary Macleod or Eve Pearce or Anna Wing (the real mother of Churchill's frequent collaborator Mark Wing-Davey), each player older than her director and playwright, and each splendidly restarting, night after night. 'I think I'm very susceptible to performers, to falling in love with what I see them do with plays', Churchill once declared to Judith Mackrell.[76] And so the challenges she sets for them continue to mount, along with the rewards.

Love and Information

For many critics, *Blue Heart* recalled the gleeful nonsense of British playwright N.F. Simpson (1919–2011), who pioneered the marriage of absurd farce and metatheatrical self-reflexivity in plays such as *A Resounding Tinkle*. Churchill's latest major offering, *Love and Information*, suggests a younger influence: Martin Crimp (b. 1956). Crimp's most celebrated and influential play, *Attempts on Her Life*, had premiered at the Royal Court in 1997, only months before *Blue Heart*. And in the ensuing years, his foremost formal innovation – the absence of a character list, speech prefixes, and stage directions, so that a director must apportion lines and construct characters without the guidance such a list, prefixes, and directions provide – was used by other playwrights, perhaps most prominently Sarah Kane in her 1999 play *4.48 Psychosis*. Having neither plot nor characters, plays such as *Attempts on Her Life* have been understood as 'postdramatic', pioneering the dramatic form that Churchill first adopted for *Seven Jewish Children*.[77] But in *Love and Information*, the conceit finds an even richer theatrical expression and a better thematic match.

Because of its form, the text of *Love and Information* can be described but not well summarised. The main text comprises over one thousand lines or speeches – many of them a single line – which unfurl in seven sections. Each section in turn includes seven subtitles, which mark discrete scenes; the exception is the seventh section, which adds additional text under the subtitle 'Last Scene: Facts'. The text thus seems to offer a rigorous dramatic equation ($7 \times 7 + 1$) with a mathematically pleasing result (50). But Churchill complicates this apparent rigour immediately. First, she offers a different challenge to linear plot than she had in the achronological *Traps* or the restlessly restarting 'Heart's Desire'. Here, she specifies that '*[t]he sections should be played in the order given but the scenes can be played in any order within each section*'.[78] Second, she appends a supplementary coda, entitled 'Random', which lists nineteen new scenes and a suite of ten partial lines (e.g. 'glass of red or'[79]) under the subheading 'Depression'. These supplementary scenes '*can happen in any section. DEPRESSION is an essential part of the play. The other random items are optional*'.[80] Compelling a production to make choices that will radically affect the play's narrative, she advocates the subversive power of play as Stoppard's Player had; at the same time, she sets constraints. In this way she underscores the tension between compulsory and voluntary that animates all theatre, a genre in which every performance is different even as the endings are predetermined. Elements of the script are mandatory, hard-wired: depression is an essential part of the play. But the vicissitudes of performance govern its contours. Thus, scenes can be played in any order; thus, some scenes are optional; thus, the dialogue awaits the casting and arrangement of an unusually free director.

Among the optional scenes we find a heuristic to the play's meaning:

> AGT TCG AGC CCT TGA CTT GAT TGT GCA TAC CGT
> GCT TGA GTC ATG TTG CAC AAC TTG TCG GTC TCA
> GTA TGC CCG TGA AAT GTA CAT GTC CGG TCC GAA
> TCT GAT TGC CCT TTG TGG AAC TGT GTG GCA TAG
> CTA GCC TGG GAC CCT TTG GGC TGC ACT TGA TTG
> TCA CCA GGT TGT TCT GTT GAA TCA TGA TCG GAC
> CCA CGT CGG CTG GCC GAC TTT GAC CGG AGT
> GGT TGT ACC TTG GTC AGG AAT TGA ACG[.][81]

A DNA sequence, the text represents a nucleotide series (the initials denote adenine, cytosine, guanine, and thymine) that constitutes an organism's genetic particularities. DNA is data. It provides the minimal textual requirement to make meaning, just, indeed, as Churchill's play does. The specific actualisation of this information – the narrative it produces, the behaviour it encourages, the emotions it incites – requires a production and especially the living bodies whose performances animate the text and therefore determine its meanings. In other words, the data awaits embodiment, as when this or that nucleotide sequence manifests in brown eyes, in dangling lobes, in sociopathic behaviour – and as this or that dramatic sequence of words causes any number of similar but particularised theatrical expressions.

The director of *Love and Information* must determine, in each scene, how many people are speaking and which of them says what, just as this director must determine the age, class, gender, and race – in short, the identity – of each speaker. Creating characters and building a narrative out of dramatic DNA, this director must provide, too, a theatrical context in which these characters can live. Many worlds are possible: Churchill has provided none but the barest of stage directions (nine in total), as when she specifies that the eponymous secret of one scene should be '*t*[*old*] *in a whisper*'.[82] What the whisper tells is left appropriately secret. That the same line might yield starkly different meanings from production to production will be clear to anyone who loves the theatre, anyone who has witnessed its radically varied and ever-proliferating Hamlets or Heddas. Churchill foregrounds this insight in the scene 'Chinese Poetry', where a poem's single line yields five different interpretations ranging from the prosaic ('A girl climbs the mountain and comes to a door') to the comically inspired ('The girl's as big as a mountain and can't get through the door').[83]

For its premiere production, which opened on the Royal Court's main stage on 6 September 2012, *Love and Information* was blessed with an unusually gifted director: James Macdonald, whose association with Churchill dates back to *Lives of the Great Poisoners* in 1991 but who became her primary director only after *A Number*, another play for which DNA suggests an organising concept. Macdonald had worked on such a radically indeterminate text before, having directed the first production of Kane's *4.48 Psychosis* (whose text he divided among three actors in an interpretive choice that has come to be seen as essential to the play's meanings).[84] For *Love and Information*, he used a diverse cast of sixteen, including stage neophytes such as Scarlett Brookes and Joshua James as well as practised interpreters of Churchill: Nikki Amuka-Bird, Amanda Drew, and Laura Elphinstone have each worked on separate revivals of *Top Girls*; and Linda Bassett is Churchill's most frequently cast collaborator. Indeed, having acted too in the premieres of *Fen*, *Serious Money*, and *Far Away*, Bassett is the only performer to work with each of Les Waters, Max Stafford-Clark, Stephen Daldry, and Macdonald. (She also performed Churchill's 'she bit her tongue' for *Plants and Ghosts*, the playwright's 2002 collaboration with choreographer Siobhan Davies.)

Macdonald divided *Love and Information*'s text among 138 characters and fifty-eight scenes, using his heterogeneous cast to emphasise – as *Cloud Nine* emphasises – the ways in which actors' specific identities shape the characters' and the scenes' meanings. In each scene, he had to establish not only its characters but also the time-and-space contexts in which they exercised their dramatic agency. For instance, he could realise a section of prose as the squabbling of gay lovers (as in 'Dinner' where he split the text between Justin Salinger and an undressing Amit Shah) or as an interracial and intergenerational friendship (as in 'Decision' where he apportioned dialogue between 78-year-old Susan Engel and 43-year-old Rhashan Stone, the basis of whose relationship was succinctly captured by dressing both in the shirts of Tate Museum guards). Context could be established by a single choice of costuming (e.g. the competitive ballroom dancing outfits worn by Drew and James in 'Dream'), of set design (e.g. the train seats that anchored Amuka-Bird and Engel in 'Spies'), or of the actors' performance (e.g. the shouting of Shah and Sarah Woodward in 'Earthquake' as they stood side by side, each holding a cocktail). The meanings of individual scenes hinged on these choices, as Stephen Daldry had taught his then-assistant, Nina Raine, a decade earlier, when he had Bassett perform the same text from *Far Away* with a series of different props and motivations.[85] And the capacity of meanings to be transformed by a changed element (as in 'Heart's Desire') was underscored by alternating one set of roles between two actors of different sexes, Billy Matthews and Nell Williams. It is instructive to learn that an even more radical contingency was attempted during the play's rehearsals: a proposal that different actors in the same scene take different lines from night to night was considered but eventually abandoned. The workable limits of *Love and Information*'s radical variability were tested and apparently reached.

Most scenes were played with two people, a decision seemingly encouraged by the text. For instance, the opening scene, 'Secret' begins –

> Please please tell me
>
> no
>
> please because I'll never
>
> don't ask don't ask[86]

– by suggesting a conversation between a couple. But Macdonald populated other scenes with three actors (as in 'Recluse', where Churchill provides contextual support in a rare stage direction, '*Two inside, one outside the door who can be heard*') or with four (as in 'Chinese Poetry', where she provides no clues whatever).[87] For 'Wedding Video' – for which '[*s*]*everal people*' are indicated[88] – Macdonald used six. Taking the licence she grants, the director arranged the scenes as he saw fit, generally using each actor once in each section and with few exceptions giving actors new scene partners in every appearance. He forewent most of Churchill's optional scenes but honoured the essential parts of 'Random' by staging eight depressive episodes, which collectively required the entire cast and thus demonstrated the impact of depression across demographics. (Uniquely, Drew appeared in two such scenes: she supported a morose Paul Jesson in one, and, in the most delightful and bizarre vignette, stood silently in a bunny costume, a glass of red wine in hand and face streaked with mascara, as Amuka-Bird enthused about the DJs and emitted celebratory whoops.[89]) A table of Macdonald's scene order and casting is provided below.

Table 5.1 James Macdonald's scene order and casting for *Love and Information* (Royal Court premiere, 2012)

	Nikki Amuka-Bird	Linda Bassett	Scarlett Brookes	Amanda Drew	Laura Elphinstone	Susan Engel	John Heffernan	Joshua James	Paul Jesson	Billy Matthews or Nell Williams	Justin Salinger	Amit Shah	Rhashan Stone	Josh Williams	Sarah Woodward
1.1: Secret	X											X			
1.2: Census													X	X	
1.3: Fan			X		X										
1.4: Torture								X			X				
1.5: Lab							X								X
Random: Depression (1)												X		X	
1.7: Remote		X		X											
1.6: Sleep						X			X						
2.1: Irrational							X	X							
2.2: Affair													X		X
2.3: Mother					X									X	
2.7: Terminal			X	X											
2.5: Message		X				X									
Random: Depression (2)										X			X		
2.6: Grass	X										X				
2.4: Fired									X			X			
3.1: Schizophrenic					X		X								
3.2: Spies	X					X									
3.4: Recluse									X		X				X
Random: Depression (3)						X	X								
3.5: God's Voice		X										X			
3.3: Dream				X				X							
3.7: Star										X				X	
3.6: The Child Who Didn't Know Fear			X										X		

4.1: Wedding Video					X			X		X	X			X	X
4.2: Savant						X						X			
4.3: Ex		X							X						
Random: Depression (4)					X			X							
4.4: Memory House				X			X								
4.5: Dinner											X	X			
4.6: Piano	X				X								X		
4.7: Flashback			X					X							
5.1: Linguist		X												X	
Random: Depression (5)				X					X						
5.3: Sex	X							X							
5.4: God						X									X
5.5: Rash			X				X								
5.2: Maths				X									X		
Random: Depression (6)		X													X
5.6: Children					X							X			
5.7: Shrink									X		X				
6.6: The Child Who Didn't Know Pain			X											X	
6.2: Climate	X	X													
6.7: Earthquake												X			X
6.3: Censor							X		X						
6.5: Decision						X							X		
Random: Depression (7)	X			X											
6.4: Wife					X						X				
6.1: The Child Who Didn't Know Sorry								X		X					
7.1: Chinese Poetry	X								X				X		X
7.3: Grief					X	X									
7.2: Manic							X					X			
Random: Depression (8)			X								X				
7.4: Fate		X						X							
7.5: Stone			X							X				X	
7.6: Virtual				X							X				
7.7: Small Thing	X								X						
Last Scene: Facts					X								X		

The production beautifully expressed the play's central conceit about dramatic data and its actualisation, since it included hundreds of unique touches and *coups de théâtre* that no reader could imagine even while it remained faithful to Churchill's text. In other words, its director maximised the licence that the script affords without overstepping its well-defined boundaries. (The only textual changes concerned 'Affair', in which three gendered pronouns were altered: an unseen spouse is female on the page but was made male in the production.) The work of Macdonald and his cast was well matched by the show's other creative personnel, including costume designer Laura Hopkins and lighting designer Peter Mumford (who had lit *Drunk Enough to Say I Love You?* in the same space). The sound was by Christopher Shutt, who previously designed *Serious Money* for Stafford-Clark and *A Dream Play* for Katie Mitchell, as well as a 2010 revival of *Far Away* at Bristol's Old Vic, directed by Simon Godwin. Shutt took the opposite approach to that taken by Arditti on *Blue Heart*, choosing to emphasise rather than mitigate the play's fractured form. After each scene, a new snatch of sound was heard: the voices of playing children, jungle noises, the theme to *The Simpsons.* Never repeating himself, Shutt honoured the play's expansive scope even as many of his choices – cellphone ringtones, subway announcements, all of them digitally transmitted via the theatre's sound system – reminded us that electronically recorded sound, too, is only data. Meanwhile, set designer Miriam Buether built a white cube that sat centre stage, as Annie Smart had when she designed *The Skriker*. But Buether's cube entirely contained the action, and each side was marked with horizontal and vertical lines, as if the actors themselves were data to be plotted on a three-dimensional coordinate grid. The sleek austerity of her design worked to underscore the quasi-scientific and minimalist elements of Churchill's text, its focus on information. Bringing it to organic life were the inhabitants: a different group of bodies in each scene, enacting a remarkable array of relationships and contexts, but always within the confines of the box that comprised the play's performance laboratory. The audience, able to see outside this structure, was thus kept mindful of Churchill's *tabula rasa* aesthetic – even if Macdonald's work may prove to have indelibly marked *Love and Information*, as happened with *4.48 Psychosis.* Certainly his premiere shadows the play's subsequent iterations, starting with his own for New York Theatre Workshop, where the play received its American premiere in February 2014 in a production at once unique and uncannily similar.

The set's contrast between the messiness of lived behaviour and an impersonal detachment undergirds *Love and Information*, whose very title sets the subjective and emotional against the factual and dispassionate. In 'Lab', the play's second-longest scene, we learn of a laboratory job involving research on chicks. (The job is clearly that of neuroscientist Steven Rose, described vividly in his book *The Making of Memory*.) Chicks are given both bitter and non-bitter stimuli, we hear, and teach themselves to avoid the former. A radioactive tracer, meanwhile, helps the researchers track the cerebral changes effected by the chicks' habituation. '[S]o you can see the memory', as the text puts it.[90] But this experiment's fascinations counterpoint its clinical practicalities:

> I hold the bird in my left hand and quickly cut off its head with a big pair of scissors
>
> aah
>
> and I drop the body in a bucket and take the head and peel back the skin and cut round the skull and there's the brain
>
> there's the brain
>
> so I put it in a dish of ice and my colleague cuts it into slabs with a razor blade and then he dissects out tiny samples that he puts into test tubes and they're immediately frozen while meanwhile I'm taking the brain out of the next chick[.][91]

Macdonald's production set the stage not for a lab but a picnic, complete with blanket and white wine. He populated the scene with two characters: a female researcher (Woodward) and her apparent date, played by John Heffernan. Rendering explicit the scene's implicit connection between love and information, his 'Lab' (from Section 1) limned the themes of the blunter 'Sex' (from Section 5) – staged as a dialogue between Amuka-Bird and James on beach towels – in which we learn that 'sex evolved to . . . get information from two sets of genes so you get offspring that's not identical to you. Otherwise you just keep getting the same thing over and over again like hydra or starfish'.[92] It is an image revisited from 1975's *Objections to Sex and Violence*, in which the prudish Madge lauds hydra for making procreation a cleaner endeavour, one that (she approves) can't be enjoyed. But she concedes that 'the child must be identical with the parent, which would stand in the way of progress'.[93] This progress has been complicated by technological innovation in the decades since. In *Love and Information*'s 'Virtual', a character claims to love a woman comprised only of digital information, computer code.

'Sex' emphasises nature: the hard-wired information written during the emotional coupling euphemised as lovemaking. But lab research proves that the brain – borne of natural information in the form of DNA – changes in response to the new information of lived experience, of nurture. Experience writes itself on the body in ways sometimes superficial (like the cryptic marks in 'Rash') and sometimes 'deep inside' (as Salter had put it in *A Number*, and as the chicks' dissected brains reveal).[94] For love, too, is memory stored in the brain, precisely as the reminiscing lovers of another scene, 'Ex', discover. The information recounted in 'Lab' ('slice the frozen brain into thin sections and put them on slides'[95]) threatened the possibility of love – or at least Woodward and Heffernan's performances suggested this meaning in one embodiment of Churchill's text. So their scene echoed 'Secret' or 'Grass' or 'Affair', each of which questions a relationship's ability to sustain a revelatory bit of information.

The vicissitudes of memory provide *Love and Information* with its second thematic throughline. In 'Savant', someone retrieves every detail of a day fifteen years earlier, a gift that seems a burden: 'Let's not do that', the character begs when asked to narrate Roland Emmerich's *Godzilla* shot by shot.[96] The prodigious memory of this scene contrasts with others that emphasise the loss or corruption of the brain's data. 'Piano' concerns an amnesiac, perpetually unfamiliar with one of his scene partners (to whom he is introduced twice) and with his skill at the piano; he can't remember that he plays it, but he can play all the same.[97] The attendant sufferings of corrupted memory also haunt 'Schizophrenic', in which the loving concern of one character goes unrecognised when another neglects to take medication. ('I stopped because it was making it hard to get the information', he or she says, having described the sinister signals received from traffic lights.[98]) And it returns in other scenes about cognitive failings, as in 'Wife', where declarations of love to a mentally ill husband are answered with 'I don't want you to love me, I don't know you'.[99] In these scenes of mental illness, love struggles to overcome the brain's faulty information.

If 'Blue Kettle' had wondered about the consequences of having no memories, *Love and Information* poses other epistemological questions. How do I know I am in love? How do I remember this apparent fact? In the absence of memory, is love possible? In 'Wedding Video' someone confesses that 'without the video I wouldn't remember hardly anything at all about it because I can't remember anything about that day that's not on the video'.[100] In its tautological circularity, the formulation replicates the mechanical workings of the video itself, which does not spur memory so much as supersede it. Meanwhile, the play's longest scene takes its name from a mnemonic exercise as old as classical Rome: 'Memory House'. As one character teaches another to populate the imagined house with objects to be remembered, we see the transmissions of cultural memory in action. But the urge to remember the past incites new recollections in the present – a surprising 'new memory'[101] – of a long-deceased father. Love has in fact transformed the brain's apparently dispassionate details.

A fundamental optimism seems to assert itself in 'Facts', the one scene whose place in the sequence Churchill mandates. The dialogue seems to conjure one character quizzing another with trivia questions, only to be answered every time. But the question 'Do you love me?' elicits only 'Don't do that'. At least until several lines later, as the play ends:

> By what name do we usually refer to Oceanus Australensis Picardia?
>
> I do yes I do. Sea anemone.[102]

Macdonald's production – a still provides this book's cover – put the cast on stage as if in a waiting room. Downstage left sat two of the evening's strongest performers: Stone asking the questions, Elphinstone answering. Absent a grisly brain experiment, love may be hard to spot in the data. But here it takes on an empirical certainty ('yes I do'), surrounded as it is by other facts. Performing the scene on the night I saw it, Stone touched Elphinstone's hand; she returned the gesture by touching his knee. They thus provided precisely the kind of performance supplement that the play invites and through which the audience might understand and even recognise, finally, the phenomenon of love. *Love and Information* seems to resolve the epistemological doubts it raises as it releases the tension between its titular terms, which – we are reminded – a conjunctive 'and' marries.

But scrutiny yields counter-information. The last scene's first question elicits a fact that research discredits. And successive facts prove absurd (duck and fennel as the traditional ingredients of 'poulash') or unverifiable. The Linnaean classification for sea anemones is, in fact, fabricated. Most telling: a nonsense equation answers the question 'What is the formula that disproves Gödel's theorem?'[103] Gödel's theorem, of course, concerns uncertainty in the first place; it asserts that an undecidable proposition can subvert any set of self-consistent axioms. So the respondent not only claims certainty where none exists but also falsely repudiates the very theorem that asserts the limits of knowledge. As one voice poses often unverifiable questions – including one about a theorem that concerns itself with unverifiable things – another voice provides wrong answers masquerading as facts. Whether the questioner is satisfied with these responses is undetermined. There are, after all, no stage directions. But by undermining her trivia whiz, Churchill suggests the limitations of information, whose proliferation may not in fact resolve love's essential mysteries. Epistemological uncertainty always lurks. It may be no accident that, in production stills for Macdonald's production, Stone wore a wedding ring in the final scene while Elphinstone did not – a bit of semiotic data that threatens to complicate the scene's apparent meanings.

The ring returns us to *Love and Information*'s most important insight: that the play's meanings are inherently indeterminate, established on this or that night and in this or that production and only in the context and the moment of performance. This fact may explain the play's polarised critical response, which ranged from grumpy irritation to rapturous praise. Among reviewers praising the play was David Benedict in *Variety*, who saw the audience's complicity in producing *Love and Information*'s story. 'The act of watching, of processing the information, is what the play is about', he wrote. 'The content . . . is indivisible from the play's unique form'.[104] His assessment seems to me exactly correct. *Love and Information* decisively positions its audience as performers, tasked – just as actors are – with making meaning from indeterminate data. And therefore it emphasises our subjective differences much more than *Traps* had, with its political utopianism. It is no surprise that the politics undergirding *Love and Information* seem bleaker, even a threat to its characters' relationships. In 'Spies', for instance, someone acidly asserts that he or she always knew that Bush and Blair were lying – 'because of what America's like' – unaware that, in asserting certainty where none exists, the bluster and blunder of those condemned have been replicated as exactly as hydras.[105]

Watching the play on 12 October 2012, I might have been unsettled by some of the data, especially in the final scene. Violating Macdonald's casting premise, Stone and Elphinstone had in fact appeared as lovers previously: the only pair of actors to do so. Visually apprehending their bodies, positioned on the set's coordinate grid, I might have been haunted by my recollections of their earlier scene, which concerned itself precisely with the workings of memory. For Stone had also played Elphinstone's amnesiac partner in 'Piano'. The semiotics of doubling intrudes as it had in *Blue Heart*. A London theatre buff, I might have been haunted by Elphinstone's performance in Stafford-Clark's revival of *Top Girls*, which had closed at Trafalgar Studios less than a year earlier, or by the unsettling theory of love that she had expressed then as she played Patient Griselda. Such extra-textual details matter: the lesson of watching J. Smith-Cameron in both *Traps* and *Owners*. Still other ghosts lurked. I might have been reminded of Stone's marriage (amply chronicled in the press) to the actress Olivia Williams, whose presence may have been symbolically conjured by a wedding band.

I can't remember. My recollections are tinged by my post-show discussion with friends at a nearby bar. And just as 'Wedding Video' theorises, my memories are coloured, too, by the mechanical aids of publicity and production photos and even video, recorded at the 11 October matinee but scrutinised by me only months later – in which Stone's costume has changed, his wedding ring disappeared. Perhaps, like the character in 'Memory House', I have invented new memories, buoyed by my unabashed love for Churchill and for a play I judge to be among her richest.

Crimp's *Attempts on Her Life* had already shown how different narratives construct and contradict one another as they attempt to represent, through performance, the absent character that is his play's subject. In her own radically indeterminate play, Churchill asks us to perform. The story of any play emerges as the spectators find meaning in what they watch, of course. But while *Traps* or *Blue Heart* sets up expectations only to refute them, *Love and Information* keeps us perpetually guessing. The play unfurls scene after scene, with new characters in each, without ever returning to a previous dramatic situation; as scenes pass, we struggle to retain them in memory and to generate understanding. At the same time, the play everywhere alerts us to the inadequacies of memory and forces us into epistemological suspicion about what we think we know. As in *Blue Heart*, actors animate the script's DNA; they make meaning even where none resides on the page in lines such as 'k bl bl bl bl' or 'AGT TCG AGC CCT TGA'.[106] As in *Traps*, these actors perform not only as characters but also in their own bodies, by their very presence, as the bathtub scene or the actual touch between Stone and Elphinstone makes poignant. If Churchill had declared herself susceptible to love for performers – with their limitless potential to do things with her plays – her latest play directs this potential outward. For in *Love and Information*, the watchful spectators engage, too, in a sensual act; and this act of presence and performance and even love proves equally essential to the theatrical experience.

CHAPTER 6
OTHER CRITICAL PERSPECTIVES

The 'Picasso' of Modern British Playwrights[1]
Elaine Aston

Elaine Aston is Professor of Contemporary Performance at Lancaster University, UK. Her monographs include *Theatre As Sign-System* (1991, with George Savona), *Caryl Churchill* (1997/2001/2010), *Feminism and Theatre* (1995), *Feminist Theatre Practice* (1999), *Feminist Views on the English Stage* (2003), *Performance Practice and Process: Contemporary [Women] Practitioners* (2008, with Geraldine Harris), and *A Good Night Out for the Girls: Popular Feminisms in Contemporary Theatre and Performance* (2013, wtih Geraldine Harris). She is the co-editor of *The Cambridge Companion to Modern British Women Playwrights* (2000, with Janelle Reinelt); *Feminist Futures: Theatre, Performance, Theory* (2006, with Geraldine Harris), *Staging International Feminisms* (2007, with Sue-Ellen Case), and *The Cambridge Companion to Caryl Churchill* (2009, with Elin Diamond). She has served as Senior Editor of *Theatre Research International*.

As the widely acclaimed dinner scene of Caryl Churchill's *Top Girls* (1982) comes to a close, Marlene's 'top girl' guests descend into a state of drunken chaos. The erudite Pope Joan spews out words of Latin, and the erstwhile monosyllabic Dull Gret breaks into her tirade about leading the peasant women's uprising against the devils from hell, as depicted in the painting by Bruegel from which her character is drawn. Directing this scene in his revival of *Top Girls* (2011 to 2012), Max Stafford-Clark, the play's original director,[2] packed a concluding, three-way political punch among Joan, Gret, and the audience: 'Let them eat bread' was the cry from the stage as Gret hurled bread rolls at Joan, who in turn batted them at spectators. While an altogether more playful note than any that I can recall from Stafford-Clark's 1991 revival of *Top Girls* at the Royal Court, it was nonetheless laced with a serious, political purpose. The *Gestus* of the revolutionary, lower-class

Gret launching her bread-roll missiles at top girl Joan made visible and palpable Churchill's overarching concern with the materialistic, individualistic drive for 'success', achieved at the expense of a disadvantaged and disempowered majority of women, while the audience was also on the receiving end of their respective angry, unhappy feelings about their lives, feelings unleashed and discharged into the auditorium. Seated near the front of the stalls for a matinee performance of *Top Girls* at the West Yorkshire Playhouse, Leeds, for instance, I was quite literally caught up in this moment: Joan was excellent 'in bat' and I was among those spectators close enough to the stage to catch the spray of flying breadcrumbs.

A major play in Churchill's canon, one that Stafford-Clark claims as the '[b]est play that I've directed'[3] and playwright Mark Ravenhill confesses to 'read . . . once a year',[4] *Top Girls* is representative not just of Churchill's commitment to a socialist-feminist politics, but more broadly to her enduring concern with a contemporary world unjustly divided between 'us' and 'them', those who have and those who have not. For over fifty years, Churchill has sought to shape and re-shape her political-theatre voice, representing and interrogating questions of social and political injustice and thereby inviting audiences to see the damaging effects of a contemporary world disfigured by capitalism.

In an essay published in 1960, Churchill identified the playwright's role as not to 'give answers' but to 'ask questions'.[5] 'We need', she argued, 'to find new questions, which may help us answer the old ones or make them unimportant, and this means new subjects and new form'.[6] The purpose of this critical perspectives essay is to historically contextualise the different 'subjects' and the 'form' Churchill's theatre has taken over the years of asking difficult, political questions of the world we have, a world that persists in the unequal distribution of wealth that means that the most basic needs (bread) remain unevenly met.

Churchill was born in London in 1938 just before the onset of World War II, but as her family relocated to Montreal, Canada in 1948, she was removed from the British experience of the post-war years. Under Clement Attlee's Labour government (1945–50) Britain transformed into a social welfare state, pursuing policies of nationalisation, public health (the National Health Service [NHS] was founded in 1948) and educational reforms (the 1944 Butler Act, under the Conservatives, established free education for all). The fifties, by contrast, dominated by three successive Conservative governments, sought, as their campaign slogan in the 1950 and 1951 general elections put it, to 'Set the People Free', by investing in privatisation, the individual (rather than the state), and market freedom.[7] A country that had 'never had it so good' was how Prime Minister Harold Macmillan described Britain at the close of the decade.

Removed from the British scene, Churchill confessed that she had an idea of England as 'little green fields and country life' and held 'a tourist's view of England as old and pageantry'.[8] Such a view was altered by her return in the late fifties to study at Lady Margaret Hall, Oxford University: from 'inside' England she began to form a very different 'perspective'.[9] Her insider's view on Britain would, in due course, come to inform her politicising, playwriting perspectives on the state of the nation, as evidenced in the opening reflections on *Top Girls*. Among her early works, many of which were for the radio, *The Ants* exemplifies an emergent concern with forming such perspectives. Originally conceived for television but, on the advice and intervention of her agent, Peggy Ramsay, broadcast on the radio (BBC 3, 27 November 1962), this play resonates with the widespread fear generated by the UK's H-bomb testing in the late fifties and the nation's failure to unilaterally disarm its nuclear weapons, as called for by the Campaign for Nuclear Disarmament (CND), founded in 1957. It represents a divorcing couple whose personal animosity towards each other eclipses their care either for their son's feelings or for the political events occurring in the world at large, a world that is at war. Core to presenting the dangers of personal concerns divorced from the bigger political (war) picture is the couple's son's struggle to gain perspective on what might be occurring in the family. The adults' 'divorce' from the atrocities happening in the world around them puts the child at risk. The subject returns, most significantly in Churchill's later, major play *Far Away* (2000); the child – the girl child in particular – comes to figure throughout Churchill's work as a repository for damaged futures (Angie in *Top Girls*, Joan in *Far Away*, or the girl in *Seven Jewish Children* [2009]).

As a young girl who was deeply troubled, 'easily reduced to tears' by the idea that half the world was starving and, moreover, frustrated by paternal explanations that this was how the world was and had to be, Churchill grew into left-wing politics as the means not only to understand but also to right and transform the social wrongs she perceived in the world around her.[10] Involving herself in a minor way in the CND protests was symptomatic of Churchill's identification with left-wing politics,[11] which, under Harold Wilson's Labour government (1964–70), were initiating widespread social reforms in the mid- to late sixties.[12] Hence it would be logical to assume that Churchill's experience of living through the sixties was a happy one. The decade witnessed countercultural and social revolution on an international scale: America experienced the rise of Black, New Left, and anti-Vietnam movements; 1962 saw Algeria achieving independence from France after the Algerian War (a subject later taken up in Churchill's *The Hospital at the Time of the Revolution*); May 1966 marked the advent of the Cultural Revolution in China; and 1968 brought worldwide student protests for social change. However, at home with three small children (she married barrister David Harter in 1961), Churchill did not feel 'a part of what was happening in the sixties'.[13] Her writing for radio was a solitary experience; her personal, domestic, and, she notes, relatively comfortable circumstance made her feel apart from rather than a part of the revolutionary zeitgeist.[14] This disjuncture between 'personal' and 'generational' axes[15] accounts for why, in brief, she suffered from the 'gloomy feeling that when the Revolution came [she] would be swept away'.[16]

Churchill's struggle to combine motherhood with a career as a professional playwright is arguably a significant factor in accounting for the time it took her to break out of radio and move into theatre, compared to the thirties-born generation of male playwrights (Alan Ayckbourn, Alan Bennett, Edward Bond, Trevor Griffiths, Harold Pinter, David Rudkin, significant among them), or those, younger still, born in the forties (Howard Barker, Howard Brenton, David Edgar, and David Hare). While playwrights of both genders had relatively few opportunities to have their work staged, the inequalities of the British theatre industry in the late sixties meant that there were even fewer opportunities for women playwrights.[17] That said, Churchill counts herself as a beneficiary of the changing landscape of British theatre in light of the advent of fringe theatre. Catherine Itzin's survey of political theatre in Britain since 1968 cites 1972 as the year when '"fringe" theatre – and particularly lunchtime theatre – had become firmly established in the landscape of London theatre'.[18] With state (Arts Council) subsidies enabling an outcrop of alternative theatre companies and the founding of new spaces for new writing, British playwrights were presented with far more opportunities. 1972 was also a landmark year for Churchill: *Owners*, her first play to be professionally produced, premiered on 6 December. The script and an interview with Churchill (in conversation with socialist playwright Steve Gooch) featured as the 'centrefold' in the theatre magazine *Plays and Players* the following month.[19] In the same issue, a feature-length round-up of plays from 1972 and the critics' awards for that year, lamented the 'dearth of new plays' that left barely any competition for Stoppard's *Jumpers* – the 'walkover winner' for the Best Play Award.[20] By contrast, however, Itzin's chronology of alternative theatre productions offers a substantial listing for 1972 (including *Owners* and Churchill's *Schreber's Nervous Illness*, which had a lunchtime production at the King's Head the same week that *Owners* opened), evidencing, perhaps, that the critics' more mainstream, West End focus had largely eclipsed a view of the new playwriting that was thriving on the alternative scene.

Situated outside of the West End in the wealthy environs of Sloane Square, the Royal Court Theatre is a subsidised venue that has a reputation for presenting hard-hitting, contemporary, and provocative plays, a tradition dating back to the regime of its pioneering Artistic Director, George Devine (1956–65). Churchill's professional theatre debut at the Court with *Owners* marked the beginning of her enduring relationship with the theatre, an association that situated her within the theatre's genealogy of socially committed drama, ranging from the kitchen-sink realism of John Osborne's *Look Back in Anger* (1956) to the Brechtian repertoire of Edward Bond.

Committed to the Court as a writer's theatre, 'the only theatre there was to work for',[21] but also to experimenting with dramatic form in the interests of interrogating urgent social questions, Churchill eschewed the tradition of social realism spawned by the success of *Look Back in Anger*.[22] *Owners*, for example, weaves the subject of owning through the fabric of an Ortonesque 'funny angle[d]' realism,[23] this to expose the absurdity of a Western investment in what Nicholas Wright, her director, termed 'emotional capitalism'.[24] Deploying the gender-reversal technique of an active woman (Marion) and inactive man (Alec), the emotional drive to own property, things, and human life (Marion) is resisted by a passively styled altruism (Alec).[25] With characters in various states of mental disrepair that encourage violent, albeit grotesquely funny, fantasies and acts of violence towards others, Churchill upends realism in the interests of defamiliarising the capitalist need and greed to own.

Seeking to expose the drama of Western capitalism, Churchill's playwriting increasingly adopted and adapted the techniques of defamiliarisation associated with a Brechtian dramaturgy, widely practised among alternative theatre-makers and politically motivated dramatists. Janelle Reinelt's study *After Brecht: British Epic Theater*, for instance, insightfully and appositely groups Churchill with those political playwrights whose theatre benefited in some ways, however obliquely, from a Brechtian legacy: Brenton, Bond, Griffiths, Hare, and John McGrath.

During the seventies, Churchill's exposure to Brechtian theatre practices came through the opportunities she had to work with alternative theatre companies. With the new alternative company Joint Stock, Churchill was to forge a relationship that would span a ten-year period from *Light Shining in Buckinghamshire* in 1976 to *A Mouthful of Birds* in 1986. Her collaboration with Joint Stock director Max Stafford-Clark, as my opening reflections on *Top Girls* attest, is even longer. Appointed as the Artistic Director of the Royal Court Theatre in 1979, a position he held until 1993, Stafford-Clark also partnered Churchill on several Court productions throughout his period of office. With Joint Stock, he introduced Churchill to workshopping processes and to a democratising practice that elicited creative thinking from all those involved – writer, director, performers, and technicians. *Light Shining* was indebted to the 'creativity' and 'commitment' of the actors;[26] to a process of dialectical enquiry that enabled her, as the writer, to distil research, ideas, and practical explorations into an historicising treatment of the seventeenth-century English Civil War, performed by the company in a Brechtian-styled ensemble.

Utterly inspired by her experience of *Light Shining*, Churchill kept faith with the Joint Stock 'method', continuing to work with the company that emerged as one of the most significant alternative theatre companies of the seventies, this alongside her commitment to the Court as a writer's theatre. She thus differed from many of her (male) leftist contemporaries who cut their political teeth on the alternative circuit but subsequently looked to make their political voices heard in more mainstream circles: the National Theatre (relocated to its South Bank premises in 1976); the RSC (which acquired a London base, the Warehouse, in 1977); or the more lucrative media of film and television. For instance, the early careers of Hare and Churchill evidence certain points of convergence. Both were writers in residence at the Court (Hare 1970 to 1971;[27] Churchill 1974 to 1975) and had works staged there in the seventies; both had productions with Joint Stock: Hare was involved in founding the company and was the writer for their 1975 production of *Fanshen,* 'one of the classic achievements of political theatre'.[28] Thereafter their careers took distinctive turns as Hare, disillusioned with his perceived limitations of political theatre as practised on the alternative scene, eschewed the revolutionary, Chinese peasant classes of *Fanshen* for dramatic critiques of the privileged middle-classes and went on to further his writing (and directing) career at the National, as well as on the small and large screens. I make this observation not to be critical of Hare's career choices but to highlight Churchill's steadfast commitment to the Court and to the fringe as a political choice. Equally, while both writers arguably shared a frustration with a Western failure to revolutionise, what keeps Churchill within a Brechtian, epic refrain is her dramaturgical capacity to realise socially transformative, politicising perspectives. Last but not least, while Hare was lamenting the inefficacies of the consciousness-raising tactics of political theatre,[29] Churchill was exploring their efficacy within a feminist, political, Brechtian-inflected framework.

The affectivity of domestic gloom that Churchill experienced in the sixties brought her to a feminist consciousness that found its way into her playwriting in the seventies. It surfaces explicitly in *Vinegar Tom*, her play for the other fringe company she worked with in the seventies: the socialist-feminist collective, Monstrous Regiment. Both *Light Shining* and *Vinegar Tom* premiered in 1976. Feminist activism is what occasioned the meeting between Churchill and the 'Monsters': company member Gillian Hanna recollects that they 'had been introduced to Caryl (in Hyde Park, after a march, NAC [National Abortion Campaign])'.[30] The discovery of a shared interest in feminism and the subject of witchcraft resulted in the commissioning of *Vinegar Tom*.

Vinegar Tom is a crucible of seventies feminism that was brought about by the Women's Liberation Movement (WLM). Its scenes locate in the seventeenth century, but songs intersperse and break up the action to insist that women's oppression is not consigned to the historical past but rather needs to be addressed as an urgent contemporary issue. Thematically, body politics, core to the WLM, come to the fore: women's reproductive control over their bodies figures as crucial to the formation of their potentially liberated selves.[31] One woman seeks advice from a local cunning woman on aborting an unwanted child. Another is condemned to marriage, while those whose bodies mark them out as socially, economically, and sexually abject – whose lives contravene patriarchal control of their sexuality and reproduction – are humiliated, punished, and condemned to death. Ultimately, the women in the play are shown as unable to achieve the kind of solidarity needed to rise up against and to resist their oppression. Achieving solidarity between women and organising collectively was core to how the WLM shaped itself politically, and this in turn influenced the structural organisation and creative practices of Monstrous Regiment. The emphasis in *Vinegar Tom* on the representation of a *community* of women at risk, rather than one woman's struggle to survive, called for ensemble-based acting, while the music served, as Hanna put it, to 'smash [the] regular and acceptable theatrical form [of a traditional play]'.[32] Overall, Churchill's socialist-feminist viewpoint, in combination with a presentational rather than representational aesthetic, aimed to raise the feminist-political consciousness of audiences: to make them see and feel their way towards the necessity of social change in the interests of women's equality.

The sixties' sexual revolution that had given rise to gay and women's activism came under further feminist scrutiny in *Cloud Nine* (1979), a play Churchill workshopped with Joint Stock. With a first act set in the colonial times of the British Empire and a second in present-day (1979), but with characters inhabiting a time-span of just twenty-five years, *Cloud Nine* offered a political perspective on the dystopian legacies of un-liberated sexualities and the utopian possibilities of transcending heterosexually constrained gender norms. It was a landmark play in Churchill's repertoire: it confirmed her as a major, innovative, and political dramatist in British theatre, and brought her to international attention when, in 1981, the play transferred to New York where it ran for two years.

In terms of British politics, however, for those on the Left such as Churchill there was little to celebrate in 1979. This year saw Margaret Thatcher elected Prime Minister of a Conservative government, a position she held until 1990. Picking up where Conservative governments of the fifties and early seventies had left off,[33] the 'Thatcher Years' systematically undermined Britain as a social welfare state, making the eighties a 'never-had-it-so-bad' decade for socialism. Implementing policies to cut back on public spending, to reduce support for education, health, and welfare, Thatcher's right-wing government brought about the state of a materially divided nation. To borrow from *Top Girls*, the eighties might have been 'stupendous' for a 'high-flying' minority like Marlene, but they were 'frightening' for the majority at the bottom of the social strata.[34]

The alternative theatre scene of the seventies was an inevitable casualty of the Thatcher regime, with cutbacks to arts subsidies seeing an erosion of the fringe companies that had formerly been able to grow and thrive. With socialism and socialist structures on the wane in theatre and in society at large, leftist playwrights sharpened their attack on Tory Britain, exemplified in Churchill's case with eighties plays such as *Top Girls*, *Fen*, and *Serious Money*, her ferocious satire of the ridiculous money that was being made on the London stock market.

Surveying the post-war history of British theatre, critic Michael Billington's snapshot of the eighties cites the 1987 production of *Serious Money* as one of a handful of 'outstanding individual events' in a decade otherwise characterised by a rise in musicals and revivals rather than new work.[35] With all theatre that relied on state subsidy, rather than just the theatre that had made up the alternative sector, feeling the economic squeeze, the opportunities for new dramatists to emerge were again reduced. Christopher Innes argues that 'the most distinctive [male] voices' in British theatre – 'marginalized, or set in their vision' – were in trouble by the nineties: Pinter 'withdrawn from the theatre'; Bond 'sacrific[ing] drama to ideology'; Barker and Brenton unable 'to develop'; Schaffer 'retreat[ing] into commercial entertainment'; Hare, Stoppard, and Ayckbourn, 'significant', but 'old guard'.[36] Bucking an otherwise seemingly dismal theatre trend, however, the eighties was the decade that saw a gradually increasing number of women playwrights coming forward, largely due to the openings and legacies created by women's companies such as Monstrous Regiment, and, in other ways, to a 'woman friendly' reception at the Royal Court under Stafford-Clark's directorship. Women playwrights to have their work staged at the Court during his regime include Sarah Daniels, April de Angelis, Andrea Dunbar, Charlotte Keatley, Sharman Macdonald, Clare McIntyre, Louise Page, Winsome Pinnock, and Timberlake Wertenbaker. The importance of Churchill to these younger generations of women dramatists cannot be overstated. She is the 'Picasso' of British playwrights, according to Daniels; she pioneered the way for women to be taken seriously as playwrights in a male-dominated profession, de Angelis attests.[37]

Churchill's politically charged capacity for theatrical reinvention that, in contrast to her male contemporaries, saw her work constantly evolving accounts for why she is held in high esteem by playwrights of both genders and across different generations. That capacity for reinvention found fertile ground not just in her text-based repertoire for the Court, but also in other of her performance collaborations with dancers and musicians. While *A Mouthful of Birds* was Churchill's last

Joint Stock project in 1986, it was also the first of several projects with the dance company Second Stride and its founder member and choreographer, Ian Spink. Experimenting with words in combination with movement, and, in the case of other collaborations, also with music (*The Lives of the Great Poisoners* [1991], *The Skriker* [1994], *Hotel* [1997]), Churchill was exceptional in moving between playwriting and the physical, visual cultures of the experimental arts scene. As a mode of experimentation that assisted with her enduring attention with how to form urgent social questions in politicising ways (ecological matters in *Poisoners*; the damaging force of global capitalism, *The Skriker*; urban alienation, *Hotel*), this interdisciplinary work also has a bearing on her text-based playwriting – with her struggle to find dramatic expression for a contemporary world in which her desire for a more socially progressive future appeared less and less obtainable given the reactionary political temperature.

Mad Forest (1990), Churchill's dramatisation of the Romanian revolution in 1989, is the last of her plays to deal with the subject of revolution and to endorse Brechtian-influenced techniques for their politicising perspectives. Capturing the zeitgeist of post-1989 Europe, the collapse of communism in Eastern European nations, *Mad Forest* puts into question democratic futures founded in neoliberal ideas, policies, and economies. Throughout the nineties and beyond, Churchill's political quarrel lies with 'emotional [global] capitalism': with attachments to capitalism occurring on a global scale, whose conditioning and control of people's lives anaesthetises a capacity for cooperation and community.

Feeling their way through the socialist theatre of the past and the Thatcherite legacies of the eighties, a new generation of British playwrights was credited with rescuing new writing from the impoverished state into which it was perceived to have fallen by the start of the nineties. Resistant to cultures of ideologically driven playwriting, this generation shaped their political discontents through experientially formed, brutal, and taboo-breaking dramas, widely characterised as in-yer-face theatre. The politicising impulse of this work has been much debated.[38] But at its best, key exponents of this new wave, such as Sarah Kane and Mark Ravenhill, effected hard-hitting critiques of a generation lost to global capitalism (Ravenhill) and a contemporary world laid to waste by the dehumanising inability to care for others (Kane).[39] Churchill's enduring concern with an acute inability to see, think, or feel the bigger political picture parallels these variously configured but uniformly dystopian outlooks, making her very much the 'contemporary' of this nineties generation.

In terms of British politics, the picture shifted. The 1997 general election brought in a New Labour government under Tony Blair, the first Labour government to be formed since Thatcher's election in 1979. However, with Blair's government distancing itself from the old Left, rebranding '*New* Labour' as a party that endorsed the global, free market economy, this election did little to rekindle the spirit of socialism. Dispirited by the lack of change, Churchill went through a 'period of writing anti-plays' in Stafford-Clark's view: he cites as examples *Blue Heart* (written for his Out of Joint company) and her short play *This Is a Chair* (Royal Court), both of which premiered in 1997.[40] At the same time, this 'anti-play' crisis over the political efficacies of theatre also marked Churchill's dramaturgical shape-shifting towards increasingly elliptical, condensed modes of dramatic writing: she began to eschew a Brechtian-styled dialectics in favour of a visceral-critical 'sensing' of the divorce between the personal and political, and of capitalism's relentless 'progress'. In this regard, the apocalyptic *Far Away* (2000) is a veritable tour de political force.

Events at the Royal Court during the 2000s occasioned celebrations of Churchill's work: in 2002, a new, full-length play, *A Number*, was presented in tandem with a series of readings from earlier works, marking her thirty-year history at the theatre; in 2008, ten playwrights directed readings of their favourite Churchill play to celebrate her seventieth birthday. Both are markers of the high esteem in which Churchill is held by the Court and the playwriting community at large. In between these two events, as part of their year-long fiftieth-anniversary-of-playwriting programme, in 2006 the Court staged *Drunk Enough to Say I Love You?*, Churchill's chilling and trenchant critique of a love affair between two men that figuratively captures the dangers of feeling and falling for the capitalist American 'dream'.

Advance press coverage of the programme highlighted plans to include contributions from Pinter (performing in *Krapp's Last Tape*) and a new play by Stoppard (*Rock 'n' Roll*), his first ever for the Royal Court and controversial in some quarters given his more mainstream career and antipathies towards the leftist sympathies that characterise the work of many of the theatre's writers.[41] Resistant to the lure of Hollywood that has seduced Stoppard and altogether eschewing opportunities to promote or publicise her theatre work, Churchill's reputation is, in the words of her erstwhile director John Tydeman, 'up there with Stoppard, although her reputation may be lower than it should be – because she has chosen to stay in the background'.[42] Whatever the merits and rankings accrued by or accorded to British dramatists writing for the stage from the mid-twentieth century onwards, none can surpass Churchill in respect to her theatrical inventiveness. Stylistically recognisable, Pinter's theatre has, for instance, engendered the term Pinteresque, but Churchill's innovative dramaturgical shifts make it comparably harder to define the Churchillian. Rather, to expect the unexpected has come to inform the horizon of Churchillian expectation. Her two most recent plays at the time of writing, both premiered at the Royal Court in 2012, evidence Churchill's continuing capacity to surprise, delight, and politicise. What might be termed emotional technology themes *Love and Information*, which has a cast of over a hundred characters (played by sixteen performers) who, through multiple scenic moments, are seen processing 'bytes' of information and feelings shaped by today's technologically driven world. It reflects Churchill's career-long obsession with the struggles for self-knowledge that can be traced back to early works such as *Lovesick* (1967) or *Schreber's Nervous Illness*, and to later works such as *A Number*, which represents the crisis in paternal identity produced by advances in bio-medical technology. The abject failure to connect personal lives to global atrocities, as essayed in *The Ants*, is also back in *Ding Dong the Wicked*, a short play that delivers a sharp, dark, political critique of warring factions: one war, two countries, two sides, two families, each resolute in their belief that militaristic right is on their side.

Seeing Stafford-Clark's revival of *Top Girls* in the same year as these two new plays served to remind of the Churchillian legacy of theatrical inventiveness – at times playful but consistently pressed into the service of forming urgent social and political questions. The question mark that punctuated feminist futures in *Top Girls*, like all other of Churchill's calls for more socially progressive futures, remains still to be answered. Yet her demand for radical intervention into the 'frightening' nightmares of a world lost to capitalism is as enduring and undiminished as her theatrical powers of reinvention. She is quite simply and deservedly the 'Picasso' of modern British playwrights.

'The Times' of Caryl Churchill's Theatre
Siân Adiseshiah

Siân Adiseshiah is Reader in English Literature and Drama at the University of Lincoln, UK. She is author of *Churchill's Socialism: Political Resistance in the Plays of Caryl Churchill* (2009) and co-editor of *Twenty-First Century Fiction: What Happens Now* (2013). She has published widely on contemporary theatre and utopianism, and is currently writing a monograph on utopian drama.

In a letter to the Chairman of the English Stage Company in November 1989, Caryl Churchill made a comment revealing of both her political disposition and the stakes of the battle between Left and Right after the election of the Conservative Party in Britain in 1979: 'There's been a lot of talk . . . about "the times" as if they were a force of nature – we are part of them just as much as the government, the city and business interests, and our opposition can be part of them'.[43] The comment makes evident her political commitment to agency and resistance. And it departs from the common refrain of the political mainstream, which inscribes inevitability into its descriptions of the political trajectory. The last forty years of Churchill's playwriting – from her first professional stage production, *Owners*, in 1972 – tells a story of competing ideas about individual and collective identities and about political agency. Ultimately, however – and tragically for the Left – it is a story of how traditional forms of resistance and opposition have been defeated by an aggressive neoliberalism, which bankrupts human cultures and economies through the processes of globalisation, consumerism, and marketisation.

This move away from socialism was less the result of a battle won by the Right and more the outcome of a steady capitulation of large sections of the Left to the seductive power of 'the times' as a 'force of nature'. For example, in a landmark book edited by Stuart Hall and Martin Jacques – *New Times: The Changing Face of Politics in the 1990s*, published in 1989 – soft Leftists and Communist Party members such as David Green, John Urry, Charlie Leadbetter, and Beatrix Campbell delivered a rethinking of socialist principles and priorities, which formed part of a wider move rightwards.[44] Instead of opposing capitalism as an entire system, the focus increasingly sought 'fairer' ways to live within the existing system – a focus very much in tune with Anthony Giddens's project of the 'third way', which emerged in practice under Neil Kinnock's leadership of the Labour Party and which Tony Blair zealously pursued in the late 1990s and 2000s.[45] The challenge of pursuing a Left agenda that posed no threat to the structures of capitalism provoked the sociologist Michael Rustin to criticise what he perceived to be 'unfortunate concessions to values that are probably better simply regarded as those of the other side'.[46] Indeed, the dissolution of clearly identifiable sides – sides marked by ideologically differentiated principles and commitments – also reflects the shift rightwards of the mainstream Left, including sections of the Labour movement, the Communist Party, and Left intellectuals.

Churchill's insistence on a clear opposition within and to 'the times', like Hall and Jacques's contrasting call to engage with the '*new* times', came in 1989. Of course, the year is pivotal: because of the fall of Soviet Communism and because the monumental events constituting this fall invigorated a developing neoliberalism. Churchill's play about the Romanian revolution, *Mad Forest* (1990), dramatises the suffocating experiences of families under the Ceauşescu regime, but it simultaneously embeds a critique of neoliberalism – most obviously through its allusions to American hyper-consumerism and its ominous depiction of the encroaching 'free' market and privatisation. Importantly, the play also takes care not to equate the Ceauşescu regime with socialism. It thus refuses to encode a structure of movement that all too easily slips from the fall of the Berlin Wall to the inevitability of global capitalism – as in Francis Fukuyama's 'end-of-history' thesis, which posits global capitalism as the telos of sociocultural and governmental evolution.[47] Outside the play, revolutionary socialist groups such as the Socialist Workers Party and Militant had developed a Trotskyist opposition to Stalinised Communism, which in their view perverted Marxism. But significant elements of the Left (various Communist Parties and sections of the Labour Party and trade union movement) bore a historical complicity with the USSR and its political project. For them, the fall of the Soviet bloc contaminated socialist politics more generally. In *New Left Review*, Mary Kaldor went as far as to question the value of the very word 'socialism', asking 'is social justice an adequate substitute for the term "socialist"?'[48]

Language, of course, is central to the ways in which the political landscape develops and is understood, and Churchill weaves this understanding into the texture of many of her plays. For example, the malignant, shape-shifting fairy in *The Skriker* (1994) speaks the language of pathology, a diseased idiom reflective of a sick disjunction between lived realities and political discourse. The move away from negotiating the political world through socialist categories, and particularly the move away from the language of social class, was helped by 'the highly successful Thatcherite endeavour to Americanise people's conception of the working-class', in the words of playwright David Edgar. This new formation separated 'the full-time employed proletariat from the part-time or unemployed section' and imported 'a new vocabulary – "the inner cities", "the underclass" – to define the latter'.[49] Marlene from *Top Girls* (1982) epitomises the Americanisation to which Edgar refers: by inhabiting a Thatcherite 'post-class' identity ('I'm original'), she frames Joyce's performance of a familiar working-class identity as anachronistic.[50]

The question of the place and importance of social class in political strategy has frequently divided socialists. Indeed, it was long before the Thatcher period that class came under scrutiny – both as an analytical category and as an identity through which to organise political opposition. From the student uprisings in Paris in 1968, for example, emerged 'The Appeal from the Sorbonne', whose Thesis 27 states:

> The proletariat, like the bourgeoisie in its time, has been revolutionary in knowing that it could have a dialogue only by radically transforming the society. The proletariat has lost this power everywhere in the world. A new ruling class has been born, a synthesis, in fact, of the proletariat and the bourgeoisie. This 'association of interests' seeks to conserve the ideology of the last century in its entirety as a guarantee of its new privileges.[51]

The working class had apparently been bought off by capitalist reforms and thus had lost its economic incentive to radicalise, at least according to the (largely middle-class) students, who authored the appeal and fashioned themselves as central agents of change. But it is significant that during the same (pre-Thatcher) period, Churchill commits firmly and repeatedly to working-class, proletarian, and plebeian agencies and to class as central to lived experience.

Churchill's *Cloud Nine* (1979) had vividly articulated the interrelatedness of colonialism, racism, capitalism, patriarchy, and homophobia, as experienced by different subjects in both historical and contemporary time-frames. But even as *Cloud Nine* was striving to make visible the connections between different forms of oppression, off stage the Left was experiencing growing sectarianism and fragmentation. In the same year that *Cloud Nine* premiered, historian Sheila Rowbotham, herself an ex-member of the International Socialists (IS), wrote: '[t]here is no conscious commitment to struggling against the forms of relationship, which are created by the division of labour under capitalism, as part of the effort to make socialism. It is assumed that the existence of the revolutionary party itself, [*sic*] can transcend the particular interests of sections within the working class'.[52] The scene was very different in 1967. Stuart Hall (then editor of *New Left Review*) along with Raymond Williams and Edward Thompson wrote a May Day Manifesto that included the following statement:

> It is our basic case, in this manifesto, that the separate campaigns in which we have all been active, and the separate issues with which we have all been concerned, run back, in their essence, to

> a single political system and its alternatives. We believe that the system we now oppose can only survive by a willed separation of issues, and the resulting fragmentation of consciousness. Our own first position is that all the issues – industrial and political, international and domestic, economic and cultural, humanitarian and radical – are deeply connected; that what we oppose is a political, economic, and social system; that what we work for is a different whole society.[53]

Like Churchill, New Left contributors were interested in forging a communistic politics that, while unambiguously anti-capitalist, did not replicate Stalinist authoritarianism. The May Day Manifesto insists on the interconnectedness of struggles; it implies that unity among socialists and Left campaigns will be central to the success of any challenge to the system. Churchill's plays of the 1970s – in particular *Owners* (1972), *The Hospital at the Time of the Revolution* (1972), *Light Shining in Buckinghamshire* (1976), and *Vinegar Tom* (1976) – similarly demonstrate a preoccupation with whole social systems and the interconnectedness of injustices and oppressions. Each populates the stage with working-class figures (often female) or makes visible the connections between class and other identities (such as race and gender).

Thatcherism, Reaganism, and the rise of the New Right – followed shortly by the fall of Soviet Communism – damaged the prospects of left-leaning politics, and this turn was no doubt isolating for a radical such as Churchill, interested in a society 'decentralised, non-authoritarian, communist, non-sexist – a society in which people can be in touch with their feelings, and in control of their lives'.[54] Twenty years after the May Day Manifesto's revolutionary call, Hall had moved his position significantly, now welcoming the 'proliferation of new points of antagonism' and the 'new social movements of resistance organised around them'. He can no longer identify an 'overall map of how these power relations connect and of their resistances' and concludes that 'perhaps there isn't, in that sense, one "power game" at all, more a network of strategies and powers and their articulations – and thus a politics which is always positional'.[55]

This transformation in political outlook was not sudden: its seeds were evident from the inception of the New Left and related counter-cultural campaigns. Keen to depart from what they perceived to be a crude Marxism – one dependent on a simple determinism between economic forces (modes of production and property relations) and the superstructure (state, family, legal, educational, and cultural practices) – New Lefts and dissident Communists such as Edward Thompson focused increasingly on the 'cultural, experiential and ideological facets of life', representing a position closer to the Marxism of the Italian political theorist Antonio Gramsci than 'an insurrectionary Leninism'.[56] This meant a move away from a focus on production (workers, trade unions, strikes, exploitation) and towards an examination of consumption (lifestyle, cultural practices, subcultural identities, individual subjectivities). Roland Muldoon of Cartoon Archetypal Slogan Theatre (CAST) characterised this move by admitting that 'by the time the working class became active and placed a demand on Theatre, CAST had become enmeshed in its self-importance. Rich situations like Heath *versus* the miners went untouched by us. We were being sidetracked into the Rock culture argument'.[57] And social philosopher André Gorz described a shift in emphasis from productive labour to the production of the self: 'This production takes place not only in the work situation but just as much in the schools, cafes, athletic fields; on voyages; in theatres, concerts, newspapers, books, expositions; in towns, neighbourhoods, discussion and action groups – in short, wherever individuals enter into relationships with one another and produce the universe of human relationships'.[58] This political development manifests itself in Churchill's work: for instance, in the fragmentation seen in the coolly dystopian *Far Away* (2000). As Todd and Joan make increasingly flamboyant hats, they demonstrate no concern for the prisoners who will wear them as part of a gruesome execution ritual. Todd says: 'you make beauty and it disappears, I love that'.[59] This neglect is framed as a deliberate 'un-seeing', an act reflective of the 'willed separation of issues' the May Day Manifesto warned against in 1967.

The deliberate absence of a legible political narrative in *Far Away* amplifies this notion of a 'willed separation of issues' even as it shows individual and collective subjectivities, production and consumption, and wider global and planetary concerns as interrelated. Marxist explanations of ways in which different forms of power interconnect and sustain each other have always been crucial to a politics seeking to challenge capitalism as a system. But some Left thinkers, influenced by the postmodernist theory of Jean-François Lyotard, became preoccupied with margins and individual subjectivities at the expense of large structures and 'grand narratives'.[60] Terry Eagleton comically dismisses one expression of this move – deconstruction – as a practice that 'like much cultural theory . . . can allow one to speak darkly of subversion while leaving one's actual politics only slightly to the left of Edward Kennedy's'. He characterised deconstructionists as treating 'the current system of power' as if it 'can be ceaselessly "interrupted", deferred or "pushed away"', while lamenting their implicit view that 'to try to get beyond it altogether is the most credulous form of utopianism'.[61] Other Left academics expressed anxiety over the knavish game-playing of the postmodernist project. For example, cultural theorist Fred Inglis claimed that 'there is something repellent in the mischievousness with which the deconstructionists toy with the loss of hope in the face of the ugliness of the times'.[62] At the same time, cultural philosopher Kate Soper saw, at least, an advantage in making visible the misdemeanours of postmodernism: it should precipitate a re-engagement with 'more than theory'.[63]

In the 1990s, in the aftermath of Thatcher's reign, the radical environmental movement represented a notable example of those engaging in 'more than theory'. The ecologically focused, non-violent strategies of direct action used by groups such as Reclaim the Streets, Earth First!, and Critical Mass demonstrated 'an "antagonistic" or "intemperate" orientation towards the normative system of production, distribution, exchange and consumption'.[64] Unlike more mainstream environmentalists such as Greenpeace, the Green Party, or Friends of the Earth, radical environmentalists located ecological concerns in broader contexts, and were thus inclined to contest not only ecologically damaging actions but also wider systemic causations. They practised a mode of politics fundamentally contrary to liberal democratic customs – in contrast, again, to the proponents of the

New Times project, who ceded Thatcherite terms. Influenced by the radical art practices of the Dadaists, Situationists, and neo-Marxists such as Henri Lefebvre and Gilles Deleuze, radical environmentalists sought to subvert and reclaim rather than to navigate and influence the political process. The form of protest was considered to be as important as the content, so to negotiate with the State and big business reinforced the power and authority of these very bodies. In contrast, for example, when Reclaim the Streets set up a volleyball court and sound system on the dual carriageway in Birmingham during the May 1988 G8 summit, they sought to reclaim and democratise space, and to make politics pleasurable, as much as they addressed the wider environmental crisis. Of course, treating the form of political protest as itself a means of radicalisation is an approach shared by Churchill in her theatre-making. *Seven Jewish Children* (2009) is a good example of the performative potential of form: aside from the poetic lyricism of the short but epic play, Churchill requires it to be performed with no admission fee but with a collection for Medical Aid to Palestinians (MAP).

Despite the vitality and subversive potential of the radical environmental movement, it remained largely irrelevant to mainstream experience. Its largely reciprocated indifference to the trade union movement and its focus on the politics of consumption rather than production meant that it remained out of the sight of most working people. What was very much in sight (but perhaps 'unseen') during the 'nasty nineties' was Western initiation and exacerbation of war around the world: the first Gulf War and the Sierra Leone conflict in 1991, followed by the Chechen war (1994–96) and the Kosovan intervention in 1999, interspersed with repeated coalition bombings of Baghdad. A growing cynicism and political evasiveness engendered a different structure of feeling, which in turn provided the context for the 'in-yer-face' theatre of Sarah Kane, Mark Ravenhill, Anthony Neilson, and others. Amelia Howe Kritzer has identified the 'deconstruction of social and political categories and goals in the perspectives of postmodern theory' as creating a 'difficult environment' that 'silenced many playwrights on the Left'.[65] The 1990s is thus unsurprisingly the decade that sees Churchill's playwriting at its most oblique. Like

The Skriker, plays such as *Lives of the Great Poisoners* (1991), *Blue Heart* (1997), and *Hotel* (1997) combine multiple forms – dance, song, drama, performance – with a left-field interest in psychology, language, and desire.

More direct forms of political expression, both on and off the stage, rapidly returned in the 2000s. Despite its premiere almost a year before the destruction of the twin towers, *Far Away* has been described by playwright Simon Stephens as the 'strongest theatrical response to 9/11'.[66] And clearly 9/11 and its aftermath catalysed a re-shaping of political consciousness. Taken together, the worldwide anti-war demonstrations on 15 February 2003 constituted the largest protest in history, according to Social Movement theorists Stefaan Walgrave and Dieter Rucht.[67] The Metropolitan Police confirmed the London demonstration to be the largest in British history with an estimated one million participants.[68] Sidney Tarrow considered the protests to be 'something new in the history of contentious politics: a concerted campaign of transnational collective action – using the new tools of the Internet and more conventional means of mobilization – which brought millions of people together around common goals and against common targets'.[69] In addition to the remarkable transnational nature of the coordinated protests, another striking feature was the diversity of those in attendance. As if in rejoinder to the social atomisation imagined in *Far Away*, a multiplicity of communities and individuals, including many who had not previously been politically active, came together collectively 'around common goals'. And this reanimation took place, too, in the theatre. Michael Billington observed in the *Guardian* that 'the disastrous Iraq invasion has galvanised political theatre', and Kate Kellaway wrote in the *Observer* that '9/11, the Iraq War and the Bush administration [have] energised playwrights'.[70]

Of course, the international cooperation evident in the Stop the War movement was helped by the pre-existing Anti-Globalization Movement (AGM), a diverse transnational movement united against the socially unjust effects of corporate capitalism or 'global neoliberalism': unfair trade; market deregulation; cultural homogenisation (so-called McDonaldisation); and the subordination of democratic politics to elitist global economic institutions, such as the World Trade Organisation (WTO). Stephen Gill identifies AGM and World Social Forum (WSF) activism 'as form[ing] part of a world-wide movement that can perhaps be understood in terms of new potentials and forms of global political agency'.[71] The AGM – or 'the movement of movements' as it has been called – involves marginalised groups, poverty and other left activists, exploited workers, environmentalists, intellectuals, and small businesses. It is anti-statist: it is not about 'seizing power' but concerned with building alternatives from the ground up. The WSF brings various communities together at a global level thanks to the Internet, which offers a permanent place of interaction unavailable to earlier anti-systemic politics. The target of the AGM – global neoliberalism – is quite obviously the same target of some of Churchill's twenty-first-century drama, most evidently *Drunk Enough to Say I Love You?* (2006), where the forces of Americanisation (or McDonaldisation) are allegorised in the relationship between Sam (America) and Guy (an everyman).

The potential of the AGM seems to have gone unfulfilled. Owen Worth and Karen Buckley state that '[i]nstead it has suffered from being a directionless series of events, whereby the working formula of "open space" has led to the creation of nothing more than a "talking shop" rather than any valid construction of counter-hegemony'.[72] They also accuse it of elitism: 'the WSF has turned itself into something of an elitist postmodern playground, whereby prominent academics and established NGOs imagine alternative futures and speak on behalf of the subaltern classes'.[73] It is also difficult to assess the potential of the more recent protest movements that have emerged in the aftermath of the 2008 global financial crisis and which were inspired by the Arab Spring, such as the Occupy Movement. Emerging in 2011 under the slogan 'We are the 99 per cent' – an allusion to the huge concentration of wealth in the top 1 per cent of the global population (and an echo of John McGrath's theatre company, 7:84, based on a similar disparity) – the movement proposes a collective (*We* are the 99%) challenge to the brutalities of economic inequality and exploitation. But the Occupy Movement has suffered a heavy and sometimes brutal crackdown by police and security services, particularly in late 2011, and has since struggled to maintain or build on its previous momentum.[74]

The political present remains precarious and uncertain. The 'austerity programmes' currently being imposed on (particularly European) populations provide cover for unprecedented cuts in welfare provisions and an aggressive expansion of privatisation to all spheres of life. Although the second decade of the twenty-first century is in many ways substantially different from the period that saw Churchill's first major plays hit the stage, some of the political problems for Left radicals remain very similar. The synthesis of separate interests, agencies, and groups into collective forms of dissent continues to be the essential but monumental challenge. Most difficult here is the necessity of forming collectives that do not reproduce experiences of marginalisation or clashes of interest, but, at the same time, are politically meaningful. Yet different forms of resistance (strikes, demonstrations, occupations) continue to offer potential for different 'times', and attempts to unify Left oppositional groups are under way.[75] At the very least, in our apparent move beyond postmodernism, we are revisiting and rehabilitating questions of agency, sincerity, and intersubjectivity – questions of interest to Churchill's *Love and Information* (2012). Returning to these concepts – so critical for imagining and enabling a (re)new(ed) Left politics – means that we are likely to witness and experience further re-shapings of our political potential both on and off the stage. This may have the kind of influence on 'the times' that Churchill desires.

EPILOGUE: EXIT THE AUTHOR

In September 2012, the Royal Court issued a surprise announcement. Even as *Love and Information* continued its successful run at the Downstairs theatre, another new play by Caryl Churchill was to receive eight performances in the same space, beginning on 1 October. The show would take place 'around' the main attraction, according to the press release; it would fit itself, in other words, into the spatial and temporal gaps left by the Court's other Churchill production. So a new cast of six came to inhabit the white cube of the *Love and Information* set, squatters in an environment not their own. And so theatregoers came to Sloane Square at odd times (4:00 p.m. on this day, 6:30 p.m. on that) to receive the latest theatrical missive from Britain's most formally daring playwright.

Ding Dong the Wicked begins with a short sharp shock as a 'Quiet Man' shoots the person he has invited to '[c]ome in': a bold announcement of the play's signal brutality.[1] Time passes before a 'Young Woman Carrying a Flower' enters the house with a 'Woman in Blue', the quiet man's sister-in-law. She joins a stage family populated also by her husband ('Overweight Man') and mother ('Woman Who Bites'), all of them gathered to send a soldier off to war: a 'Pale Young Man' who is son to the woman in blue and lover to the flower-carrying young woman. But a television report interrupts their farewell by announcing the death of (we presume) the play's titular despot. Their explosion of triumph culminates in a chant: 'Zig zig zig, zag zag zag, zig zig zig, zag zag zag'.[2] There is no closure. Instead, a second act moves to '[*a*]*nother country*' and an identical living room in which the same furniture is rearranged.[3] So is the cast, re-appearing to embody new roles constellated as a new family: a 'Drunk Woman' and her mother ('Woman with a Limp'), daughter ('Young Woman with a Cigarette'), and son-in-law ('Man Who Bites His Nails'). They too inhabit a setting suffused with aggression and menace. And they too prepare a man for battle: the nail-biting man's brother, a 'Speedy Young

Man' costumed in a different military uniform. Their gathering similarly climaxes in a television assassination and incites the same zig-zag chant, at once nonsensical and unmistakably bellicose. After a 'Man Who is a Wreck' arrives, the act ends with a ringing doorbell that provokes an invitation: '[c]ome in'.[4] It is, of course, the line that opened the play, spoken – per the magic of doubling – by a different character and yet recognisably the same actor.

The play's *mise-en-scène* mimics the writing constraints that govern its *mise-en-page*. For just as *Ding Dong the Wicked* repurposes its first-act furniture and actors, so too does the first-act dialogue reappear in its entirety, its every line now reconfigured and resituated in the landscape of the second act. The shuffling and redistribution of words alters their meanings and turns monologues into dialogues. Changes in punctuation reshape affirmations into inquisitions. Syntactic variations prove transformative: for instance, 'the body' 'by the road' mutates disturbingly from a dead dog to a dead person.[5] Yet revenant words ('jellybelly', 'lefthandedness') and images (a faltering marriage, a locked-away child) serve as beacons. They signal Churchill's method of construction and conjure the first act's world, now putatively far away. Adopting arbitrary constraints better known to experimental poetry, Churchill seems to comment on the diminished political possibilities of the present day. Progressive action appears straitened: 'I think people should try to forgive each other' is twice declared, twice rebuked.[6] Clichés are recycled like old hostilities: '[t]hey want to destroy us', '[s]he was asking for it'.[7] Xenophobia triumphs. Each of the play's two tribes fears others deemed worthy of punishment and dismissed as 'bastards', an epithet that appears ten times in twenty-two pages. Thus the play alloys the oblique politics of Churchill's later work with her signature metatheatricality. As in *Blue Heart*, the author's hand reveals itself, her structural conceits controlling a diptych text. And as in *Far Away*, an allegorical world – here conveyed by unnamed settings and characters – reveals itself as our own, as in the film from which Churchill recycled her title. Unlike Oz, however, our world is riven by antagonisms that no dictator's deposition can quell. The play cannot move past its lexicon of alleged heroes and retributive killing. It ends as it begins.

Close scrutiny of the text – my copy is now annotated, highlighted, and cut up almost to illegibility – reveals fissures in an apparently rigid construction. For example, the first act's assertion that 'the government want to take that away', with its relative pronoun reaching back to the overweight man's money, reappears in the second act as 'the government wants to take that away', referring to the drunk woman's pastoral view.[8] Note the grapheme <s>, newly trailing 'want'. Thematically, the letter shifts the setting from a speech community in which collective nouns are plural (such as the United Kingdom) to one in which one they are singular (such as the United States). This may seem just another tribal difference. But by slyly undermining her play's governing constraint, Churchill offers an escape from an apparently closed system. Smattered words from Act 1 never recur as expected (e.g. *who*, *yes*, *so*); and Act 2 introduces a compensatory smattering of its own (e.g. *did*, *can*, *out*). A single line from Act 1 ('He'll be down in a minute') lacks a twin entirely, even if it is shadowed by a different line which makes its sole appearance in Act 2 ('That's dead, that's really dead').[9] The variation seems to replace anticipation and futurity with deadly certitude. But if the play's limited lexicon exposes the inadequacy of contemporary political discourse, these cracks in its limits may make room for political difference. Death may not be certain. There is no indication whether the man who bites his nails will shoot the doorbell-ringer at the play's end, for instance, as the quiet man had done in the opening scene – even if (recalling Chekhov's famous dictum) the first act's gun has already been re-introduced in the second.

A lot depends on performance. After all, even as the text generates an undeniable anxiety with its cryptic references to killing and threatened ways of life, the precise meanings of its lines depend on the conditions of their utterance. This is the lesson, of course, of the play's constant repetitions with difference, its second act's repeated citations of its first. But as in other late plays such as *Drunk Enough to Say I Love You?* or *Seven Jewish Children*, the supplementary work of performers proves essential. In *Ding Dong the Wicked*'s premiere at the Royal Court, for example – directed by its outgoing Artistic Director, Dominic Cooke – the overweight man asked '[w]hat's happening out there?' in the first act, as the script requires.[10] But the ambiguous line's meanings were determined by the actor Stuart McQuarrie, and these differed from those imposed by Daniel Kendrick when he uttered the same line, in a revised dramatic situation, as the second act's speedy young man. The line will manifest still other meanings when the play is performed anew in future productions and future contexts. In *Love and Information*, Churchill had required directors and actors to generate sense for themselves, denying them stage directions or even characters. And in this sense, too, *Ding Dong the Wicked* may have taken place 'around' the larger play, serving as its thematic complement. The main attraction directs our attention to interpersonal micropolitics, even as its absent speech prefixes demand that we invent the relationships for ourselves. The interstitial play inhabits the negative space: it orients us to the macropolitics of nationalism and to the zigzagging lurches of foreign policy that so easily alter individual lives. Or at least that's my reading of a work which, even more than most, commands me to perform one.

As I was waiting to enter the theatre on 11 October 2012 – *Ding Dong the Wicked*'s curtain that day was 4:15 p.m. – I spotted Churchill in the Royal Court's downstairs bar. I managed to eke out a few star-struck sentences before I took my seat and was immersed in the play's unsettling twinned worlds, inhabited by a cast including John Marquez (one of Churchill's *Identical Twins* at the Court ten years earlier, in a production also directed by Cooke) and Jennie Stoller (a performer in his production of *Seven Jewish Children*, as well as *Fen*'s inaugural Val in 1983). Leaving the theatre twenty-five minutes later, I saw the playwright again, standing apart from the crowd as it snaked out the Downstairs theatre and up toward Sloane Square. I might have asked her about the play's precise relationship to *Love and Information* – less clear, certainly, than that between *Icecream* and its curtain-raiser, *Hot Fudge*. I might have asked her about the play's resonance with *The Ants*, the early radio drama with which it shares thematic affinities but whose political meanings prove easier to apprehend. I might have asked her about that opening shot, a rare act of onstage violence for a writer whose guns (whether Joshua's in *Cloud Nine* or the soldiers' in *Mad Forest*) usually remain undischarged or offstage.[11] But even before

I had much interpretive traction on *Ding Dong the Wicked*, I knew that it would rebuke such grasping after authorial intent. After all, Churchill best prepared us for her cryptic twenty-first-century plays decades ago, when she stopped commenting on her work.[12] And the meanings that this work generates – and the political energies that this work inspires – belong, finally, to its performers and audiences. Accordingly, I asked her no questions. I said goodbye, I climbed the stairs, and I stepped out of the theatre and onto the street.

APPENDIX A
ALPHABETICAL LIST OF CHURCHILL WORKS DISCUSSED

Note: Parenthetical dates indicate *first* performance and publication.

Abortive (production 1971; publication 1990). In Caryl Churchill, *Shorts*, London: Nick Hern Books, 1990, pp.21–36.

The After-Dinner Joke (production 1978; publication 1990). In Churchill, *Shorts*, pp.165–221.

The Ants (production 1962; publication 1969). In Irving Wardle (ed.), *New English Dramatists 12: Radio Plays*, Harmondsworth: Penguin Books, 1969, pp.89–103.

Bliss [translation of Olivier Choinière's *Félicité*] (production and publication 2008). London: Nick Hern Books, 2008.

Blue Heart (production and publication 1997). In Caryl Churchill, *Plays: Four*, London: Nick Hern Books, 2008, pp.59–129.

The Brown Bride (unproduced and unpublished, c. 1962).

Cloud Nine (production and publication 1979). In Caryl Churchill, *Plays: One*, London: Methuen Drama, 1985, pp.243–320.

Crimes (production 1982; unpublished).

The Death of Tintagiles [after Maurice Maeterlinck] (unproduced and unpublished, 1998).

The Demonstration (unfinished; unproduced and unpublished, c. 1962).

Ding Dong the Wicked (production and publication 2012). London: Nick Hern Books, 2012.

Downstairs (amateur production 1958; unpublished).

A Dream Play [after August Strindberg] (production and publication 2005). In Churchill, *Plays: Four*, pp.207–65.

Drunk Enough to Say I Love You? (production and publication 2006). In Churchill, *Plays: Four*, pp.267–309.

Easy Death (amateur production 1962; unpublished).

Far Away (production and publication 2000). In Churchill, *Plays: Four*, pp.129–59.
Fen (production and publication 1983). In Caryl Churchill, *Plays: Two*, London: Methuen Drama, 1990, pp.143–92.
The Finnsburg Fragment (unproduced and unpublished, c. 1961).
Floorshow [contributor to Monstrous Regiment cabaret, with David Bradford, Bryony Lavery, and Michelene Wandor] (production 1978; unpublished).
Fugue [with Ian Spink] (production 1988; unpublished).
Having a Wonderful Time (amateur production 1960; unpublished).
Henry's Past (production 1972; unpublished).
The Hospital at the Time of the Revolution (publication 1990; production 2013). In Churchill, *Shorts*, pp.95–146.
Hot Fudge (production and publication 1989). In Churchill, *Shorts*, pp.275–304.
Hotel (production and publication 1997). In Churchill, *Plays: Four*, pp.1–36.
Icecream (production and publication 1989). In Caryl Churchill, *Plays: Three*, London: Nick Hern Books, 1998, pp.55–102.
Identical Twins (production 1968; unpublished).
Interior [after Maurice Maeterlinck] (unproduced and unpublished, 1998).
The Intruder [after Maurice Maeterlinck] (unproduced and unpublished, 1998).
Iraq.doc (production 2003; unpublished).
The Judge's Wife (production 1972; publication 1990). In Churchill, *Shorts*, pp.147–63.
Lee (unproduced and unpublished, 1963).
The Legion Hall Bombing (production 1978; unpublished).
Light Shining in Buckinghamshire (production 1976; publication 1978). In Churchill, *Plays: One*, pp.181–241.
Lives of the Great Poisoners (production 1991; publication 1993). In Churchill, *Plays: Three*, pp.183–237.
Love and Information (production and publication 2012). London: Nick Hern Books, 2012.

The Love Salesman (unfinished; unproduced and unpublished, c. 1962).

Lovesick (production 1967; publication 1990). In Churchill, *Shorts*, pp.1–19.

Mad Forest: A Play from Romania (production and publication 1990). In Churchill, *Plays: Three*, pp.101–81.

The Magic Ring (unfinished; unproduced and unpublished, c. 1962).

The Marriage of Toby's Idea of Angela and Toby's Idea of Angela's Idea of Toby (unproduced and unpublished, 1968).

Midday Sun [with Geraldine Pilgrim and Pete Brooks] (production 1984; unpublished).

A Mouthful of Birds [with David Lan] (production and publication 1986). In Churchill, *Plays: Three*, pp.1–53.

Moving Clocks Go Slow (production 1975; unpublished).

Not Not Not Not Not Enough Oxygen (production 1971; publication 1990). In Churchill, *Shorts*, pp.37–55.

A Number (production and publication 2002). In Churchill, *Plays: Four*, pp.161–206.

Objections to Sex and Violence (production 1975; publication 1985). In Michelene Wandor (ed.), *Plays by Women: Volume 4*, London: Methuen, 1985, pp.11–51.

Owners (production 1972; publication 1973). In Churchill, *Plays: One*, pp.1–67.

Perfect Happiness (production 1973; unpublished).

Portrait of an Artist (unproduced and unpublished, c. 1961).

A Ring a Lamp a Thing [libretto for Orlando Gough] (production 2010; unpublished).

Save It for the Minister [with Mary O'Malley and Cherry Potter] (production 1975; unpublished).

Schreber's Nervous Illness (production 1972; publication 1990). In Churchill, *Shorts*, pp.57–93.

Seagulls (publication 1990; production 2002). In Churchill, *Shorts*, pp.223–43.

Serious Money (production and publication 1987). In Churchill, *Plays: Two*, pp.193–309.

Seven Jewish Children (production and publication 2009). Available at http://graphics8.nytimes.com/packages/pdf/world/SevenJewishChildren.pdf

'she bit her tongue' [monologue for Siobhan Davies's *Plants and Ghosts*] (production and publication 2002). Available at http://www.siobhandaviesreplay.com/media2/UserType/00000000/00000000/00000589.pdf

A Shout in the Street (unproduced and unpublished, c. 1961).

The Skriker (production and publication 1994). In Churchill, *Plays: Three*, pp.239–91.

Softcops (production and publication 1984). In Churchill, *Plays: Two*, pp.1–49.

Strange Days [with Joan Mills] (amateur production 1975; partial publication 2008). In Philip Roberts, *About Churchill: The Playwright and the Work*, London: Faber, 2008, pp.172–7.

This Is a Chair (production and publication 1997). In Churchill, *Plays: Four*, pp.37–58.

Three More Sleepless Nights (production 1980; publication 1990). In Churchill, *Shorts*, pp.245–73.

Thyestes [after Seneca] (production 1994; publication 1995). In Churchill, *Plays: Three*, pp.293–344.

Top Girls (production and publication 1982). In Churchill, *Plays: Two*, pp.51–141.

Traps (production 1977; publication 1978). In Churchill, *Plays: One*, pp.69–125.

Turkish Delight (production 1974; unpublished).

Vinegar Tom (production 1976; publication 1978). In Churchill, *Plays: One*, pp.127–79.

We Turned on the Light [libretto for Orlando Gough] (production 2006; publication 2008). In Roberts, *About Churchill*, p.268.

You've No Need to Be Frightened (amateur production 1961; unpublished).

Linda Fitzsimmons's *File on Churchill*, London: Methuen Drama, 1989, notes four other early plays – *The Swimming Club, The Loonies, Comic Strips from the Chinese*, and *Angel* – that remain unproduced and unpublished. The absence of these plays from the BBC Written Archives Centre suggests that they were not circulating in the Scripts Department as other Churchill plays of the period – whether written for radio, television, or stage – were.

APPENDIX B
CHRONOLOGICAL LIST OF CHURCHILL PRODUCTIONS DISCUSSED

Note: Opening nights indicate first public showing for shows with previews.

Downstairs, dir Wilfred De'Ath. Opened 4 Nov. 1958, Oriel College Dramatic Society, Oxford University.

Having a Wonderful Time, dir E. Gilbert. Opened 5 Aug. 1960, Questors Theatre, Ealing.

Easy Death, dir Paul Burge. Opened 9 Mar. 1962, Experimental Theatre Club, Oxford University.

The Ants, dir Michael Bakewell. Broadcast on BBC Radio 3, 27 Nov. 1962.

Lovesick, dir John Tydeman. Broadcast on BBC Radio 3, 8 Apr. 1967.

Identical Twins, dir John Tydeman. Broadcast on BBC Radio 3, 21 Nov. 1968.

Abortive, dir John Tydeman. Broadcast on BBC Radio 3, 4 Feb. 1971.

Not Not Not Not Not Enough Oxygen, dir John Tydeman. Broadcast on BBC Radio 3, 31 Mar. 1971.

Schreber's Nervous Illness, dir John Tydeman. Broadcast on BBC Radio 3, 25 July 1972.

The Judge's Wife, dir James Ferman. Broadcast on BBC 2, 2 Oct. 1972.

Schreber's Nervous Illness, dir Kenneth Haigh. Opened 5 Dec. 1972, King's Head Theatre, London.

Henry's Past, dir John Tydeman. Broadcast on BBC Radio 3, 5 Dec. 1972.

Owners, dir Nicholas Wright. Opened 6 Dec. 1972, Royal Court Theatre Upstairs.

Owners, dir Terese Hayden. Opened 14 May 1973, Mercer-Shaw Theatre, New York.

Perfect Happiness, dir John Tydeman. Broadcast on BBC Radio 3, 30 Sept. 1973.

Turkish Delight, dir Herbert Wise. Broadcast on BBC 2, 22 Apr. 1974.

Objections to Sex and Violence, dir John Tydeman. Opened 2 Jan. 1975, Royal Court Theatre Downstairs.

Moving Clocks Go Slow, dir John Ashford. Opened 15 June 1975, Royal Court Theatre Upstairs.

Save It for the Minister (with Mary O'Malley and Cherry Potter), dir Piers Haggard. Broadcast on BBC 2, 26 July 1975.

Light Shining in Buckinghamshire, dir Max Stafford-Clark for Joint Stock. Opened 7 Sept. 1976, Traverse Theatre, Edinburgh. Transferred 21 Sept. 1976, Royal Court Theatre Upstairs.

Vinegar Tom, dir Pam Brighton for Monstrous Regiment. Opened 12 Oct. 1976, Humberside Theatre, Hull. Transferred 14 Dec. 1976, ICA, London. Transferred 17 Jan. 1977, Half Moon Theatre, London.

Traps, dir John Ashford. Opened 27 Jan. 1977, Royal Court Theatre Upstairs.

Floorshow (with David Bradford, Bryony Lavery, and Michelene Wandor), dir David Bradford. Opened 18 Jan. 1978, Theatre Royal, Stratford East.

The After-Dinner Joke, dir Colin Bucksey. Broadcast on BBC 1, 14 Feb. 1978.

The Legion Hall Bombing, dir Roland Joffe. Broadcast on BBC 1, 22 Aug. 1978.

Cloud Nine, dir Max Stafford-Clark for Joint Stock. Tour opened 14 Feb. 1979, Dartington College. Opened 27 Mar. 1979, Royal Court Theatre Downstairs.

Three More Sleepless Nights, dir Les Waters. Opened 9 June 1980, Soho Poly Theatre, London. Transferred 5 Aug. 1980, Royal Court Theatre Upstairs.

Cloud Nine, dirs Max Stafford-Clark and Les Waters for Joint Stock. Opened 4 Sept. 1980, Royal Court Theatre Downstairs.

Cloud Nine, dir Tommy Tune. Opened 18 May 1981, Theatre de Lys (now Lucille Lortel), New York.

Crimes, dir Stuart Burge. Broadcast on BBC 1, 13 Apr. 1982.

Top Girls, dir Max Stafford-Clark. Opened 23 Aug. 1982, Royal Court Theatre Downstairs. Transferred 21 Dec. 1982, Public Theater, New York (Newman).

Fen, dir Les Waters for Joint Stock. Tour opened 20 Jan. 1983, University of Essex. Opened 16 Feb. 1983, Almeida Theatre, London. Transferred 24 May 1983, Public Theater, New York (LuEsther). Transferred 29 July 1983, Royal Court Theatre Downstairs.

Top Girls, dir Max Stafford-Clark. Opened 24 Feb. 1983, Public Theater, New York (Newman).

Traps, dir William Petersen. Opened 10 Mar. 1983, Remains Theatre, Chicago.

Softcops, dir Howard Davies. Opened 2 Jan. 1984, Barbican Pit, London.

Fen, dir Les Waters. Opened 23 Feb. 1984, Public Theater, New York (Newman).

Midday Sun (with Geraldine Pilgrim and Pete Brooks), dir John Ashford. Opened 8 May 1984, ICA, London.

Fen, dir Rita Giomi. Opened 3 Dec. 1985, Empty Space Theater (Second Space), Seattle.

Fen, dir Tony Taccone. Opened 4 Dec. 1985, Eureka Theatre, San Francisco.

A Mouthful of Birds (with David Lan), dirs Ian Spink and Les Waters for Joint Stock. Tour opened 29 Aug. 1986, Birmingham Repertory Theatre. Opened 26 Nov. 1986, Royal Court Theatre Downstairs.

Fen, dir Dan LaMorte. Opened 26 Feb. 1987, Center Theater, Chicago.

Serious Money, dir Max Stafford-Clark. Opened 21 Mar. 1987, Royal Court Theatre Downstairs. Transferred 6 July 1987, Wyndham's Theatre, London. Transferred 22 Nov. 1987, Public Theater, New York (Newman).

Owners, dir Annie Castledine. Opened 6 Apr. 1987, Young Vic, London.

Serious Money, dir Max-Stafford Clark. Opened 20 Jan. 1988, Royale Theatre, Broadway.

Traps, dir John Stix. Opened 22 Mar. 1988, Theater Upstairs, St John's in the Village, New York.

Fugue (with Ian Spink), dir Ian Spink. Broadcast on Channel Four, 26 June 1988.

Icecream, dir Max Stafford-Clark. Opened 11 Apr. 1989, Royal Court Theatre Downstairs.

Icecream with Hot Fudge, dir Les Waters. Opened 3 May 1990, Public Theater, New York (Newman).

Mad Forest: A Play from Romania, dir Mark Wing-Davey. Opened 25 June 1990, Embassy Theatre, Central School for Speech and Drama, London. Transferred 17 Sept. 1990, National Theatre, Bucharest. Transferred 9 Oct. 1990, Royal Court Theatre Downstairs.

Lives of the Great Poisoners (with Ian Spink and Orlando Gough), dir James Macdonald. Tour opened 13 Feb. 1991, Arnolfini, Bristol.

Light Shining in Buckinghamshire, dir Lisa Peterson. Opened 16 Feb. 1991, Perry Street Theatre (for New York Theatre Workshop).

Top Girls, dir Max Stafford-Clark. Tour opened 5 Mar. 1991, Warwick Arts Centre. Opened 10 Apr. 1991, Royal Court Theatre Downstairs.

Top Girls, dir Max Stafford-Clark (film for television). Broadcast on BBC 1, 2 Nov. 1991.

Mad Forest: A Play from Romania, dir Mark Wing-Davey. Opened 22 Nov. 1991, Perry Street Theatre (for New York Theatre Workshop). Transferred 22 Sept. 1992, Manhattan Theatre Club.

Owners, dir Mark Wing-Davey. Opened 5 Mar. 1993, New York Theatre Workshop.

Traps, dir Lisa Peterson. Opened 12 Mar. 1993, New York Theatre Workshop.

The Skriker, dir Les Waters. Opened 20 Jan. 1994, National Theatre Cottesloe.

Thyestes, dir James Macdonald. Opened 7 June 1994, Royal Court Theatre Upstairs.

The Skriker, dir Mark Wing-Davey. Opened 26 Apr. 1996, Public Theater, New York (Newman).

Light Shining in Buckinghamshire, dir Mark Wing-Davey. Tour opened 7 Nov. 1996, Gulbenkian Theatre, Canterbury. Opened 9 Jan. 1997, National Theatre Cottesloe.

Cloud Nine, dir Tom Cairns. Opened 10 Mar. 1997, Old Vic, London.

Hotel (with Orlando Gough and Ian Spink), dir Ian Spink. Opened 15 Apr. 1997, Schauspielhaus, Hanover, Germany. Opened 22 Apr. 1997, The Place, London.

This Is a Chair, dir Stephen Daldry. Opened 25 June 1997, Royal Court at Duke of York's Theatre.

Blue Heart, dir Max Stafford-Clark. Opened 14 Aug. 1997, Theatre Royal, Bury St Edmunds. Transferred 19 Aug. 1997, Traverse Theatre, Edinburgh. Transferred 17 Sept. 1997, Royal Court at Duke of York's Theatre.

Blue Heart, dir Max Stafford-Clark. Opened 27 Jan. 1999, Brooklyn Academy of Music, New York.

Our Late Night (by Wallace Shawn), dir Caryl Churchill. Opened 20 Oct. 1999, Royal Court at New Ambassadors Theatre, London.

Far Away, dir Stephen Daldry. Opened 24 Nov. 2000, Royal Court Jerwood Theatre Upstairs. Transferred 18 Jan. 2001, Albery Theatre, London.

Far Away, dir Peter Brook. Opened 22 Jan. 2002, Théâtre des Bouffes du Nord, Paris.

A Number, dir Stephen Daldry. Opened 23 Sept. 2002, Royal Court Jerwood Theatre Downstairs.

Identical Twins, dir Dominic Cooke. Opened 1 Oct. 2002, Royal Court Jerwood Theatre Downstairs.

Seagulls, dir Caryl Churchill (rehearsed reading). Opened 3 Oct. 2002, Royal Court Jerwood Theatre Downstairs.

Not Not Not Not Not Enough Oxygen, dir Ian Rickson. Opened 7 Oct. 2002, Royal Court Jerwood Theatre Upstairs.

Far Away, dir Ron Sossi. Opened 15 Nov. 2003, Odyssey Theatre Ensemble, Los Angeles.

Far Away, dir Simon Cox. Opened 2 June 2004, Studio Theatre, Sheffield.

Fen, dir Simon Cox. Opened 2 June 2004, Studio Theatre, Sheffield.

Fen, dir Jimmy Fay. Opened 30 June 2004, Project Arts Centre, Dublin.

A Number, dir James Macdonald. Opened 16 Nov. 2004, New York Theatre Workshop.

A Dream Play, dir Katie Mitchell. Opened 4 Feb. 2005, National Theatre Cottesloe.

We Turned on the Light (with Orlando Gough), conductors Martyn Brabbins and Orlando Gough. Opened 29 July 2006, Royal Albert Hall, London for BBC Proms.

Drunk Enough to Say I Love You?, dir James Macdonald. Opened 10 Nov. 2006, Royal Court Jerwood Theatre Downstairs.

A Dream Play, dir Allison Arkell Stockman. Opened 16 June 2007, Source Theatre, Washington.

Cloud Nine, dir Thea Sharrock. Opened 25 Oct. 2007, Almeida Theatre, London.

Drunk Enough to Say I Love You?, dir James Macdonald. Opened 5 Mar. 2008, Public Theater, New York (Newman).

Bliss (by Olivier Choinière), dir Joe Hill-Gibbons. Opened 28 Mar. 2008, Royal Court Jerwood Theatre Upstairs.

Top Girls, dir James Macdonald. Opened 7 May 2008, Biltmore Theatre, New York.

Light Shining in Buckinghamshire, dir Mark Ravenhill (rehearsed reading). Opened 17 Sept. 2008, Royal Court Jerwood Theatre Downstairs.

Icecream, dir Wallace Shawn (rehearsed reading). Opened 23 Sept. 2008, Royal Court Jerwood Theatre Downstairs.

Seven Jewish Children, dir Dominic Cooke. Opened 6 Feb. 2009, Royal Court Jerwood Theatre Downstairs.

Serious Money, dir Jonathan Munby. Opened 8 May 2009, Birmingham Repertory Theatre.

A Thought in Three Parts (by Wallace Shawn), dir Caryl Churchill (rehearsed reading). Opened 19 June 2009, Royal Court Jerwood Theatre Downstairs.

The Skriker, dir Alix Sobler. Opened 2 Feb. 2010, Echo (Beach) Theatre, Winnipeg.

Far Away, dir Simon Godwin. Opened 24 May 2010, Bristol Old Vic.

A Ring a Lamp a Thing (with Orlando Gough), dir James Macdonald. Opened 18 June 2010, Linbury Studio Theatre, Royal Opera House, London.

Light Shining in Buckinghamshire, dir Polly Findlay. Opened 14 July 2010, Arcola Theatre, London.

Serious Money, dir Eda Holmes. Opened 31 July 2010, Shaw Festival Studio Theatre, Niagara-on-the-Lake, Canada.

The Skriker, dirs Amy Wyllie and Sally Waters. Opened 27 Jan. 2011, Theatre Royal, Bury St Edmunds.

Fen, dir Ria Parry. Opened 1 Mar. 2011, Finborough Theatre, London.

Top Girls, dir Max Stafford-Clark. Opened 23 June 2011, Minerva Theatre, Chichester. Transferred 16 Aug. 2011, Trafalgar Studios, London. Tour opened 18 Jan. 2012, Warwick Arts Centre.

Serious Money, dir Cheryl Faraone. Opened 5 July 2012, Atlantic Theater Company, New York. Revived 3 July 2013.

Love and Information, dir James Macdonald. Opened 6 Sept. 2012, Royal Court Jerwood Theatre Downstairs.

Ding Dong the Wicked, dir Dominic Cooke. Opened 1 Oct. 2012, Royal Court Jerwood Theatre Downstairs.

The Hospital at the Time of the Revolution, dir James Russell. Opened 31 Mar. 2013, Finborough Theatre, London.

Love and Information, dir James Macdonald. Opened 4 Feb. 2014, Minetta Lane Theatre (for New York Theatre Workshop).

NOTES AND REFERENCES

Preface and Acknowledgements: The Theatre of Caryl Churchill

1. Caryl Churchill, *Turkish Delight*, unpublished typescript, p.6.
2. *Ibid.*, p.27, p.28.
3. *Ibid.*, p.32, p.34.
4. *Ibid.*, p.18.
5. Churchill interviewed by Emily Mann in Kathleen Betsko and Rachel Koenig (eds), *Interviews with Contemporary Women Playwrights*, New York: Beech Tree Books, 1987, pp.75–84, at p.78.
6. Elaine Aston, *Caryl Churchill* (3rd edn), Horndon: Northcote House Publishers, 2010, p.43.
7. David Greig, 'The Best Performance I've Ever Seen', *Observer*, 29 May 2011.
8. Churchill, *Turkish Delight*, p.35.
9. *Ibid.*, p.2.
10. Gertrude Stein, 'Plays' in *Last Operas and Plays*, Baltimore: Johns Hopkins University Press, 1995, pp.xxix–lii, at p.xxxvi.

Chapter 1

1. Qtd in Jim Hiley, 'Revolution in Miniature', *The Times*, 10 Oct. 1990.
2. Qtd in Heidi Stephenson and Natasha Langridge (eds), *Rage and Reason: Women Playwrights on Playwriting*, London: Methuen, 1997, p.6.
3. Qtd in Sarah Lyall, 'The Mysteries of Caryl Churchill', *New York Times*, 5 Dec. 2004.
4. August Strindberg, Preface to *Miss Julie*, Michael Robinson (trans.), Oxford: Oxford University Press, 1998, p.56.

5. See Hanna's remarks in Philip Roberts, *About Churchill: The Playwright and the Work*, London: Faber, 2008, p.209.
6. See Lynn Truss, 'A Fair Cop', *Plays and Players*, No. 364 (Jan. 1984), pp.8–10, at p.8.
7. See Roberts, *About Churchill*, p.81.
8. The fact is recorded in Stafford-Clark's diary, held at the British Library.
9. Caryl Churchill, *Top Girls* in *Plays: Two*, London: Methuen Drama, 1990, pp.51–141, at p.137.
10. *Ibid.*, p.113.
11. *Ibid.*, p.67.
12. *Ibid.*, p.122.
13. *Ibid.*, p.120.
14. *Ibid.*, p.141.
15. See a 1986 letter qtd in Linda Fitzsimmons (ed.), *File on Churchill*, London: Methuen Drama, 1989, p.63.
16. On changes in social mobility after Thatcher, see Jo Blanden et al., 'Changes in Intergenerational Mobility in Britain' in Miles Corak (ed.), *Generational Income Mobility in North America and Europe*, Cambridge: Cambridge University Press, 2004, pp.122–46.
17. Churchill, *Top Girls*, p.140, p.138; Margaret Thatcher, *The Downing Street Years*, London: HarperCollins, 1993, p.626.
18. Churchill, *Top Girls*, p.139.
19. *Ibid.*, p.137.
20. The remark, made in 1960, is qtd in Tessa ten Tusscher, 'Patriarchy, Capitalism and the New Right' in Judith Evans et al. (eds), *Feminism and Political Theory*, London: Sage Publications, p.66–84, at p.79. For her discovery of this detail I am grateful to Janet E. Gardner (who misquotes it slightly). Thatcher appointed the first (and only) woman to cabinet in 1982: the unelected Baroness Young, now best remembered for her unbending prejudice against gays and lesbians. Comparing British Parliaments since World War II, only 1951 elected fewer women than 1979; Thatcher's 339-strong caucus contained only seven others.
21. Churchill, *Top Girls*, p.138.
22. *Ibid.*, p.130

23. *Ibid.*, p.127.
24. *Ibid.*, p.138.
25. Janet E. Gardner, 'Caryl Churchill's *Top Girls*: Defining and Reclaiming Feminism in Thatcher's Britain', *New England Theatre Journal*, Vol. 10 (1999), pp.89–110, at p.106.
26. Churchill, *Top Girls*, p.129, p.121, p.91. Stafford-Clark's diary for 21 July (MS 79554, p.124) takes up this theme when he wonders 'Y is Joyce such a horrid mum'?
27. See Lisa Merrill, 'Monsters and Heroines: Caryl Churchill's Women' in Phyllis R. Randall (ed.), *Caryl Churchill: A Casebook*, New York: Garland Publishing, 1988, pp.71–89, at pp.86–7.
28. Churchill, *Top Girls*, p.140.
29. *Ibid.*
30. Caryl Churchill, *Crimes*, unpublished typescript, p.12.
31. Churchill, *Top Girls*, p.94.
32. Trevor R. Griffiths, 'Waving Not Drowning: The Mainstream, 1979–88' in Trevor R. Griffiths and Margaret Llewellyn-Jones (eds), *British and Irish Women Dramatists Since 1958: A Critical Handbook*, Buckingham: Open University Press, 1993, pp.47–76, at p.53.
33. Churchill, *Top Girls*, p.141.
34. Qtd in Laurie Stone, 'Caryl Churchill Makes Room at the Top', *Village Voice*, 1 Mar. 1983.
35. Qtd in Roberts, *About Churchill*, p.86.
36. Churchill, *Top Girls*, p.100.
37. Lizbeth Goodman and Juli Thompson Burk, 'Contemporary Women's Theatre: *Top Girls*' in Lizbeth Goodman (ed.), *Literature and Gender*, London: Routledge, 1996, pp.229–51, at p.232.
38. The letter, addressed to John Tydeman and dated 22 Feb. 1966, is held at the BBC Written Archives Centre in Reading, Folder RCont. 12 [Caryl Churchill Scriptwriter File II: 1963–67].
39. Churchill had been referred to Ramsay by her erstwhile Oxford colleague, the playwright John McGrath, and had sent to the agent *Downstairs*, her first produced play; *Having a Wonderful Time*, her first staged outside of Oxford; and *A Shout in the Street*, an unproduced teleplay about pacifism. See Colin Chambers,

Peggy: The Life of Margaret Ramsay, Play Agent, London: Methuen, 1997, p.268.

40. *Ibid.*, p.241.
41. See the letter from Churchill to Tydeman, dated 8 May 1966 and held at the BBC Written Archives Centre, in which she describes her upset work schedule.
42. Qtd in Goodman and Burk, 'Contemporary', p.232.
43. Chambers, *Peggy*, p.272.
44. Stafford-Clark, MS 79553, 1 Mar. 1982, p.266.
45. Stafford-Clark has sometimes perpetrated this myth himself. In an interview in the *Guardian*, for instance, he claimed, 'She wrote the scene in the form of monologues, and I said, "Caryl, that's too difficult". So she cut the monologues together'. See Melissa Denes, 'How We Made: Max Stafford-Clark and Lesley Manville on *Top Girls*', *Guardian*, 16 Jan. 2012. The article was amended eight days later, at Stafford-Clark's own request and faulting his memory.
46. My analysis draws on two typescripts: the initial rehearsal script in London (held at Blythe House) and a later draft sent to Joseph Papp, which appears among his papers in the Billy Rose Theatre Division, New York Public Library for the Performing Arts. Churchill confirms the change in Lizbeth Goodman, 'Overlapping Dialogue in Overlapping Media: Behind the Scenes of *Top Girls*' in Sheila Rabillard (ed.), *Essays on Caryl Churchill: Contemporary Representations*, Winnipeg: Blizzard Publishing, 1998, pp.69–101, at p.91.

    She and director James Macdonald would revert to her original beginning decades later, for the play's 2008 Broadway revival.
47. See Manville's remarks in Denes, 'How We Made'.
48. Stafford-Clark, MS 79554, pp.160–1.
49. *Ibid.*, p.182.
50. Francis King, 'Top Heavy', *Sunday Telegraph*, 5 Sept. 1982; Carol Rumens, 'The Price of Success', *Times Literary Supplement*, 24 Sept. 1982.
51. Ned Chaillet, Rev. of *Top Girls*, *The Times*, 2 Sept. 1982.
52. Robert Cushman, 'Churchill at the Court', *Observer*, 5 Sept. 1982.

53. See Churchill interviewed by Emily Mann in Kathleen Betsko and Rachel Koenig (eds), *Interviews with Contemporary Women Playwrights*, New York: Beech Tree Books, 1987, pp.75–84, at p.77. The location of the visit is revealed in Helene Keyssar, 'The Dramas of Caryl Churchill: The Politics of Possibility', *Massachusetts Review: A Quarterly of Literature, the Arts, and Public Affairs*, Vol. 24, No. 1 (1983), pp.198–216, at p.215.
54. Churchill, *Top Girls*, p.129.
55. Frank Rich, 'Caryl Churchill's *Top Girls*, at the Public', *New York Times*, 29 Dec. 1982.
56. All details of the Joseph Papp-produced transfer and subsequent production are taken from their production records.
57. See the helpful chronology at Fitzsimmons, *File on Churchill*, pp.8–9.
58. Qtd in Goodman, 'Overlapping', p.78.
59. The piece is currently installed at the Brooklyn Museum of Art in New York, where I first experienced it.
60. Churchill, *Top Girls*, p.62.
61. *Ibid.*, p.80.
62. *Ibid.*, p.57.
63. *Ibid.*, p.60.
64. For this point I am indebted to Victoria Bazin, '"[Not] Talking 'Bout My Generation": Historicizing Feminisms in Caryl Churchill's *Top Girls*', *Studies in the Literary Imagination*, Vol. 39, No. 2 (Fall 2006), pp.115–34, at p.132.
65. Churchill, *Top Girls*, p.74.
66. See Linda Fitzsimmons, '"I Won't Turn Back for You or Anyone": Caryl Churchill's Socialist-Feminist Theatre', *Essays in Theatre*, Vol. 6, No. 1 (1987), pp.19–29.
67. Churchill, *Top Girls*, p.58, p.61.
68. *Ibid.*, p.82.
69. For a reading of Dull Gret's 'naïve assault upon hell' as a parody of 'radical and bourgeois forms of feminism', see, for example, Joseph Marohl, 'De-realised Women: Performance and Identity in *Top Girls*', *Modern Drama*, Vol. 30, No. 3 (1987), pp.366–88, at p.388. The Flemish proverb behind Bruegel's painting – and a

counter-reading to Marohl's – is provided in Sharon Ammen, 'Feminist Vision and Audience Response: Tracing the Absent Utopia in Caryl Churchill's *Top Girls*', *Utopian Studies: Journal of the Society for Utopian Studies*, Vol. 7, No. 1 (1996), pp.86–102, at p.90.

70. Caryl Churchill, *Cloud Nine* in *Plays: One*, London: Methuen Drama, 1985, pp.243–320, at p.251.
71. Churchill, *Top Girls*, p.81.
72. *Ibid.*, p.82.
73. *Ibid.*, p.60.
74. Stafford-Clark, MS 79553, 1 Mar. 1982, p.266.
75. See Elaine Aston, *Feminist Views on the English Stage: Women Playwrights, 1990–2000*, New York: Cambridge University Press, 2003, p.22.
76. Churchill, *Top Girls*, p.67, p.86, p.102.
77. *Ibid.*, p.100.
78. *Ibid.*, p.106.
79. *Ibid.*, p.81.
80. My translations are taken from Lucretius, *On the Nature of Things*, Frank O. Copley (trans.), New York: W. W. Norton and Company, 1977, p.29. The playwright, of course, gives only the Latin of this line, at Churchill, *Top Girls*, p.81: 'quibus ipse malis careas quia cernere suave est'.
81. Churchill, *Top Girls*, p.72.
82. *Ibid.*, p.83.
83. See Truss, 'Fair Cop', p.10; Goodman, 'Overlapping', p.92.
84. See Aston, Elaine, *Caryl Churchill* (3rd edn), Horndon: Northcote House Publishers, 2010, p.40.
85. Caryl Churchill, *Perfect Happiness*, unpublished typescript, p.1.
86. *Ibid.*, p.27.
87. Qtd in Stone, 'Caryl Churchill'.
88. Caryl Churchill, *The Skriker* in *Plays: Three*, London: Nick Hern Books, 1998, pp.239–91, at p.243. Despite the critical tendency to gender the Skriker as female, I adopt the pronoun 'it', following Churchill's own practice when discussing the play with producers.
89. *Ibid.*

90. *Ibid.*, p.246.
91. *Ibid.*, p.243.
92. *Ibid.*, p.247.
93. *Ibid.*, p.258.
94. *Ibid.*, p.257.
95. The notes appear in *T-MSS 1993-028, Box 138, Folder 2.
96. Churchill, *Skriker,* p.254.
97. *Ibid.*, p.250.
98. *Ibid.*, p.279.
99. *Ibid.*, p.243.
100. *Ibid.*, p.246.
101. See Katherine Perrault, 'Beyond Patriarchy: Feminism and the Chaos of Creativity', *Journal of Dramatic Theory and Criticism*, Vol. 17, No. 1 (2002), pp.45–67, at p.54.
102. Churchill, *Skriker,* p.269.
103. *Ibid.*, p.246; compare *ibid.*, p.259.
104. *Ibid.*, p.246, p.291.
105. See *ibid.*, p.253 ('none but the brave'), p.244 ('all go into the dark'), p.244 ('a bushel and a peck').
106. *Ibid.*, p.246.
107. *Ibid.*, p.256.
108. *Ibid.*, p.290.
109. See Sheila Rabillard, 'On Caryl Churchill's Ecological Dramas: Right to Poison the Wasps?' in Elaine Aston and Elin Diamond (eds), *The Cambridge Companion to Caryl Churchill*, Cambridge: Cambridge University Press, 2009, pp.88–104, at p.99. The libretto is published in Roberts, *About Churchill*, p.268.
110. Churchill, *Skriker,* p.271.
111. *Ibid.*, p.256.
112. Caryl Churchill, *Light Shining in Buckinghamshire* in *Plays: One*, London: Methuen Drama, 1985, pp.181–241, at p.192.
113. On this point, see Geraldine Cousin, 'Owning the Disowned: *The Skriker* in the Context of Earlier Plays by Caryl Churchill' in Rabillard, *Essays*, pp.189–204, at pp.197–8.
114. Churchill's treatment for *The Magic Ring* can be found in the archives of the BBC.

115. Claudia Barnett, '"Reveangance Is Gold Mine, Sweet": Alchemy and Archetypes in Caryl Churchill's *The Skriker*', *Essays in Theatre*, Vol. 19, No. 1 (2000), pp.45–57, at p.46.
116. See Churchill, *Plays: Three*, p.184.
117. See Ian Spink and Richard Allen Cave, 'Collaborations' in *Border Tensions: Dance and Discourse, Proceedings of the Fifth Study of Dance Conference at the University of Surrey*, Guildford: University of Surrey, 1995, pp.293–303, at p.299.
118. Giraudeau had performed in *A Mouthful of Birds* and *Fugue*; Goff, in both, as well as *Lives of the Great Poisoners.*
119. Churchill made these remarks in a public talk with Nicholas Wright (who had directed *Owners* over twenty years earlier) held on 29 Jan. 1994. Excerpts appeared in the New York programme and were published as Caryl Churchill and Nicholas Wright, 'Fairy Stories', *Public Access*, 1 Mar. 1996, p.32. The quotation above was edited out and is cited from the transcript (*T-MSS 1993-028, Box 138, Folder 2).
120. The line is 'Alfred and the cakes', a shorthand for ninth-century history, used both in Churchill, *Skriker*, p.257, and in Caryl Churchill, *Icecream* in *Plays: Three*, pp.55–102, at p.58.
121. See Churchill and Wright, 'Fairy Stories', n.p.
122. Ralf Erik Remshardt, Rev. of *The Skriker, Theatre Journal*, Vol. 47 (1995), pp.121–3, at p.121.
123. Stafford-Clark, MS 79570, p.169.
124. The Echo Theatre production in Winnipeg, Canada – staged as part of an annual 'Master Playwright Festival' whose other honorees have included Bertolt Brecht, Eugene O'Neill, and Harold Pinter – premiered on 2 Feb. 2010. In the UK, the Theatre Royal in Bury St Edmunds also used multiple performers for the Skriker in a production of its Young Company that premiered on 27 Jan. 2011.
125. Stafford-Clark, MS 79570, p.169.
126. *Ibid.*, p.310.
127. Here, as elsewhere in this chapter, I draw on the play's production files in the archives of the National Theatre.
128. See Spink and Cave, 'Collaborations', pp.299–300.

129. See Paul Taylor in the *Independent*, Charles Spencer in the *Daily Telegraph*, and Nicholas de Jongh in the *Evening Standard*, all in *Theatre Record*, Vol. 14 (15–28 Jan. 1994), pp.93–8, at p.94, p.96, p.97.
130. De Jongh; Spencer; Benedict Nightingale in *The Times* (in *ibid.*, p.93). Hindsight (and archival video held at the National) confirms these assessments, especially of Spink's movement and Smart's design.
131. The quotation is from Stafford-Clark's diary (24 July 1992), MS 79571, p.8. The National's production records leave some confusion about the precise rehearsal period, which Churchill had described as two months in her discussion with Wright, cited at n.119, above.
132. *T-MSS 1993-028, Box 292, Folder 5.
133. Ben Brantley, 'A Land of Fairy Tales Creepily Come True', *New York Times*, 16 May 1996; Donald Lyons, 'Demons, Real and Imagined', *Wall Street Journal*, 16 May 1996.
134. Jeremy Gerard, 'Rude mechanicals', *Variety*, 20 May 1996; Linda Winer, 'Forget "Victor" Let's Talk "Skriker"', *Newsday*, 24 May 1996.
135. Whereas the Shriker appears in any reference book of fairy lore – such as K.M. Briggs, *The Fairies in Tradition and Literature*, London: Routledge and Kegan Paul, 1967, p.90 – Skriker spottings are rarer. A full tale is told in James Bowker, *Goblin Tales of Lancashire*, London: W. Swan Sonnenschein, 1883, pp.27–36.
136. The first etymology is asserted by Barbara Norden, 'When the Kelpie Rides and the Spriggan Stalks', *Times Literary Supplement*, 4 Feb. 1994; the second, by the *OED*.
137. *Noah* in David Bevington (ed.), *Medieval Drama*, Atlanta: Houghton Mifflin Company, pp.290–307, at p.297; Edmund Spenser, *The Faerie Queene*, A.C. Hamilton (ed.), Harlow: Longman Group, 1992, p.650.
138. Churchill, *Skriker*, p.268.
139. Qtd in Matt Wolf, 'A Damaged World in Which Nature is a Weirdo Killer', *New York Times*, 5 May 1996.

140. The foundational work of Elin Diamond, 'Caryl Churchill: Feeling Global' in Mary Luckhurst (ed.), *A Companion to Modern British and Irish Drama, 1880-2005*, Malden, MA: Blackwell Publishing, 2006, pp.476–87, has been built on by Candice Amich, 'Bringing the Global Home: Caryl Churchill's *The Skriker*', *Modern Drama*, Vol. 50, No. 3 (2007), pp.394–413, and by Jean E. Howard, 'On Owning and Owing: Caryl Churchill and the Nightmare of Capital' in Aston and Diamond, *Cambridge Companion*, pp.36–51. Diamond gives this quotation from Deleuze and Guattari's *Anti-Oedipus* at p.483.
141. Harvey's theory, discussed in my third chapter, appears in his 1989 *The Condition of Postmodernity*.
142. Churchill, *Skriker*, p.270.
143. *Ibid.*, p.270.
144. *Ibid.*, p.288.
145. *Ibid.*, p.283.
146. *Ibid.*, p.243.
147. Qtd in Peter Wells, 'Scary Fairies', *Time Out New York*, 15–22 May 1996.
148. See Elaine Aston, 'But Not That: Caryl Churchill's Political Shape Shifting at the Turn of the Millennium', *Modern Drama*, Vol. 56, No. 2 (2013), pp.145–64. The quotation from Stafford-Clark, which I have not been able to verify, appears in different forms in Roberts, *About Churchill*, p.135, and in Philip Roberts and Max Stafford-Clark, *Taking Stock: The Theatre of Max Stafford-Clark*, London: Nick Hern Books, 2007, p.175.
149. This argument is mounted, too, in Amelia Howe Kritzer, 'Political Currents in Caryl Churchill's Plays at the Turn of the Millennium' in Marc Maufort and Franca Bellarsi (eds), *Crucible of Cultures: Anglophone Drama at the Dawn of a New Millennium*, Brussels: Peter Lang, 2002, pp.57–67.
150. Caryl Churchill, *This Is a Chair* in *Plays: Four*, London: Nick Hern Books, 2008, pp.37–58, at p.45.
151. Caryl Churchill, *Far Away* in *Plays: Four*, pp.129–59, at p.133.
152. *Ibid.*, p.139, p.140.
153. *Ibid.*, p.142.

154. Caryl Churchill, *The Judge's Wife* in *Shorts*, London: Nick Hern Books, 1990, pp.147–63, at p.159.
155. Churchill, *Far Away*, p.137, p.141, p.140.
156. Caryl Churchill, *Softcops* in *Plays: Two*, pp.1–49, at p.5.
157. Churchill, *Far Away*, p.142.
158. *Ibid.*, p.143, p.143, p.147.
159. *Ibid.*, p.149.
160. *Ibid.*, p.150.
161. Churchill, *Softcops*, p.14.
162. See Diamond, 'Feeling Global', p.485. Churchill's *Portrait of an Artist* was rejected by the BBC and went unproduced.
163. Churchill, *Far Away*, p.150.
164. *Ibid.* Rick Fisher, who designed the lights for *Far Away*, rendered explicit Churchill's implicit analogy: 'We all spend our time working on these little gossamer works of art and then they all get burned', qtd in Aston, 'But Not That', p.157.
165. Una Chaudhuri, 'Different Hats', *Theater*, Vol. 33, No. 3 (Fall 2003), pp.132–4, at p.132.
166. Churchill, *Far Away*, p.153, p.155.
167. *Ibid.*, p.152.
168. *Ibid.*, p.159.
169. *Ibid.*
170. Stafford-Clark, MS 79564, 25/26 July 1987, p.77.
171. Stafford-Clark, MS 84047, 6 Dec. 1999, p.88.
172. Details of discussions of the Royal Court script meeting are revealed at *ibid.*, p.130.
173. *Ibid.*, pp.129–30.
174. Stephens qtd in Aleks Sierz, *Rewriting the Nation: British Theatre Today*, London: Methuen Drama, 2011, p.75.
175. Qtd in Michael R. Gordon and Kareem Fahim, 'Kerry Says Egypt's Military Was "Restoring Democracy" in Ousting Morsi', *New York Times*, 1 Aug. 2013.
176. Churchill, *Far Away*, p. 158.
177. *Ibid.*, p.159.
178. *Ibid.*, p.135.
179. Stafford-Clark, MS 84047, 11 Dec. 1999, p.89.

180. On this point, see Aston, *Caryl Churchill*, p.117.
181. Churchill, *Far Away*, p.133.
182. *Ibid.*, p.141.
183. *Ibid.*, p.132.
184. Qtd in Roberts, *About Churchill*, p.261.
185. The connection between *Far Away* and the rhetoric of terror receives a coruscating treatment in Elin Diamond, 'On Churchill and Terror' in Aston and Diamond, *Cambridge Companion*, pp.125–43; to it, my analysis here is generally indebted.
186. Churchill, *Far Away*, p.150.
187. Sierz, *Rewriting*, p.75.
188. See Sam Marlowe in *What's On*, Georgina Brown in the *Mail on Sunday*, Michael Billington in the *Guardian*, and Charles Spencer in the *Telegraph*, all in *Theatre Record*, Vol. 20 (18 Nov.–1 Dec. 2000), pp.1574–8, at p.1574, p.1577, p.1578, p.1576.
189. Churchill, *Far Away*, p.134.
190. The production is described in Yael Prizant, Rev. of *Far Away*, *Theatre Journal*, Vol. 56, No. 3 (Oct. 2004), pp.504–5.
191. The production is described in Helen Meany, Rev. of *Far Away*, *Guardian*, 6 July 2004.
192. Churchill, *Top Girls*, p.66.
193. Caryl Churchill, *The Ants* in Irving Wardle (ed.), *New English Dramatists 12: Radio Plays*, Harmondsworth: Penguin Books, 1969, pp.89–103, at p.93, p.95.
194. Churchill, *Judge's Wife*, p.149.
195. Roberts, *About Churchill*, p.259 (Tozer); interview, 8 Apr. 2013 (Bassett).
196. Churchill, *Far Away*, p.157.
197. *Ibid.*, p.153.
198. Qtd in Roberts, *About Churchill*, p.261.
199. Interview, 8 Apr. 2013.
200. Details appear in Roberts, *About Churchill*, p.150.
201. Details appear in Annemarie Jacir, 'For Cultural Purposes Only' in Hamid Dabashi (ed.), *Dreams of a Nation*, London: Verso Books, 2006, pp.23–31, at p.26.

202. Caryl Churchill, 'Not Ordinary, Not Safe: A Direction for Drama?' in *The Twentieth Century*, Vol. 168 (Nov. 1960), pp.443–51, at p.446.
203. Qtd in Lyall, 'Mysteries'.
204. Qtd in David Savran, 'Tony Kushner Considers the Longstanding Problems of Virtue and Happiness', *American Theatre*, Vol. 11, No. 8 (Oct. 1994), pp.20–7, at p.24.
205. Mark Ravenhill, 'Dramatic Moments', *Guardian*, 9 Apr. 1997.

Chapter 2

1. Caryl Churchill, *The After-Dinner Joke* in *Shorts*, London: Nick Hern Books, 1990, pp.165–221, at p.169.
2. Caryl Churchill, introduction to *Shorts*, n.p.
3. Churchill, *After-Dinner Joke*, p.190.
4. *Ibid.*, p.208.
5. The book is real: a compendium of occasionally racist and sexist anecdotes from 'important' Britons starting with its (unwittingly appropriate) foreword-writer, Prince Philip. See Christian Brann (ed.), *Pass the Port: The Best After-Dinner Stories of the Famous*, Cirencester: Christian Brann Limited for Oxfam, 1976.
6. Churchill, *After-Dinner Joke*, p.221.
7. Tape of the programme can be viewed at the British Film Institute's National Archive.
8. See http://www.tvcream.co.uk/?p=7620
9. My discussion of the play is indebted to its records at the BBC Written Archives Centre in Reading.
10. Caryl Churchill, *Plays: One*, London: Methuen Drama, 1985, p.xi.
11. John Heilpern, *John Osborne: The Many Lives of the Angry Young Man*, New York: Alfred A. Knopf Books, 2007, pp.370–2.
12. Caryl Churchill, *Owners* in *Plays: One*, pp.2–67, at p.21.
13. See Steve Gooch, 'Caryl Churchill, Author of This Month's Playtext, Talks to P & P', *Plays and Players*, Vol. 20, No. 4 (1973), p.40 and inset p.I, at p.I.
14. Churchill, *Owners*, p.18.

15. *Ibid.*, p.19.
16. *Ibid.*, p.51.
17. *Ibid.*, p.5.
18. Qtd in Gooch, 'Caryl Churchill', p.I.
19. Qtd in John Hall, 'Angled Islington', *Guardian*, 12 Dec. 1972.
20. Churchill, *Owners*, p.36.
21. *Ibid.*, p.23, p.25.
22. *Ibid.*, p.18.
23. *Ibid.*, p.31.
24. *Ibid.*, p.53, p.52.
25. *Ibid.*, p.42.
26. *Ibid.*, p.60.
27. *Ibid.*, p.63.
28. *Ibid.*, p.56.
29. *Ibid.*, p.20.
30. Alisa Solomon, 'Witches, Ranters and the Middle Class: The Plays of Caryl Churchill', *Theater*, Vol. 12, No. 2 (Spring 1981), pp.49–55, at p.50.
31. Churchill, *Owners*, p.30. Clegg likens Marion to a dog at *ibid.*, p.11.
32. *Ibid.*, p.5.
33. Elaine Aston, *Caryl Churchill* (3rd edn), Horndon: Northcote House Publishers, 2010, p.21.
34. Churchill, *Owners*, p.13, p.30.
35. *Ibid.*, p.35.
36. Qtd in Hall, 'Angled Islington'. See also Gooch, 'Caryl Churchill', p.I.
37. Catholic doctrine holds that Mary, having been conceived free of sin by Anne, experienced no birth pains, labour being God's curse on Eve.
38. Jean E. Howard, 'On Owning and Owing: Caryl Churchill and the Nightmare of Capital' in Elaine Aston and Elin Diamond (eds), *The Cambridge Companion to Caryl Churchill*, Cambridge: Cambridge University Press, 2009, pp.36–51.
39. Churchill, *Owners*, p.67.
40. *Ibid.*, p.4.

41. *Ibid.*, p.8.
42. Churchill called *Owners* (a bit conservatively) her twentieth play at *Plays: One*, p.xi. The proposal for *The Love Salesman* appears in the archives of the BBC.
43. Churchill, *Owners*, p.11.
44. Ian Spink and Richard Allen Cave, 'Collaborations' in *Border Tensions: Dance and Discourse, Proceedings of the Fifth Study of Dance Conference at the University of Surrey*, Guildford: University of Surrey, 1995, pp.293–303, at p.302n.7.
45. Details about the play and its rights can be verified in production records held in the Theatre and Performance Collections of the Victoria and Albert Museum at Blythe House.
46. Robert Brustein, 'Subjects of Scandal and Concern', *Observer*, 17 Dec. 1972.
47. See, for instance, Charles Lewsen in *The Times* (13 Dec. 1972); Jeremy Kingston in *Punch* (20 Dec. 1972); Benedict Nightingale in the *New Statesman* (22 Dec. 1972); or Michael Billington in the *Guardian* (14 Dec. 1972).
48. Qtd in Gresdna A. Doty and Billy J. Harbin (eds), *Inside the Royal Court Theatre, 1956-1981: Artists Talk*, Baton Rouge: Louisiana State University Press, 1990, p.200.
49. The letter is qtd in Philip Roberts, *About Churchill: The Playwright and the Work*, London: Faber, 2008, p.45.
50. An exception is Helene Keyssar, 'The Dramas of Caryl Churchill: The Politics of Possibility', *Massachusetts Review: A Quarterly of Literature, the Arts, and Public Affairs*, Vol. 24, No. 1 (1983), pp.198–216, at p.205, who describes the dismissiveness of New York's critics and Hayden's poor production.
51. The exception is Linda Fitzsimmons (ed.), *File on Churchill*, London: Methuen Drama, 1989, p.19.
52. Robert Brustein, 'Birds and Beasts of the West', *New Republic*, 18 Jan. 1988, pp.27–8, at p.27.
53. My reading here draws on two excellent articles on capital and *Serious Money*: Daniel Jernigan, '*Serious Money* Becomes "Business by Other Means": Caryl Churchill's Metatheatrical Subject', *Comparative Drama*, Vol. 38, No. 2/3 (2004), pp.291–313; and

Linda Kintz, 'Performing Capital in Caryl Churchill's *Serious Money*', *Theatre Journal*, Vol. 41, No. 3 (1999), pp.251–65. Kintz invokes Marx's 'cash nexus' at p.255. Unlike earlier critics, I had access to the play's production records from its Royal Court, Wyndham's, Public Theater, and Broadway runs. All details – stage manager reports, contracts, box office tallies – are taken from these records, held at Blythe House in London and in the Billy Rose Theatre Division, New York Public Library for the Performing Arts.

54. Caryl Churchill, *Serious Money* in *Plays: Two*, pp.193–309, at p.231.
55. *Ibid.*, p.224.
56. *Ibid.*, p.221.
57. *Ibid.*, p.207.
58. Qtd in Fitzsimmons, *File on Churchill*, p.84.
59. Churchill, *Serious Money*, p.197.
60. For a fuller discussion of *Serious Money*'s debt to Brecht, see Janelle Reinelt, *After Brecht: British Epic Theater*, Ann Arbor: University of Michigan Press, 1996, pp.97–101.
61. Thomas Shadwell, *The Volunteers, or the Stock-Jobbers*, London: James Knapton, 1693, p.24.
62. Churchill, *Serious Money*, p.197, p.196, p.196; see also, almost identically, Shadwell, *Volunteers*, p.24.
63. Churchill, *Serious Money*, p.210.
64. *Ibid.*, p.236, p.222.
65. The date is often given as 27 Sept. (which was a Saturday), including by Philip Roberts and Stafford-Clark himself in their *Taking Stock: The Theatre of Max Stafford-Clark*, London: Nick Hern Books, 2007, p.124. But Stafford-Clark's own diary, held at the British Library, confirms the correct date.
66. Qtd in Don Nelsen, 'Delirious Money', *New York Daily News*, 24 Jan. 1988.
67. Norman St John Stevas (soon to be replaced by Thatcher), qtd in D. Keith Peacock, *Thatcher's Theatre: British Theatre and Drama in the Eighties*, Westport, CT: Greenwood Press, 1999, p.36.
68. Stafford-Clark, MS 79563, p.52.

69. On the first point, see Jernigan, '*Serious Money*', p.296; on the second, Roberts, *About Churchill*, p.115.
70. Peacock, *Thatcher's Theatre*, p.28.
71. Howard Brenton, *Hot Irons: Diaries, Essays, Journalism*, London: Nick Hern Books, p.75.
72. The former quotation is from Neil Collins in the *Telegraph*, 30 Mar. 1987; the latter, from Michael Coveney in the *Financial Times*, 30 Mar. 1987.
73. Qtd in Andy Lavender (ed.), 'Theatre in Thatcher's Britain: Organizing the Opposition' (*NTQ* Symposium), *New Theatre Quarterly*, Vol. 5, No. 18 (1989), pp.113–23, at p.121.
74. Qtd in *ibid.*, pp.121–2.
75. Qtd in *ibid.*, p.119.
76. Qtd in Michael Darvell, 'Money Movers', *What's On and Where To Go*, 9 July 1987.
77. See Thomas Sutcliffe, 'Four Plays for Your Money this Summer', *Independent*, 15 July 1987; Jeremy Kingston, Rev. of *Serious Money*, *The Times*, 7 July 1987.
78. Qtd in Peter Lewis, 'Serious Money Cleans Up', *The Times*, 30 July 1987.
79. Churchill, *Serious Money*, p.225.
80. *Ibid.*, p.235.
81. *Ibid.*, p.235.
82. *Ibid.*, p.211.
83. Jernigan, '*Serious Money*', p.304.
84. Qtd in Lewis, 'Serious Money'.
85. Churchill, *Serious Money*, p.196; see also Shadwell, *Volunteers*, p.24.
86. See Jerry Tallmer, 'B'way not "Serious"', *New York Post*, 20 Feb. 1988.
87. Churchill, *Serious Money*, p.244.
88. *Ibid.*
89. *Ibid.*, p.255.
90. *Ibid.*, p.306.
91. *Ibid.*, p.215.
92. *Ibid.*, p.306.

93. *Ibid.*, p.307.
94. *Ibid.*, p.308.
95. Clive Barnes, 'After the "Big Bang"', *New York Post*, 4 Dec. 1987.
96. Churchill, *Serious Money*, p.229.
97. The donation (Boesky's largest, but not only) paid for the cast recording of the Papp-produced musical 'The Human Comedy'. See Meg Cox, 'The Crash of '87 Proves Fortunate for "Serious Money"', *Wall Street Journal*, 20 Nov. 1987.
98. Qtd in Ruth Little and Emily McLaughlin, *The Royal Court Inside Out*, London: Oberon Books, 2007, p.254.
99. Actor Christine Dunford qtd in Susan Antilla, '"Serious Money" to Open Wallets', *USA Today*, 8 Feb. 1988.
100. The report, dated 11 Dec. 1987, can be found in *T-MSS 1993-028, Box 4-27, Folder 9.
101. Both actors are qtd in Drew Fetherson, 'Getting Serious to Make "Money" Funny', *Newsday*, 6 Dec. 1987.
102. Qtd in James Sterngold, 'Party Time: Wall St. Goes Broadway', *New York Times*, 10 Feb. 1988.
103. Qtd in *ibid.*
104. Karl Marx and Friedrich Engels, *The Communist Manifesto*, Samuel Moore (trans.), David McLennan (ed.), Oxford: Oxford University Press, 2008, p.5.
105. Churchill, *Serious Money*, p.212, p.213.
106. *Ibid.*, p.283, p.281.
107. The Broadway rewrites are held in *T-MSS 1993-028, Box 4-27, Folder 26.
108. See, for example, Diana Maychick, '"Serious Money" for Broadway', *New York Post*, 9 Dec. 1987.
109. Qtd in *ibid.*
110. Stafford-Clark, MS 79564, p.202.
111. Stafford-Clark, MS 79563, p.132.
112. Stafford-Clark, MS 79564, p.218.
113. Details of the royalty pool, and the letter, appear in *T-MSS 1993-028 Box 5-86, Folder 29.
114. Churchill, *Serious Money*, p.287.

115. *Ibid.*, p.236.
116. *Ibid.*, p.302.
117. See Harold James, 'When Sid Turns Vicious', *Telegraph*, 6 Sept. 1987.
118. Stafford-Clark paraphrases Barker's warning in his diary, at MS 79563, p.112.
119. See the unsigned '700G "Serious Money" Drops Ditto; Subject Too Painful, Says Papp', *Variety*, 24 Feb. 1988.
120. Jernigan, '*Serious Money*', p.294.
121. See Roberts, *About Churchill*, p.142.
122. The report appears in *T-MSS 1993-028, Box 4-27, Folder 28.
123. Collins, *Telegraph*, 30 Mar. 1987.
124. Churchill, *Serious Money*, p.244.
125. Robert L. King, 'Recent Drama', *The Massachusetts Review*, Vol. 29, No. 1 (1988), pp.87–97, at p.89.
126. Strindberg's text is translated into English and prefaced to Caryl Churchill, *A Dream Play* in *Plays: Four*, London: Nick Hern Books, pp.207–65, at p.212.
127. My own translation of an original found at August Strindberg, *Ett Drömspel* in *Till Damaskus och Ett Drömspel*, Stockholm: Albert Bonniers Förlag, 1962, pp.79–145, at pp.144–5.
128. Churchill, *Dream Play*, p.264.
129. Caryl Churchill, 'she bit her tongue', p.2. Available online at http://www.siobhandaviesreplay.com/media2/UserType/00000000/00000000/00000589.pdf
130. Churchill, *Dream Play*, p.261.
131. *Ibid.*, p.215. Strindberg's flower-topped *slott* would be more literally rendered as 'castle'.
132. *Ibid.*, p.264.
133. *Ibid.*, p.211.
134. See Sue Prideaux, *Strindberg: A Life*, New Haven: Yale University Press, 2012, especially pp.302–8.
135. Churchill, *Dream Play*, p.249.
136. *Ibid.*
137. *Ibid.*, p.220.

138. All production details can be verified in the records held at the National Theatre Archives. There I also watched video of Mitchell's production (which I had seen live in 2005) and generated a performance script to compare with Churchill's text.
139. Angus Wright qtd in Roberts, *About Churchill*, p.265.
140. Churchill, *Dream Play*, p.215.
141. *Ibid.*, p.245.
142. *Ibid.*, p.216.
143. Amelia Howe Kritzer, 'A Dream Play', *Theatre Journal*, Vol. 57, No. 3 (2005), pp.502–4, at p.503.
144. Churchill, *Dream Play*, p.237.
145. Qtd in Roberts, *About Churchill*, p.265.
146. Churchill, *Dream Play*, p.252.
147. Nicholas de Jongh, 'Stockbroker Belted', *Evening Standard*, 16 Feb. 2005.
148. Charles Spencer, 'Haunting Theatre of Dreams', *Telegraph*, 17 Feb. 2005; David Benedict, Rev. of *A Dream Play*, *Bloomberg News*, 6 Feb. 2005.
149. Carole Woddis, Rev. of *A Dream Play*, *Glasgow Herald*, 23 Feb. 2005.
150. Alistair Macaulay, Rev. of *A Dream Play*, *Financial Times*, 22 Feb. 2005.
151. Churchill, *Dream Play*, p.211, p.210.
152. See Katie Mitchell, 'Throwing Light on Strindberg', *Evening Standard*, 15 Feb. 2005.
153. Churchill's dialogue originated from the verbatim transcript of a Diplock trial in Belfast. But the playwright wrote a voiceover narration for the teleplay's beginning and ending, which were removed by the BBC whose executives found them inappropriately editorialising. Details can be found in the teleplay's voluminous records held at the BBC Written Archives Centre.
154. Caryl Churchill, *Plays: Three*, London, Nick Hern Books, 1998, p.viii.
155. Churchill, *Owners*, p.36.
156. Qtd in Catherine Sheehy, 'Time and Again: Caryl Churchill's New/Old Plays at NYTW', *Village Voice*, 23 Mar. 1993.

Chapter 3

1. Caryl Churchill, *Identical Twins*, unpublished typescript, p.3.
2. *Ibid.*, p.6. The typescript's typographical error 'Reddy' has been here corrected.
3. Caryl Churchill, *Cloud Nine* in *Plays: One*, London: Methuen Drama, 1985, pp.243–320, at p.251.
4. *Ibid.*, p.275.
5. Caryl Churchill, *Softcops* in *Plays: Two*, London: Methuen Drama, 1990, pp.1–49, at p.41.
6. An early article setting out the feminist theory that informs Churchill's play (especially Gayle Rubin's groundbreaking anthropology) is still the best. See John M. Clum, '"The Work of Culture": *Cloud Nine* and Sex/Gender Theory' in Phyllis R. Randall (ed.), *Caryl Churchill: A Casebook*, New York: Garland Publishing, 1988, pp.91–116.
7. Judith Butler, *Gender Trouble: Feminism and the Subversion of Identity*, New York: Routledge, 1990, p.92.
8. Churchill, *Cloud Nine*, p.276.
9. *Ibid.*
10. The reference appears on the first page of Stafford-Clark's 22 July to 6 Oct. 1978 diary (MS 79545) held at the British Library.
11. Churchill, *Cloud Nine*, p.245.
12. *Ibid.*, p.251.
13. James M. Harding, 'Cloud Cover: (Re)Dressing Desire and Comfortable Subversions in Caryl Churchill's *Cloud Nine*', *PMLA*, Vol. 113, No. 2 (1998), pp.258–72, at p.265. Similar concerns are raised by Loren Kruger, 'The Dis-play's the Thing: Gender and Public Sphere in Contemporary British Theater', *Theatre Journal*, Vol. 42, No. 1 (1990), pp.27–48, especially at p.34.
14. Caryl Churchill, *Cloud Nine* unpublished typescript held in the Theatre and Performance Collections of the Victoria and Albert Museum at Blythe House, p.I–41.
15. Churchill, *Cloud Nine*, p.278.
16. Churchill, *Cloud Nine* unpublished typescript, p.I–34. The line was redacted during the play's rehearsals.

17. Churchill, *Cloud Nine*, p.255.
18. *Ibid.*, p.256.
19. *Ibid.*, p.257.
20. *Ibid.*
21. *Ibid.*, p.254.
22. Churchill, *Cloud Nine* unpublished typescript, p.I–14.
23. *Ibid.*, p.II–26, p.II–27. Here as elsewhere, the typescript's missing apostrophes have been inserted
24. Churchill, *Cloud Nine*, p.271.
25. Churchill, *Cloud Nine* unpublished typescript, p.I–38.
26. Churchill, *Cloud Nine*, p.281.
27. See Elaine Aston, *Caryl Churchill* (3rd edn), Horndon: Northcote House Publishers, 2010, p.33.
28. Churchill, *Cloud Nine*, p.266.
29. *Ibid.*, p.277.
30. *Ibid.*, p.260.
31. *Ibid.*, p.268.
32. *Ibid.*, p.261.
33. *Ibid.*, p.262.
34. *Ibid.*, p.273.
35. *Ibid.*, p.274.
36. *Ibid.*, p.262.
37. *Ibid.*, p.280.
38. *Ibid.*, p.263.
39. *Ibid.*, p.286.
40. *Ibid.*, p.274, p.287.
41. *Ibid.*, p.246.
42. *Ibid.*, p.307, p.306.
43. *Ibid.*
44. Churchill, *Cloud Nine* unpublished typescript, p.II–24.
45. Churchill, *Cloud Nine*, p.246.
46. Amelia Howe Kritzer, *The Plays of Caryl Churchill: Theatre of Empowerment,* New York: St Martin's Press, 1991, p.123.
47. Churchill, *Cloud Nine*, p.302.
48. See Joseph Roach, *Cities of the Dead: Circum-Atlantic Performance*, New York: Columbia University Press, 1996, pp.1–31.

49. Aston, *Caryl Churchill*, p.32.
50. Roach, *Cities*, p.2.
51. Churchill, *Cloud Nine*, p.314.
52. *Ibid.*, p.303.
53. *Ibid.*, p.308.
54. Qtd in Aston, *Caryl Churchill*, p.31.
55. See Apollo Amoko, 'Casting Aside Colonial Occupation: Intersections of Race, Sex, and Gender in *Cloud Nine* and *Cloud Nine* Criticism', *Modern Drama*, Vol. 42, No. 1 (1999), pp.45–58.
56. Churchill, *Cloud Nine*, p.277, p.263. Freud: 'We know less about the sexual life of little girls than boys. But we need not feel ashamed of this distinction; after all, the sexual life of adult women is a "dark continent" for psychology'. Sigmund Freud, 'The Questions of Lay Analysis' in *The Standard Edition of the Complete Psychological Works*, Vol. 20, James Strachey et al. (eds and trans.), London: Hogarth Press, 1959, pp.179–258, at p.212.
57. Qtd in John Simon, 'Sex, Politics, and Other Play Things,' *Vogue*, Aug. 1983, pp.126, 130, at p.126.
58. Churchill qtd in Amoko, 'Casting', p.52; Stafford-Clark, MS 79545, 14 Sept. 1978, p.93.
59. Churchill qtd in Amoko, 'Casting', p.52.
60. See Stafford-Clark, MS 79545, pp.65–7, p.69.
61. I draw here on the argument of Mary F. Brewer, *Staging Whiteness*, Middletown, CT: Wesleyan University Press, 2005, p.142.
62. See the reviews of Paul Taylor in the *Independent* ('a touch dated'), Julie Carpenter in the *Daily Express* ('outdated'), and Patrick Marmion in the *Daily Mail* ('now-fusty'), all in *Theatre Record*, Vol. 27, No. 22 (22 Oct.–4 Nov. 2007), p.1316.
63. Churchill, *Cloud Nine*, p.292.
64. Philip Roberts and Max Stafford-Clark, *Taking Stock: The Theatre of Max Stafford-Clark,* London: Nick Hern Books, 2007, p.96. Roberts and Stafford-Clark erroneously date the revival to 1999.
65. *Ibid.*, p.68.
66. Qtd in Philip Roberts, *About Churchill: The Playwright and the Work*, London: Faber, 2008, p.202. The incredibly intimate

nature (and the sheer volume) of the actors' revelations at the workshop is confirmed in Stafford-Clark's journals.

67. See Sher's testimony in Roberts and Stafford-Clark, *Taking Stock*, p.78.
68. Churchill, *Cloud Nine*, p.246.
69. The workshops are described at Roberts and Stafford-Clark, *Taking Stock*, pp.63–88.
70. Qtd in Kritzer, *Plays*, p.128.
71. While several sources cite 14 Dec., a second reading of the script was held already on 13 Dec., according to Stafford-Clark's journal.
72. Stafford-Clark, MS 79546, p.116.
73. *Ibid.*, p.126, p.139.
74. Roberts and Stafford-Clark, *Taking Stock*, p.90. The director's journal quotes Sher as saying, on 13 Dec., that the play is 'one of the most brilliant pieces of political theatre I've ever read . . . one is constantly surprized in 1st 1/2 . . . shame that we h[a]v[e] to l[ea]v[e] jungle at all' (MS 79546, p.100).
75. *Ibid.*, p.158.
76. See Gresdna A. Doty and Billy J. Harbin (eds), *Inside the Royal Court Theatre, 1956-1981: Artists Talk*, Baton Rouge: Louisiana State University Press, 1990, p.15, p.21.
77. Stafford-Clark, MS 79551, p.24.
78. Churchill interviewed by Emily Mann in Kathleen Betsko and Rachel Koenig (eds), *Interviews with Contemporary Women Playwrights*, New York: Beech Tree Books, 1987, pp.75–84, at p.83.
79. *Cloud Nine* joined a New York theatre season featuring Tune's productions of the musicals *Best Little Whorehouse in Texas* and *A Day in Hollywood/A Night in the Ukraine*; he would later add *Nine* and, off-Broadway, David Williamson's straight play *The Club*.
80. Curt Davis, 'Churchill's Cloud and Clear', *Other Stages*, 3 Dec. 1981.
81. Churchill, *Cloud Nine*, p.247.
82. Don Shewey, 'Box Office Bombshells', *Soho News*, 4 Aug. 1981. Shewey likens Churchill to Joe Orton, an important influence on her *Owners*. See also Terry Helbing, 'The Gay's the Thing', *New York Native*, 19 Oct. 1981.

83. The event was held on 23 Mar. 1983; its promotional material can be found at the Billy Rose Theatre Division, New York Public Library for the Performing Arts.
84. Stephen M. Silverman, 'Churchill's "Cloud 9" Has a Silver Lining', *New York Post*, 24 Oct. 1981.
85. Jennifer Dunning, '"Cloud 9", Viewed by Those Floating on It', *New York Times*, 6 Nov. 1981.
86. See, e.g., Richard Winton, 'Actor Gets Probation for Inducing Boy to Pose Nude', *Los Angeles Times*, 9 July 2003. Twice since the actor's sentencing – first in 2004 and again in 2010 – Jones has been arrested for failing to update his registration as a sex offender.
87. Qtd in Jill Lynne, 'Tuned up on "Cloud 9"', *After Dark*, July 1981.
88. Stafford-Clark, MS 79567, p.11.
89. *Ibid.*, p.8.
90. See Kritzer, *Plays*, p.111.
91. Caryl Churchill, *Icecream* in *Plays: Three*, London: Nick Hern Books, 1998, pp.55–102, at p.57.
92. The lyrics they intend – the song's chorus – read as follows: 'Sure, by Tummel and Loch Rannoch and Lochaber I will go, / By heather tracks wi'heaven in their wiles; / If it's thinkin' in your inner heart braggart's in my step, / You've never smelt the tangle o' the Isles'.
93. Qtd in Roberts, *About Churchill*, p.113.
94. Churchill, *Icecream*, p.58.
95. Michael Billington, Rev. of *Icecream* in *London Theatre Record*, Vol. 9, No. 8 (9–22 Apr. 1989), p.450.
96. Stafford-Clark, MS 79567, p.7.
97. *Ibid.*, p.18.
98. Churchill, *Icecream*, p.65.
99. *Ibid.*, p.63. Indeed, the characters even celebrate clichés. See, for example, Vera: 'clichés are just what's true, what millions of people have already realised is true. Like proverbs are true. A stitch in time does in fact save nine'. *Ibid.*, p.68.
100. The Broadmoor example is highlighted at Kritzer, *Plays*, p.186.

101. Churchill, *Icecream*, p.96.
102. See the performance reports for 11 May and 18 May 1989, held at Blythe House.
103. Kritzer, *Plays*, p.184, p.186.
104. Qtd in Laurie Winer, 'Caryl Churchill, Ex-Ideologue, Trusts to Luck', *New York Times*, 29 Apr. 1990.
105. Stafford-Clark, MS 79567, p.21.
106. Qtd in Roberts, *About Churchill*, p.112.
107. Churchill, *Icecream*, p.59.
108. *Ibid.*, p.60.
109. *Ibid.*, p.61.
110. *Ibid.*, p.99.
111. Qtd in Winer, 'Caryl Churchill'.
112. See the reviews of Michael Coveney and Peter Kent in *London Theatre Record*, Vol. 9, No. 8 (9–22 Apr. 1989), p.448, p.449.
113. Churchill, *Icecream*, p.59.
114. *Ibid.*, p.62.
115. David Harvey, *The Condition of Postmodernity*, Oxford: Blackwell Publishing, 1989, p.303.
116. Churchill, *Icecream*, p.102.
117. In an article promoting the New York production, Churchill was paraphrased as saying 'her new work should be viewed simply as a story. Theatergoers should not look for either theme or message'. Enid Nemy, 'On Stage', *New York Times*, 30 Mar. 1990.
118. Roberts and Stafford-Clark, *Taking Stock*, p.105. The fuller context of Stafford-Clark's journal reveals how agonised the director felt about this decision – and how much work he had put into *Hot Fudge* – before his final decision, made on 15 Mar. 1989, to omit the play.
119. Caryl Churchill, *Hot Fudge* in *Shorts*, London: Nick Hern Books, 1990, pp.275–304, at p.280, p.282.
120. *Ibid.*, p.288, p.289.
121. See John Urry, *The Tourist Gaze* (2nd edn), London: Sage Publications, 2002, especially at pp.50–6.
122. Churchill, *Hot Fudge*, p.290.
123. *Ibid.*, p.293.

124. *Ibid.*, p.294.
125. *Ibid.*, p.292.
126. Although *The Love Salesman* found favour with a BBC script reader in May 1962, the project went uncommissioned and the play remained unwritten. I here quote from Churchill's undated treatment, held at the BBC Written Archives Centre in Reading, Folder RCont. 1 [Scriptwriters Caryl Churchill File I: 1959–96].
127. Mimi Kramer, 'Rocky Road', *New Yorker*, 21 May 1990, p.69.
128. Frank Rich, '2 Caryl Churchill Plays Show Dark Side of 1980s', *New York Times*, 4 May 1990.
129. The outlying reviewer weirdly complained that 'her technique is so perfect that you can see the actors . . . criss-crossing and swerving and stopping and starting until it all slots together perfectly'. Jonathan Myerson, 'Clones Crafted So Perfectly They Lack Humanity', *Independent*, 27 Sept. 2002.
130. Spencer's disparagement came in a review of the 1997 Old Vic revival of *Cloud Nine*, in which he judged it 'a tiresomely tendentious, unpleasantly man-hating play which scarcely merits revival on the gay and feminist fringe, let alone at the Old Vic'. Charles Spencer, Rev. of *Cloud Nine* in *Theatre Record*, Vol. 17, No. 6 (12–25 Mar. 1997), p.328. See, by contrast, Charles Spencer, Rev. of *A Number* in *Theatre Record*, Vol. 22, No. 20 (24 Sept.–7 Oct. 2002), pp.1280–1.
131. See the reviews of Nicholas de Jongh and John Peters in *Theatre Record*, Vol. 22, No. 20 (24 Sept.–7 Oct. 2002), p.1279, p.1278.
132. Ada Calhoun, 'Sam Shepard, the Silent Type', *New York*, 13 Sept. 2004.
133. Caryl Churchill, *A Number* in *Plays: Four*, London: Nick Hern Books, 2008, pp.161–206, at p.189.
134. *Ibid.*, p.170.
135. *Ibid.*, p.190.
136. *Ibid.*, p.164.
137. *Ibid.*, p.165.
138. *Ibid.*, p.169.
139. *Ibid.*, p.168.

140. *Ibid.*, p.176, p.197.
141. *Ibid.*, p.197, p.204.
142. *Ibid.*, p.172.
143. Churchill, *Plays: Four*, p.iv.
144. Qtd in Roberts, *About Churchill*, p.263. Daldry's assistant director, Sarah Wooley, claimed that even a simple change of shoes was rejected as 'signalling too much' at *ibid.*, p.264.
145. Churchill, *A Number*, p.177.
146. See, for example, Matt Wolf, 'Gotham-bound', *Variety*, 10 Mar. 2003 (on the likelihood of a Broadway transfer) or Matt Wolf, 'The Winning "Number"', *Variety*, 2 Dec. 2002 (on the rumour that Gene Hackman would star in a Broadway remount).
147. Churchill, *A Number*, p.187.
148. *Ibid.*, p.192.
149. *Ibid.*, p.202.
150. *Ibid.*
151. *Ibid.*, p.204.
152. Churchill, *Cloud Nine*, p.271.
153. *Ibid.*, p.291.
154. The line, used as jacket copy on the play's print editions, appears also at Churchill, *Plays: Two*, p.x.
155. Stafford-Clark, MS 79568, p.45. Barclays's investment in South Africa ended only in 1986, and after extraordinary public pressure.
156. *Ibid.*, p.46.
157. Qtd in Roberts, *About Churchill*, p.117, p.115.
158. Churchill, *A Number*, p.193.
159. *Ibid.*, p.205.
160. *Ibid.*, p.206.

Chapter 4

1. Elaine Aston, 'On Collaboration: "Not Ordinary, Not Safe"' in Elaine Aston and Elin Diamond (eds), *The Cambridge Companion to Caryl Churchill*, Cambridge: Cambridge University Press, 2009, pp.144–62, at p.144.

2. Caryl Churchill, *Plays: One*, London: Methuen Drama, 1985, p.xiii.
3. Caryl Churchill, *Light Shining in Buckinghamshire* in *Plays: One*, pp.181–241, at p.183.
4. See the unattributed pamphlet [Abiezer Coppe,] *A Second Fiery Flying Roule: To All the Inhabitants of the Earth; Specially to the Rich Ones* (London: no press, 1649), pp.3–4. Churchill (who spells his surname Cobbe) quotes him with elisions in Rob Ritchie (ed.), *The Joint Stock Book: The Making of a Theatre Collective*, London: Methuen, 1987, p.119.
5. Churchill, *Light Shining*, p.183.
6. The term comes from one of Churchill's contemporary sources: Christopher Hill, *The World Turned Upside Down: Radical Ideas During the English Revolution*, New York: The Viking Press, 1972, p.13.
7. Janelle Reinelt, *After Brecht: British Epic Theater*, Ann Arbor: University of Michigan Press, 1996, pp.85–6.
8. Qtd in Geraldine Cousin, *Churchill, the Playwright*, London: Methuen Drama, 1989, p.20.
9. See, for example, Churchill, *Light Shining*, p.205.
10. *Ibid.*, p.219.
11. These details are derived from Stafford-Clark's journal from the period (MS 79537), held in the British Library, starting with the entries for 26 Apr. 1976.
12. See Churchill's account in Ritchie, *Joint Stock*, p.118–9, supplemented by Siân Adiseshiah, 'Utopian Space in Caryl Churchill's History Plays: *Light Shining in Buckinghamshire* and *Vinegar Tom*', *Utopian Studies*, Vol. 16, No. 1 (2005), pp.3–26, at p.10.
13. Richie, *Joint Stock*, p.119.
14. Amelia Howe Kritzer, *The Plays of Caryl Churchill: Theatre of Empowerment*, New York: St Martin's Press, 1991, p.86.
15. Owing to competing commitments – for Joint Stock's actors were at the time not paid during the gap between workshops, causing them to seek other work – Ian Charleson, Jenny Cryst, Carole Hayman, Annie Raitt, and David Rintoul left the cast. They were

replaced by Janet Chappell and Nigel Terry. Once the production was mounted, Chappell would herself have to leave, at which point Hayman returned.

16. The first quotation is from an interview with Michael Oliver on 'Kaleidoscope', a programme broadcast on Radio 4 on 28 Sept. 1976 (a transcript is held in the Theatre and Performance Collections of the Victoria and Albert Museum at Blythe House). The phrase 'common imagination' appears in a print interview with Churchill: Geraldine Cousin, 'The Common Imagination and the Individual Voice', *New Theatre Quarterly*, Vol. 4, No. 13 (Feb. 1988), pp.3–16, at p.16. The emphasis is mine.
17. Churchill qtd in Oliver, 'Kaleidoscope'. *The Demonstration* went uncommissioned by the BBC despite positive reader reports.
18. See Churchill's remarks in Helene Keyssar, 'The Dramas of Caryl Churchill: The Politics of Possibility', *Massachusetts Review*, Vol. 24, No.1 (1983), pp.198–216, at p.208.
19. Qtd in Ritchie, *Joint Stock*, p.120.
20. The historical transcript is published in A. S. P. Woodhouse (ed.), *Puritanism and Liberty: Being the Army Debates (1647-9) from the Clarke Manuscripts with Supplementary Documents*, Chicago: University of Chicago Press, 1951. Compare Woodhouse, *Puritanism*, p.10 to Churchill, *Light Shining*, p.210.
21. For instance, Sexby's 'put to a question' is changed to 'put to a vote', and Cromwell's 'put this paper to the question' is changed to 'a vote': compare Woodhouse, *Puritanism*, pp.75–6 with Churchill, *Light Shining*, p.217. Churchill changes Rainborough's and Ireton's individual uses of 'burgesses' to 'members': compare Woodhouse, *Puritanism*, p.56 and p.60 to Churchill, *Light Shining*, p.213 and p.214.
22. Compare Woodhouse, *Puritanism*, p.67 to Churchill, *Light Shining*, p.215; compare Woodhouse, *Puritanism*, p.71 to Churchill, *Light Shining*, p.216.
23. Churchill, *Light Shining*, p.218.
24. I have located no archival trace of the project, discussed in Colin Chambers, *Peggy: The Life of Margaret Ramsay, Play Agent*, London: Methuen, 1997, p.268. BBC records do reveal that

Churchill had been commissioned to adapt Laurie Lee's *Cider with Rosie* around 1965. The project was never completed.

25. Churchill had her name removed in protest of changes made by the broadcaster. She and her husband had received the transcript from a sympathetic party whose identity, now declassified, was kept secret by the BBC.
26. The decision is recorded in Stafford-Clark's diary.
27. Churchill, *Light Shining*, p.187.
28. *Ibid.*, p.220.
29. See *ibid.*, pp.184–5: 'This seems to reflect better the reality of large events like war and revolution. . . . When different actors play the parts what comes over is a large event involving many people, whose characters resonate in a way they wouldn't if they were more clearly defined'. Churchill amplified these sentiments in Ritchie, *Joint Stock*, pp.118–21.
30. Wandor, discussing the workshop for *Cloud Nine*, is qtd in Linda Fitzsimmons (ed.), *File on Churchill*, London: Methuen Drama, 1989, p.46.
31. Michael Billington, 'Light Shining', *Guardian*, 28 Sept. 1976.
32. Bowen appeared on Oliver, 'Kaleidoscope', cited above.
33. Quotations appear in the transcript of the Philip French's 'Critic's Forum', 2 Oct. 1976.
34. Bertolt Brecht, *Brecht on Theatre: The Development of an Aesthetic*, John Willett (ed. and trans.), London: Methuen Drama, 1990, at pp.210–11.
35. Qtd in Ritchie, *Joint Stock*, p.119.
36. Adiseshiah, 'Utopian Space', p.11.
37. Qtd in Ritchie, *Joint Stock*, p.105.
38. Churchill's work (with Mills and the Young People's Theatre Scheme) with nine- and ten-year-olds in Islington produced a play that was performed at their school. Details are provided in Dan Rebellato, 'On Churchill's Influences' in Aston and Diamond, *Cambridge Companion*, pp.163–79, at p.170. Churchill has noted that critics – and even she – have tended to forget *Strange Days*, whose workshops preceded *Light Shining* by a year: see Philip Roberts, *About Churchill: The Playwright and the*

Work, London: Faber, 2008, p.52. Roberts also published the play's first seven scenes at *ibid.*, pp.172–7.

39. A BBC memo retroactively assessed the collaborative venture – directed by Piers Haggard and broadcast on 26 July 1975 – thus: 'Three writers tended either to over stimulate each other so that the resulting writing was over-rich or to wrestle much of the time over how they should collaborate'. The memo is at the BBC Written Archives Centre, Folder T62/223/1.
40. See, for example, Joyce Devlin, 'Joint Stock: From Colorless Company to Company of Color', *Theatre Topics*, Vol. 2, No. 1 (Mar. 1992), pp.63–76.
41. Qtd in *ibid.*, p.65.
42. Qtd in Ritchie, *Joint Stock*, p.110.
43. As it happens, the remark reconstructs history a bit, too. It is published in Philip Roberts and Max Stafford-Clark, *Taking Stock: The Theatre of Max Stafford-Clark*, London: Nick Hern Books, 2007, p.211, ostensibly as a transcription of Stafford-Clark's diary from 27 Sept. 1999. In fact, his diary from that date – MS 84047, p.43 – records Hayman's comments and his irritation with them. But his analysis about 'reconstructing history' has been silently introduced into the published entry.
44. Churchill, *Light Shining*, p.233.
45. *Ibid.*, p.207.
46. *Ibid.*
47. Churchill interviewed by Emily Mann in Kathleen Betsko and Rachel Koenig (eds), *Interviews with Contemporary Women Playwrights*, New York: Beech Tree Books, 1987, pp.75–84, at p.78.
48. Elaine Aston, *Caryl Churchill* (3rd edn), Horndon: Northcote House Publishers, 2010, p.25.
49. Qtd in Aston, 'On Collaboration', p.145.
50. Caryl Churchill, *Vinegar Tom* in *Plays: One*, pp.127–79, at p.136.
51. My report has been built deductively: Churchill mentions inventing the part of Betty for Cupido in an interview excerpted at Fitzsimmons, *File on Churchill*, p.34. She mentions recycling the bleeding scene, cut from *Light Shining*, at Roberts, *About*

Churchill, p.183. The scene itself is at Churchill, *Vinegar Tom*, p.149.

52. *Abortive*, directed by John Tydeman and starring Prunella Scales, was broadcast on 4 Feb. 1971 on BBC Radio 3.
53. Churchill, *Plays: One*, p.131.
54. Churchill, *Light Shining*, p.205.
55. *Ibid.*
56. *Ibid.*, p.198.
57. *Ibid.*, p.223.
58. *Ibid.*, p.226.
59. Qtd in Ritchie, *Joint Stock*, p.105.
60. See, for example, the remarks of Simon Callow – 'what was all this nonsense about a collective? By far the largest group within the collective were actors, but did they have any say in the style of the productions? Just let them try' – qtd in Devlin, 'Joint Stock', p.65. Callow had joined Joint Stock the autumn that *Light Shining* was produced; his first of several shows with the group was *The Speakers*, which opened even as *Light Shining* continued its successful run, which after a tour returned to the Royal Court, where it was extended into 1977.
61. Stafford-Clark, MS 79537, 11 June 1976, n.p.
62. Brighton had directed the first production of *Stones in His Pockets* and has claimed to have made atypical creative contributions to its script, which later achieved enormous creative and commercial success. But after a lawsuit she was found to have no authorial or other ongoing interest in the play. For a legal analysis of the case and its ramifications, see Lior Zemer, *The Idea of Authorship in Copyright*, Aldershot: Ashgate Publishing, 2007, at pp.212–13.
63. Jean E. Howard, 'On Owning and Owing: Caryl Churchill and the Nightmare of Capital' in Aston and Diamond, *Cambridge Companion*, pp.36–51, at p.43.
64. *Ibid.*
65. Caryl Churchill, *Fen* in *Plays: Two*, London: Methuen Drama, 1990, pp.143–92, at p.147.
66. Caryl Churchill, *Fen* unpublished typescript, p.1. The typescript can be seen at the Billy Rose Theatre Division of the New York

Public Library for the Performing Arts, *T-MSS 1993-028, Box 3-163.

67. Churchill, *Fen*, p.163.
68. *Ibid.*, p.162, p.177.
69. Churchill, *Fen* unpublished typescript, p.6.
70. Churchill, *Fen*, p.161.
71. *Ibid.*, p.147.
72. Initially entitled *Blocks, Parks, Fanatics*, the play was astutely recognised by the BBC's readers as one of Churchill's finest radio plays. Some of its plot points (charges for driving, or fanatics killing civilians, in central London) seem remarkably prescient – even if Mick, bizarrely to contemporary eyes, sends a telegram. One of the play's other plot points – Mick's nineteen-year-old son Claude is celebrated for being the last child born in London – would reappear in P. D. James's dystopian novel, *Children of Men*, in 1992. *Not Not Not Not Not Enough Oxygen* received a stage production without décor, directed by Ian Rickson at the Royal Court and starring Sophie Okonedo, on 7 Oct. 2002.
73. Stafford-Clark, MS 79553, 13 Dec. 1981, p.163.
74. My description of the workshop draws on my interview with Bassett on 8 Apr. 2013, supplemented by Jennifer Dunning, '*Fen*, Unusual On-the-Spot Creation', *New York Times*, 21 June 1983; by Jennie Stoller in Ritchie, *Joint Stock*, pp.150–2; and by Churchill's interviews in Betsko and Koenig, *Interviews*, pp.80–1, and in Cousin, 'Common Imagination', p.6.
75. Qtd in Cousin, 'Common Imagination', p.6.
76. Qtd in Betsko and Koenig, *Interviews*, p.80.
77. See Jennifer Dunning, '*Fen* with an American Cast', *New York Times*, 2 Mar. 1984.
78. Qtd in Betsko and Koenig, *Interviews*, p.80. Churchill connects domestic violence to the region's economic upheavals at Roberts, *About Churchill*, p.89.
79. See Betsko and Koenig, *Interviews*, p.80.
80. Compare Churchill, *Fen*, pp.157–8 and Mary Chamberlain, *Fenwomen: A Portrait of Women in an English Village*, London: Virago, 1975, pp.112–14.

81. Churchill, *Fen* unpublished typescript, p.38.
82. The first quotation is from Betsko and Koenig, *Interviews*, p.80; the second, from Churchill, *Fen*, p.ix.
83. Churchill, *Fen*, p.145.
84. *Ibid.*, p.151.
85. *Ibid.*, p.162.
86. *Ibid.*, p.163.
87. *Ibid.*, p.187.
88. *Ibid.*, p.181.
89. *Ibid.*, p.154.
90. *Ibid.*, p.157.
91. *Ibid.*, p.165.
92. *Ibid.*, p.174.
93. *Ibid.*, p.169.
94. *Ibid.*, p.151.
95. *Ibid.*, pp.159–60.
96. Churchill, *Fen* unpublished typescript, pp.15–16.
97. Here, as elsewhere, I rely on the production records held in New York.
98. Qtd in Cousin, *Churchill, the Playwright*, p.47.
99. *Fen*, p.171. Churchill attributes the insight to their Upwell workshop at Cousin, 'Common Imagination', p.6.
100. Interview, 9 Apr. 2013.
101. Ritchie, *Joint Stock*, p.152.
102. Rabillard follows the ecofeminist Vandana Shiva: see Sheila Rabillard, '*Fen* and the Production of a Feminist Ecotheater', *Theater*, Vol. 25, No. 1 (1994), pp.62–71, at p.65.
103. Qtd in Dunning, 'American Cast'.
104. Elin Diamond, *Unmaking Mimesis: Essays on Feminism and Theatre*, New York: Routledge, 1997, p.93.
105. Churchill, *Fen*, p.190.
106. *Ibid.*, p.180.
107. *Ibid.*, p.172.
108. Churchill, *Fen* unpublished typescript, p.41.
109. Churchill, *Fen*, p.189.
110. Ritchie, *Joint Stock*, p.28.

111. See, for example, Cushman, who praises the play but finds that the 'restless doubling . . . actually works against a sense of community; there are simply never enough people around' in the *Observer* (20 Feb. 1983); or Wardle in *The Times* (17 Feb. 1983), who describes the play as 'the theatrical equivalent of a landscape painting' but finds the doubling too confusing.
112. The letter can be found in *T-MSS 1993-028, Box 2-57, Folder 7.
113. *Ibid.*
114. Laurie Stone, 'Labor of Love', *Village Voice*, 7 June 1983.
115. The undated memo appears in *T-MSS 1993-028, Box 4-26, Folder 7.
116. Churchill did draw some dialogue from Pat Barr's Isabella Bird biography, *A Curious Life for a Lady*, and Lady Nijo's autobiographical *The Confessions of Lady Nijo.*
117. Ramsay's letter, dated 2 June 1983, appears in *T-MSS 1993-028, Box 5-135, Folder 13.
118. Rabillard, '*Fen*', p.68.
119. Clive Barnes, 'Churchill's *Fen* is the Place to Be', *New York Post*, 12 Mar. 1984.
120. Churchill, *Fen*, p.145.
121. Qtd in Mary Luckhurst, 'On the Challenge of Revolution' in Aston and Diamond, pp.52–87, at p.63.
122. See Ceridwen Thomas, 'Not Out of the Wood', *Plays and Players*, No. 441 (Aug. 1990), pp.18–19.
123. Mark Wing-Davey, 'England: The Power of Paranoia', *Journal of Stage Directors and Choreographers*, Vol. 8, No. 1 (Spring/Summer 1994), pp.43–6 at p.45. Strangely, Romanian and British actors alike could fool their compatriots more easily than their foreign collaborators.
124. See, for example, Benedict Nightingale, Rev. of *Mad Forest, The Times*, 26 June 1990.
125. Caryl Churchill, *Mad Forest: A Play from Romania* in *Plays: Three*, London: Nick Hern Books, 1998, pp.101–81, at p.123.
126. *Ibid.*, p.126.
127. *Ibid.*, p.108.
128. *Ibid.*, p.109, p.111.

129. On the connection between the resistance of *Mad Forest*'s young characters to their parents and their resistance to Ceauşescu, see Tony Mitchell, 'Caryl Churchill's *Mad Forest*: Polyphonic Representations of Southeastern Europe', *Modern Drama*, Vol. 36, No. 4 (1993), pp.499–511, at p.506.
130. Churchill, *Mad Forest*, p.126.
131. Qtd in Jim Hiley, 'Revolution in Miniature', *The Times*, 10 Oct. 1990.
132. Qtd in Carl Miller, 'Romanian Rhapsody', *City Limits*, 11–18 Oct. 1990.
133. Churchill, *Mad Forest*, p.132.
134. *Ibid.*, p.141, p.142.
135. *Ibid.*, p.175.
136. *Ibid.*, p.153.
137. *Ibid.*, p.145.
138. Qtd in Hiley, 'Revolution'.
139. Alison Light, '*Mad Forest* (Royal Court Theatre, London)', *Feminist Review*, Vol. 39 (1991), pp.204–10, at p.207, p.206.
140. See Andrei Oţetea and Andrew MacKenzie, *A Concise History of Romania*, London: Robert Hale, 1985, p.12, used as an epigraph at Churchill, *Mad Forest*, p.103.
141. Wing-Davey, 'England', p.45.
142. Churchill, *Mad Forest*, p.107.
143. *Ibid.*
144. *Ibid.*, p.166.
145. *Ibid.*, p.139.
146. *Ibid.*, p.119.
147. *Ibid.*, p.157.
148. Churchill, *Light Shining*, p.183.
149. Churchill, *Mad Forest*, p.181.
150. *Ibid.*, p.181. Compare *ibid.*, p.139.
151. Louis Althusser, *For Marx*, Ben Brewster (trans.), London: Allen Lane, 1960, p.146.
152. Churchill, *Mad Forest*, p.104.
153. *Ibid.*, p.163.
154. *Ibid.*, p.164.

155. *Ibid.*, p.136.
156. *Ibid.*, p.131.
157. *Ibid.*, p.149.
158. Amelia Howe Kritzer, 'Dionysus in Bucharest: Caryl Churchill's *Mad Forest*', *In-Between: Essays and Studies in Literary Criticism*, Vol. 4, No. 2 (1995), pp.151–61, at p.152.
159. Churchill, *Mad Forest*, p.146, p.142.
160. Here and elsewhere, I draw on the play's British and American production records, held at Blythe House in London and at the Billy Rose Theatre Division of the New York Public Library for the Performing Arts.
161. *Fen*'s inability to return to Upwell is claimed at Rabillard, '*Fen*', p.68.
162. See Caryl Churchill, 'To Romania with Love', *Guardian*, 13 Oct. 1990.
163. Details are found in Marc Robinson, 'Bracing Grace: Wing-Davey's Approach to *Mad Forest*', *Village Voice*, 24 Dec. 1991.
164. Mel Gussow, 'A Play That Improves as It Travels from Place to Place', *New York Times*, 25 Jan. 1992.
165. Frank Rich, 'After Ceausescu, Another Kind of Terror', *New York Times*, 5 Dec. 1991.
166. John Simon, 'Finding the Tone', *New York*, 16 Dec. 1991.
167. John Simon, Rev. of *Mad Forest, New York*, 12 Oct. 1992.
168. Rocco Sisto replaced Joseph Siravo, who left to do Herb Gardner's *Conversations with My Father* on Broadway. Sisto thus inherited the roles inaugurated, in London, by Iain Hake.
169. Caryl Churchill, *This Is a Chair* in *Plays: Four*, London: Nick Hern Books, 2008, pp.37–58, at p.58.
170. Qtd in Fitzsimmons, *File on Churchill*, p.62.
171. Churchill, *Mad Forest*, p.166.
172. Qtd in Roberts, *About Churchill*, p.270.

Chapter 5

1. Caryl Churchill, *Hotel* in *Plays: Four*, London: Nick Hern Books, 2008, pp.1–36, at p.3.

2. Caryl Churchill, *Drunk Enough to Say I Love You?* in *Plays: Four*, pp.267–309, at p.271.
3. The denunciation is cited in Tony Kushner and Alisa Solomon, '"Tell Her the Truth": On Caryl Churchill's *Seven Jewish Children: A Play for Gaza*', *The Nation*, 13 Apr. 2009, pp.11, 13, 14, 16, at p.11.
4. Caryl Churchill, *Traps* in *Plays: One*, London: Methuen Drama, 1985, pp.69–125, at p.72.
5. *Ibid.*, p.71.
6. *Ibid.*, p.108.
7. *Ibid.*, p.74, p.86, p.100.
8. *Ibid.*, p.71.
9. *Ibid.*, p.87.
10. Aristotle, *On Poetry and Style*, G.M.A. Grube (trans.) Indianapolis: Hackett Publishing Company, 1989, p.7.
11. Churchill, *Traps*, p.76.
12. Philip Roberts, *About Churchill: The Playwright and the Work*, London: Faber, 2008, p.54.
13. Churchill, *Traps*, p.90.
14. *Ibid.*, p.88.
15. Caryl Churchill, *Turkish Delight*, unpublished typescript, p.37.
16. Elin Diamond, *Unmaking Mimesis: Essays on Feminism and Theatre*, New York: Routledge, 1997, p.87.
17. Schechner distinguishes among 'event time' (when an activity is over after a predetermined sequence of events ends), 'set time' (an arbitrary limit, as in Marina Abramović's 736½-hour performance *The Artist is Present*), and 'symbolic time' (as in most plays, where one span of time represents another). See Richard Schechner, *Performance Theory*, New York: Routledge, 1988, pp.6–7.
18. Churchill, *Traps*, p.125.
19. Caryl Churchill, *Henry's Past*, unpublished typescript, p.34.
20. Peter Handke, *Offending the Audience* in *Plays: One*, Michael Roloff (trans.), London: Methuen Drama, 1997, pp.1–32, at p.9.
21. Peter Handke, *Kaspar* in *Plays: One*, pp.51–141, at pp.53–4.
22. The keen observation appears in Amelia Howe Kritzer, *The Plays of Caryl Churchill: Theatre of Empowerment*, New York: St Martin's Press, 1991, p.80.

23. Peter Handke, *The Ride Across Lake Constance* in *Plays: One*, pp.163–233, at p.166.
24. Catherine Sheehy, 'Time and Again: Churchill's New/Old Plays at NYTW', *Village Voice*, 23 Mar. 1993.
25. *Ibid.*
26. On the connection between Handke and Beckett, see Jonas Barish, *The Antitheatrical Prejudice*, Berkeley: University of California Press, 1981, at pp.457–64. Beckett's line about Joyce was: 'His writing is not *about* something; *it is that something itself*'. See Samuel Beckett, *Disjecta: Miscellaneous Writings and a Dramatic Fragment*, Ruby Cohn (ed.), New York: Grove Press, 1984, p.27.
27. Sam Shepard, *Buried Child* in *Seven Plays*, Toronto: Bantam Books, 1981, pp.61–132, at p.125.
28. Churchill, *Traps*, p.80.
29. See Churchill's comments – in Rob Ritchie (ed.), *The Joint Stock Book: The Making of a Theatre Collective*, London: Methuen, 1987, p.119 – about *Light Shining in Buckinghamshire*. Its run extended, *Light Shining* had closed only a month before *Traps*' premiere.
30. Gillian Hanna (ed.), *Monstrous Regiment: Four Plays and a Collective Celebration*, London: Nick Hern Books, 1991, p.xxxvii.
31. Churchill, *Traps*, p.76.
32. Michael Billington, Rev. of *Traps, Guardian*, 28 Jan. 1977.
33. Records for both Stix productions can be found at the Billy Rose Theatre Division, New York Public Library for the Performing Arts.
34. The exception was David Alford, who played Jack in *Traps* but did not appear in *Owners*; its cast requires one less man and two more women.
35. Qtd in Sheehy, 'Time and Again'.
36. Handke, *Ride Across Lake Constance*, p.164.
37. Churchill, *Traps*, p.87.
38. *Ibid.*, p.125.
39. Jill Dolan, *Utopia in Performance: Finding Hope at the Theater*, Ann Arbor: University of Michigan Press, 2005, p.65.
40. *Ibid.*, p.59.

41. Charles Spencer, Rev. of *Blue Heart* in *Theatre Record*, Vol. 17, No. 19 (10–23 Sept. 1997), p.1191; Ben Brantley, 'Finding Appalling Sense in a Giddy Anarchy', *New York Times*, 1 Feb. 1999. A stark exception to all the praise in Edinburgh, London, and New York was a reviewer for *The Times*, who sourly assessed that 'Churchill seems to be addressing no one but herself, with her meticulously crafted mind games being too exclusive to let ordinary folk in'. See Neil Cooper, Rev. of *Blue Heart* in *Theatre Record*, Vol. 17, No. 19 (10–23 Sept. 1997), p.1191.
42. Brantley, 'Finding'; Gerard Raymond, 'Play and Anti-Play', *Village Voice*, 2 Feb. 1999. Stafford-Clark reports Churchill's description of *Blue Heart* as 'anti-plays' in the same article.
43. Raymond, 'Play'.
44. *Ibid.*
45. Caryl Churchill, *Blue Heart* in *Plays: Four*, London: Nick Hern Books, 2008, pp.60–128, at p.65.
46. *Ibid.*, p.77.
47. *Ibid.*, p.77, p.91.
48. *Ibid.*, p.92. Churchill underscores the significance of this particular interruption not only by positioning it where she does but also by repeating it twice. See also *ibid.*, p.95: 'You are my heart's –', where Brian is cut off, mid-line, for the final reset.
49. *Ibid.*, p.95.
50. *Ibid.*, p.103.
51. *Ibid.*, p.128.
52. *Ibid.*, p.74.
53. *Ibid.*, pp.81–2.
54. See *ibid.*, p.120. David Benedict was the only critic to identify Blyton's importance to Churchill's play; see his perceptive review (from the Edinburgh Festival) in *Theatre Record*, Vol. 17, No. 17 (13–26 Aug. 1997), p.1054.
55. Churchill, *Blue Heart*, p.115.
56. I make this argument, too, and connect *Traps* to *Blue Heart*, in the article from which this chapter draws: R. Darren Gobert, 'Performance and Selfhood in Caryl Churchill' in Elaine Aston and Elin Diamond (eds), *The Cambridge Companion to Caryl*

Churchill, Cambridge: Cambridge University Press, 2009, pp.105–24, especially at pp.115–16.
57. Churchill, *Blue Heart*, p.86.
58. *Ibid.*, p.117.
59. *Ibid.*, p.118.
60. *Ibid.*, p.128.
61. The quotation is related in Raymond, 'Play'.
62. Tom Stoppard, *Rosencrantz and Guildenstern Are Dead*, New York: Grove Press, 1967, p.25.
63. Churchill, *Blue Heart*, p.99.
64. *Ibid.*, p.69. See also *ibid.*, p.71, p.72, p.76, p.93.
65. *Ibid.*, p.78, p.85.
66. *Ibid.*, p.74.
67. All details about the production can be verified in the play's archival documents in the Theatre and Performance Collections of the Victoria and Albert Museum held at Blythe House.
68. Churchill, *Blue Heart*, p.128.
69. Charles Isherwood, Rev. of *Blue Heart, Variety*, 8–14 Feb. 1999.
70. Qtd in Elaine Aston, *Caryl Churchill* (3rd edn), Horndon: Northcote House Publishers, 2010, p.113.
71. Churchill's friendship with the American playwright goes back several decades, and (despite being an active presence in many rehearsals of her own plays) she has largely restricted her directorial forays to his work. She also staged a reading of his *A Thought in Three Parts* on 19 June 2009, also for the Royal Court.
72. Churchill, *Blue Heart*, p.71.
73. *Ibid.*, p.91.
74. Herbert Blau, *Blooded Thought: Occasions of Theatre*, New York: PAJ Press, 1982, p.134.
75. Stoppard, *Rosencrantz and Guildenstern*, p.115.
76. Qtd in Judith Mackrell, 'Flights of Fancy', *Independent*, 20 Jan. 1994.
77. The term 'postdramatic theatre' was coined in the book of that name by Hans-Thies Lehmann, who ties the director-driven spectacles of troupes such as the Wooster Group to the radical postmodernism of writers such as Heiner Müller. Especially since

the translation of *Postdramatische Theater* (1999) to English – by Karen Jürs-Munby in 2006 for Routledge – the term has been deployed so broadly that its analytic value is now compromised. I am therefore reluctant to use it as shorthand for *Love and Information*'s radical indeterminacy.

78. Caryl Churchill, *Love and Information*, London: Nick Hern Books, 2012, p.2.
79. *Ibid.*, p.74.
80. *Ibid.*
81. *Ibid.*, p.76.
82. *Ibid.*, p.5.
83. *Ibid.*, p.62.
84. Macdonald discusses his work on Kane's blank-slate play in R. Darren Gobert, 'Finding a Physical Language: Directing for the Nineties Generation', *New Theatre Quarterly* 24.2 (May 2008), pp.141–57, especially at pp.151–2. The director had also hoped to do the premiere production of *Attempts on Her Life*, but a conflict prevented it.
85. Details can be found in Nina Raine, 'Whose Line Is It Anyway', *Guardian*, 9 Dec. 2006.
86. Churchill, *Love and Information*, p.4.
87. *Ibid.*, p.26.
88. *Ibid.*, p.34.
89. Amuka-Bird's line in this scene, along with Amit Shah's line in the production's sixth (about a documentary on the Amazon River) represent the only bits of dialogue written too late in the process to be included in *Love and Information*'s first edition.
90. *Ibid.*, p.12.
91. *Ibid.*, p.11.
92. *Ibid.*, p.49.
93. Caryl Churchill, *Objections to Sex and Violence* in Michelene Wandor (ed.), *Plays by Women: Volume Four*, London: Methuen, 1985, pp.11–53, at p.17.
94. Caryl Churchill, *A Number* in *Plays: Four*, London: Nick Hern Books, 2008, pp.161–206, at p.202.

95. Churchill, *Love and Information*, p.11.
96. *Ibid.*, p.36.
97. Unusually, Churchill has provided one clue to the character's identity in this scene, since her stage direction genders the unremembering character as male. See *ibid.*, p.45.
98. *Ibid.*, p.24.
99. *Ibid.*, p.56.
100. *Ibid.*, p.35.
101. *Ibid.*, p.43.
102. *Ibid.*, p.71.
103. *Ibid.*
104. David Benedict, Rev. of *Love and Information, Variety*, 24–30 Sept. 2012.
105. Churchill, *Love and Information*, p.25.
106. Churchill, *Blue Heart*, p.128; Churchill, *Love and Information*, p.76.

Chapter 6

1. 'Picasso' is attributed to Churchill on account of her theatrical inventiveness: see 'Sarah Daniels's [interview] in Heidi Stephenson and Natasha Langridge (eds), *Rage and Reason: Women Playwrights on Playwriting*, London: Methuen, 1997, pp.1–8, at p.6.
2. The revival was a co-production between Stafford-Clark's Out of Joint theatre company and Chichester Festival Theatre. The play toured nationally from 2011 to 2012. Stafford-Clark was the original director of *Top Girls* in 1982 at the Royal Court and directed the play's Court revival in 1991. His commentary on the revival at Chichester can be heard at: http://www.outofjoint.co.uk/prods/top-girls-in-conversation.html
3. See Stafford-Clark's diary qtd in this book's first chapter, n.49.
4. Mark Ravenhill, 'Dramatic Moments', *Guardian*, 9 Apr. 1997.
5. Caryl Churchill, 'Not Ordinary, Not Safe: A Direction for Drama?', *The Twentieth Century*, Vol. 168 (Nov. 1960), pp.443–51, at p.446.
6. *Ibid.*

7. Conservative governments were led by Winston Churchill, 1951; Antony Eden, 1955; Harold Macmillan, 1957. Macmillan took prime ministerial office on the resignation of Eden in 1957, won the 1959 election, and remained Prime Minister until 1963.
8. *Omnibus on Caryl Churchill*, BBC 1, broadcast 11 Apr. 1988.
9. *Ibid.*
10. *Ibid.*
11. The majority of CND supporters were leftist in outlook, while the movement looked to the Labour Party as a source of political support for its cause.
12. Significant were the 1967 Abortion and Sexual Offences Acts.
13. Qtd in Catherine Itzin, *Stages in the Revolution: Political Theatre in Britain Since 1968*, London: Eyre Methuen, 1980, p.279.
14. Interview with Mel Gussow, 'Genteel Playwright, Angry Voice', *New York Times*, 22 Nov. 1987. Those circumstances were to change when her husband 'left the bar and started working for a law centre'. As Churchill puts it, 'We did not want to shore up a capitalist system that we didn't like', qtd in Itzin, *Stages*, p.279.
15. I draw here on E. Ann Kaplan's distinction between the 'age: personal/longitudinal axis' and the 'generation: cultural axis': 'Feminism, Aging and Changing Paradigms', *Surfaces*, Vol. 12, No. 110: http://www.pum.umontreal.ca/revues/surfaces/pdf/vol7/kaplan.pdf
16. Qtd in Gussow, 'Genteel Playwright'.
17. For a survey of the industry's sexual politics through the sixties and seventies, see Michelene Wandor, *Understudies: Theatre and Sexual Politics*, London: Eyre Methuen, 1981.
18. Itzin, *Stages*, p.135.
19. See Steve Gooch, 'Caryl Churchill, Author of This Month's Playtext, Talks to P & P', *Plays and Players*, Vol. 20, No. 4 (1973), p.40 and inset p.I. The script follows at pp.II–XVI.
20. *Ibid.*, p.22.
21. Churchill qtd in Philip Roberts, *About Churchill: The Playwright and the Work*, London: Faber, 2008, p.xxv.

22. 1956 and the premiere of Osborne's *Look Back in Anger* constituted Churchill's first encounter with the Royal Court Theatre. This was after her return to England from Canada; she was seventeen at the time. For further details see Gresdna A. Doty and Billy J. Harbin (eds), *Inside the Royal Court Theatre, 1956-1981: Artists Talk*, Baton Rouge: Louisiana State University Press, 1990, pp.144–5.
23. Churchill explained that 'the playing [of *Owners*] has to be kept sharp, or parts of the play could seem like clichéd naturalistic scenes, whereas things which might be naturalistic should really be thrown up at funny angles'. Gooch, 'Caryl Churchill', p.I.
24. *Ibid.*
25. Turning 'to Chinese philosophical mysticism, Taoism' helped Churchill to find an alternative to 'western capitalistic individualism, puritanism, and everything which came out of Christianity', *ibid.*
26. Qtd in Ronald Hayman, 'Partners: Caryl Churchill and Max Stafford-Clark', *Sunday Times Magazine*, 2 Mar. 1980, pp.25–7, at p.27.
27. Hare was also literary manager at the Royal Court prior to being a dramatist in residence.
28. Itzin, *Stages*, p.330.
29. Delivered in his 1978 Cambridge lecture on political theatre. For a digest see Itzin, *Stages*, pp.330–6.
30. Gillian Hanna (ed.), *Monstrous Regiment: Four Plays and a Collective Celebration,* London: Nick Hern Books, 1991, p.xxxvii.
31. In Britain, the WLM organised around four key demands: for equal pay, equal education and opportunity, twenty-four-hour nurseries, and free contraception and abortion on demand.
32. Gillian Hanna, *Feminism and Theatre*, Theatre Papers, 2nd series, No. 8, Dartington, Devon: Dartington College, 1978, p.9.
33. A Conservative government under Edward Heath was in power from 1970 to 1974.
34. Caryl Churchill, *Top Girls* in *Plays: Two,* London: Methuen Drama, 1990, pp.51–141, at p.137, p.137, p.141.

35. Michael Billington, 'The Players', *Guardian*, 6 July 2002.
36. Christopher Innes, *Modern British Drama: 1890-1990*, Cambridge: Cambridge University Press, 1992, p.448.
37. Qtd in Jane Edwardes, 'Celebrating Caryl Churchill', *Time Out London*, 14 Nov. 2006.
38. See, for example, Rebecca D'Monté and Graham Saunders (eds), *Cool Britannia?: British Political Drama in the 1990s*, Basingstoke: Palgrave Macmillan, 2008.
39. I have their respective debut plays particularly in mind: *Shopping and Fucking* (Ravenhill); *Blasted* (Kane).
40. http://www.outofjoint.co.uk/prods/top-girls-in-conversation.html
41. Objections came from former Royal Court director, William Gaskill. See Nuala Calvi, 'Stoppard's Place in Anniversary Season Defended by Royal Court', *The Stage.Co.Uk*, 28 Dec. 2005: http://www.thestage.co.uk/news/2005/12/stoppards-place-in-anniversary-season-defended-by-royal-court/
42. Qtd in Mark Lawson, 'Feminist, Pioneer, Shaman', *Guardian*, 4 Oct. 2012.
43. Qtd in Roberts, *About Churchill*, p.116.
44. Stuart Hall and Martin Jacques (eds), *New Times: The Changing Face of Politics in the 1990s*, London: Lawrence and Wishart in association with *Marxism Today*, 1989.
45. See Anthony Giddens, *The Third Way: The Renewal of Social Democracy*, London: Polity, 1998.
46. Michael Rustin, 'The Trouble with "New Times"' in Hall and Jacques, *New Times*, pp.303–20, at p.313.
47. Francis Fukuyama, 'The End of History', *The National Interest*, Vol. 16 (Summer 1989), pp.3–18.
48. Mary Kaldor, 'After the Cold War', *New Left Review*, Vol. 180 (Mar./Apr. 1990), pp.25–37, at p.37.
49. David Edgar, *The Second Time as Farce*, London: Lawrence and Wishart, 1988, p.124.
50. Caryl Churchill, *Top Girls* in *Plays: Two*, London: Methuen Drama, 1990, pp.51–141, at p.140.
51. 'The Appeal from the Sorbonne' in Carl Oglesby (ed.), *The New Left Reader*, New York: Grove Press, 1969, pp.267–73, at p.272.

52. Sheila Rowbotham, 'Leninism in the Lurch' in *Dreams and Dilemmas*, London: Virago Press, 1983, pp.119–23, at p.122.
53. Stuart Hall, Raymond Williams, and Edward Thompson, 'From *The May Day Manifesto*' in Oglesby, *New Left Reader*, pp.113–43, at pp.113–14.
54. Caryl Churchill, Interview by Judith Thurman, *Ms* (May 1982), p.54.
55. Stuart Hall, 'The Meaning of New Times' in Hall and Jacques, *New Times*, p.130.
56. On this point, see John Callaghan, *The Far Left in British Politics*, Oxford: Blackwell, 1987, p.71.
57. Roland Muldoon, 'Cast Revival', *Plays and Players*, Vol. 24, No. 4 (Jan. 1977), pp.40–1, at p.41.
58. André Gorz, 'From Strategy For Labour' in Oglesby, *New Left Reader*, pp.41–2.
59. Caryl Churchill, *Far Away* in *Plays: Four*, pp.129–59, at p.150.
60. See Jean-François Lyotard, *The Postmodern Condition: A Report on Knowledge*, Geoffrey Bennington and Brian Massumi (trans.), Minneapolis: University of Minnesota Press, 1984.
61. Terry Eagleton, 'In the Gaudy Supermarket', Rev. of Gayatri Chakravorty Spivak, *A Critique of Post-Colonial Reason: Toward a History of the Vanishing Present, London Review of Books*, 13 May 1999, pp.3–6, at p.6.
62. Fred Inglis, 'The Figures of Dissent', *New Left Review*, Vol. 215 (Jan./Feb. 1996), pp.83–92, at p.91.
63. Kate Soper, 'Postmodernism, Subjectivity, Value', *New Left Review*, Vol. 186 (Mar./Apr. 1999), pp.120–8, at p.123.
64. The assessment is that of Graeme Chesters, 'Resist to Exist?' *ECOS*, Vol. 20, No. 2 (1999), pp.19–25, at p.20.
65. Amelia Howe Kritzer, 'Political Currents in Caryl Churchill's Plays at the Turn of the Millennium' in Marc Maufort and Franca Bellarsi (eds), *Crucible of Cultures: Anglophone Drama at the Dawn of the New Millennium*, Brussels: Peter Lang, 2002, pp.57–67, at p.57.
66. Qtd in Aleks Sierz, *Rewriting the Nation: British Theatre Today*, London: Methuen Drama, 2011, p.75.

67. Stefaan Walgrave and Dieter Rucht (eds), *The World Says No to War: Demonstrations Against the War on Iraq*, Minneapolis: University of Minnesota Press, 2010, p.xiii.
68. Rajeev Syalm, Andrew Alderson, and Catherine Milner, 'One Million March Against War', *Telegraph*, 16 Feb. 2003.
69. Sidney Tarrow, Preface in Walgrave and Rucht, *World Says No*, pp.i–xi, at p.viii.
70. Michael Billington, Theatre Blog, *Guardian*, 3 May 2007; Kate Kellaway, 'Theatre of War', *Observer*, 29 Aug. 2004.
71. Stephen Gill, 'Toward a Postmodern Prince? The Battle in Seattle as a Moment in the New Politics of Globalisation', *Millennium: Journal of International Studies*, Vol. 29 (2000), pp.131–40, at p.137.
72. Owen Worth and Karen Buckley, 'The World Social Forum: Postmodern Prince or Court Jester?' *Third World Quarterly*, Vol. 30, No. 4 (2009), pp.649–61, at p.650.
73. *Ibid.*, p.659.
74. Naomi Wolf, 'Revealed: How the FBI Coordinated the Crackdown on Occupy', *Guardian*, 29 Dec. 2012.
75. Recent developments in the UK include the emergence of the organisation Left Unity with filmmaker Ken Loach as its figurehead. Its inaugural conference was on 30 Nov. 2013, where it sought to form a 'coalition for change'. The website reads: 'The need for unity is paramount as attacks on the living and working conditions of ordinary people intensify, and the very fabric of our welfare state is being destroyed. We need to open a dialogue of the left, as a matter of urgency, to ensure that we do not remain outside of these developments': http://leftunity.org/about/

    There is also The People's Assembly, involving many of the same organisations and figures, such as Tariq Ali. The People's Assembly endorsed a declaration and action plan campaigning against austerity cuts in June 2013: http://thepeoplesassembly.org.uk/

Epilogue: Exit the Author

1. Caryl Churchill, *Ding Dong the Wicked*, London: Nick Hern Books, 2012, p.4.
2. *Ibid.*, p.13.
3. *Ibid.*, p.15.
4. *Ibid.*, p.25.
5. Compare *ibid.*, p.8 and p.18.
6. *Ibid.*, p.14, p.21.
7. *Ibid.*, p.6 and p.24; *ibid.*, p.5 and p.18.
8. Compare *ibid.*, p.10 and p.20.
9. *Ibid.*, p.10, p.21.
10. *Ibid.*, p.7. Compare *ibid.*, p.22.
11. An exception occurs in Churchill's teleplay *The Judge's Wife* from 1972, which opens on the judge's shooting.
12. The unique exception came in 1997, when she spoke to journalist David Benedict to promote the enigmatic *Hotel.* See David Benedict, 'The Mother of Reinvention', *Independent*, 19 Apr. 1997.

INDEX